UNDERSTANDING N
PRODUCTION

Using in-depth analysis of film, TV, news and online productions, *Understanding Media Production* shows how media theory helps aspiring producers understand good practice in media production.

With detailed contemporary examples, including *Pirates of The Caribbean*, *Game of Thrones*, *Love Island* and PewDiePie's "letsplay" videos, Dwyer highlights similarities and differences in the production strategies and styles used for a wide range of media products. The book tracks the evolution of these entertainment formats and the emergence of the media businesses which produce them. Chapters describe the key production practices associated with each format, including single and multi-camera filming, news reporting, three-point lighting and gameplay animation. They also explain the development of the production roles associated with these content forms; directors, producers, reporters, correspondents etc. The book goes on to explain how media businesses have used new technologies and production innovations to reduce costs and increase profits, resulting in dramatic changes to established production practices and roles.

By comparing media production across media industries, in the UK and US, and illustrating the links between economic, sociopolitical and cultural influences on production, *Understanding Media Production* opens up a constructive debate between media practitioners and theorists about key questions of creativity and innovation in production.

Paul Dwyer is Director of the Creative Enterprise Centre, a Course Leader and a member of the CAMRI research group at the University of Westminster, UK. He is a former producer and director of factual, news and drama TV and radio programmes.

UNDERSTANDING MEDIA PRODUCTION

Paul Dwyer

Routledge
Taylor & Francis Group

LONDON AND NEW YORK

First published 2019
by Routledge
2 Park Square, Milton Park, Abingdon, Oxon OX14 4RN

and by Routledge
52 Vanderbilt Avenue, New York, NY 10017

Routledge is an imprint of the Taylor & Francis Group, an informa business

British Library Cataloguing-in-Publication Data
A catalogue record for this book is available from the British Library

Library of Congress Cataloging-in-Publication Data
A catalog record has been requested for this book

ISBN: 978-1-138-23813-8 (hbk)
ISBN: 978-1-138-23814-5 (pbk)
ISBN: 978-1-315-29805-4 (ebk)

Typeset in Bembo
by Swales & Willis Ltd, Exeter, Devon, UK
Printed and bound by CPI Group (UK) Ltd, Croydon, CR0 4YY

CONTENTS

FIGURES

INTRODUCTION

Theorists vs practitioners

Can media theories help us make a good film, radio, or TV show, news report or YouTube video? Can a detailed understanding of these processes produce ground-breaking research? In a recent answer, a successful Hollywood producer, seemed to suggest not. David Weddle (*Battle Star Galactica*, *CSI* and *Star Trek: Deep Space 9*) contrasted the current teaching of media theory, with his own film school education decades earlier: "yes, students read theoretical essays and books. But they were about the nuts and bolts of moviemaking" (Weddle, 2003). Weddle's practitioner critique of academic theory noted its often obscure terminology, its "negative" portrayal of the industries many students want to work in, its "political agendas", and its tendency to focus on philosophical debates, making the practical work of production subordinate. A recent answer to the second question suggested that it is the very requirement to understand, and teach, these practices which holds back communication research by burdening the field with a "vocational taint" (Pooley, 2008).

At the heart of this debate is an argument about the purpose of education and the nature of learning. While some practitioners (see Hensher, 2014) believe the essential skills of media production are innate talents which can't be taught, others, like Weddle, suggest that creative skills follow a "craft" model, best learned through observation, practice and reading "how-to" books describing practical examples. Since the origins of the mass media, there have been many attempts to pass on such "trade secrets", through interviews with practitioners about their working practices (e.g. Rooney and Lou Belli, 2011), practitioners' books detailing their experiences of production (the classic is Goldman, 1983) or documentaries describing the "making of" specific productions (such as Coppola, 1991). However, as Becker (1982:199) notes, there is a fundamental problem with this approach:

> artists find it difficult to verbalize the general principles on which they make their choices, or even to give any reasons at all. They often resort to such non-communicative statements as "it sounds better that way," "it looked good to me," or "it works." That inarticulateness frustrates the researcher.

The film theorists Weddle spoke to argued that the purpose of film or media theory, and of an education in these fields, should not simply be to pass on the production knowledge contained in "how-to" books. Indeed, from this theoretical perspective, the "nuts and bolts" knowledge of production is the key intellectual problem media theories should address. Rather than passing on these production practices, the purpose of media theories should be to "problematise" them. Since the origin of the Hollywood feature, film theorists have argued that this cultural form and its associated production knowledge is ideological; "it is an apparatus destined to obtain a precise ideological effect, necessary to the dominant ideology" (Baudry and Williams, 1974:46). As Rodowick (1995:xiii) notes, the argument is that "Hollywood films efface the materiality of the film medium and through this transparency of form promote an identification with, and unquestioning acceptance of, the fictional world offered by the film". Such theorists identify an alternative tradition of oppositional filmmaking techniques: "that from Eisenstein to Godard is concerned with problematizing cinematic illusionism by exploiting, through various montage strategies, the heterogeneity of the semiotic channels available to film" (op. cit.:4). This critique has influenced broader theories, studying the practices of news reporting and TV production, which portray media production as "the production of consent" (Hall, 1982:83). While media producers may perceive themselves to be applying techniques designed to create "objective" news reports, or "impartial" representation of society, in fact; "the discourse has spoken itself through him/her. Unwittingly, unconsciously, the broadcaster has served as a support for the reproduction of a dominant ideological discursive field" (op. cit.:84).

Weddle's argument expresses a hostility to academic media theories which is common among practitioners. But it also exists, often below the surface, in many media and film schools – in debates and conflicts between academics, former practitioners and students. Responding to Weddle's argument, Maras (2005) concluded; "for many media departments, the integration of theory and a practice is a priority, and represents a 'problem' that requires serious attention". This book tries to address this problem by showing how media theories can be used to understand, explain and help improve media practice. The aim is to provide a common language, a set of concepts, which allows people on either side of this debate to express their views in a way which helps those on the other side to understand and learn from them. Chapter 1 outlines this theory. The rest of this introduction briefly reviews the alternative approaches to studying media production to explain the reasons for the theoretical approach developed in Chapter 1.

Academic studies of media production

Studies of media production are less common than studies of audience reception, analysis of media content or economic studies of media corporations. Nonetheless, since the 1950s, academics have studied newsrooms, production studios and TV executive suites (see White, 1950, Elliott, 1972, Mayer et al., 2009). A key focus has been the role of media producers in decisions which set political agendas or represent different social groups:

> how does it happen that decisions made strictly for business, in a land of business contain elements of – O forbidden word! – ideology? What is the genesis of TV's images of men and women, blacks and whites, families and workplaces, authority and rebellion.
>
> *Gitlin, 1983:9–10*

Lotz's (2004) interest in studying production is as "a tool for understanding discursive and ideological features related to telling stories about gender and ethnicity". Her study of *Any Day Now* – a series about the lives of black women four decades after their involvement in the civil rights movement – identified how commissioning and promotion practices limited the range of discursive and ideological features permissible in the show.

Other studies have drawn on theories of "business" in analysing the origins of the "trade secrets" of media producers and executives. Since the early writings of the Frankfurt school (see Adorno, 2001), academics have argued that the tried and trusted "formulas" of the Hollywood community are simply the cultural equivalent of the standardised products of manufacturing industry. Theories of the political economy of communication (PEC) draw attention to the power of global media corporations to determine the media products which are produced, and the profit motive which drives these decisions. Some studies trace the relationship between these quasi-monopolies and the "labour process" of media production (Staiger, 1985). The parallel between media and manufacturing corporations is observed in the way media managers devise standardised, formulaic products and then routinise and supervise the media workers in "mass production" of this content. A variant of this theory argues that while mass production of media content was once the norm, the media industries had seen a, "transition from Fordist mass production to 'flexible specialization'; from slothful, hierarchical bureaucracies to loose, dynamic networks of small production companies" (McKinlay and Quinn, 1999). Keane and Moran (2008:157) identified the spread of this paradigm in a "post-Fordist format economy" across TV industries around the world. This, in turn, appeared to explain the transition of the status of media producers from permanent employees to "precarious" freelancers (Hesmondhalgh and Baker, 2011).

Between the studio or newsroom floor and the boardroom of the global media conglomerate is the individual media organisation. Studies of the BBC (Born, 2004, Schlesinger, 1978) draw attention to the variety of ways the creative imagination and autonomy of media workers is constrained by a range of "factors" (financial, legal and technical) emanating from its bureaucratic structure. These limits constrain innovation and creativity in some genres more than others: "Compared to prime time, soaps face unique constraints to developing innovative programming, with a narrower audience, more conservative advertising sponsors, and genre restrictions that emphasise continuity and respect for history over innovation" (Bielby and Harrington, 2008:87).

A further avenue of academic critique came from theories which argued that the problem with media producers' knowledge was not, primarily, its ideological nature, its commercial compromises or its bureaucratic boundaries; the real problem was that media producers did not actually know much at all. What Gitlin's (1983:22) interviews with TV executives revealed was: "the higher I got, the more likely I was to hear important people half-joke that they couldn't explain how their business operated . . . (and so) real doubt exists about what it is a TV executive *knows*" (original emphasis). Writers like Caldwell (2008) argue that media producers' knowledge is a, largely self-serving, attempt to convince others that they know how to produce content which will attract the attention of large audiences, when in fact what they face is radical uncertainty about this process. Some practitioners, like Goldman (1983), have been happy to reveal the secret that "nobody knows" how to make a successful movie. Indeed Caves (2000) argues that this "nobody knows" uncertainty is a definitive feature, differentiating the creative industries from "humdrum" industries.

One response practitioners like Weddle might make to these academic critiques of the commercial influences, ideological subtexts or bureaucratic constraints on media prosecution practices, is that that they contain very few practical proposals – short of some emancipatory social transformation – for resolving the problems with these practices. As Pöttker (2003:507) notes; "many researchers take it for granted that there is a fundamental contradiction between the commercial interests of the mass media and journalistic quality". But as he points out "not only the principle of creating publicness and public discourse . . . but also the rules of journalistic professionalism developed not despite but because of the dynamics of capitalism".

The outline of this book

This book tries to use media theory to understand media practice. The first step, illustrated by this brief review, is to understand the relationships between different levels of analysis – from the studio or newsroom, to the individual media organisation, to the level of the global media conglomerate. In a recent debate on this subject (see Dwyer 2015b, 2016, Fuchs, 2016, Garnham, 2011, 2016), Murdock and Golding (2016) argued that "the central challenge for theories of media production then is to move between levels of analysis and to integrate them". As Mayer (2009:15) noted "it is this connection between the micro contexts and the macro forces . . . that is so frequently lost in the efforts to describe the current media landscape, its interconnected industries and its networks of professionals". This book, therefore, tries to develop a theory showing the causal relationships between these levels – macro (economics and political economy), meso (organisation studies) and micro (production studies). In another intervention, Murdock (2018) added that "we need comparative studies" showing the similarities and differences between different types of media production. This book compares six types of production; feature films, radio and TV studio shows, filmed TV series, news reports, entertainment formats and letsplay YouTube videos. The book also outlines the coevolution of US and UK media industries, allowing comparisons between them.

The first chapter outlines the theory to be used to specify the different levels of analysis and show the relationships between them. This involves examining the economic and media studies literature to identify four key models of production; the neoclassical "production function"; production as a system of transactions; the division of labour; and production as "process innovation" in producing a "dominant design". The chapter concludes by developing an integrated model of production which combines elements of each of the models.

Each of the following chapters begins with an analysis of an example of each of these forms of content; a feature (*Pirates of The Caribbean*), a studio show (*Friends*), a filmed series (*Game of Thrones*), a news report (the Harvey Weinsten story and #MeToo campaign), an entertainment format (*Love Island*) and a YouTube let-splay video (PewDiePie's *Uncharted #1*).

Second, the chapters describe the evolution of these forms and outline how industry sectors and regulatory structures emerged to produce them. The chapters identify the moments when these industries are more competitive and when they are controlled by a few large companies. This helps answer a range of questions: why do so many media organisations continue to produce these types of content? Is this evidence of the 'homogenisation' of a commercialised mass culture? Does it reflect and reinforce ideologies of race, class, gender and sexuality? Is it the stand-ardised output of Fordist mass production? The chapters also outline the changing structures of the companies themselves – when they employ staff, buy technology and build facilities to produce content (vertical integration) and when they con-tract these things out to independent producers, suppliers or freelances (vertical dis-integration). This also allows us to see whether or not one of these forms of organisation is likely to be more creative or innovative than the other.

Each chapter then connects these (macro and meso) levels with the level of the production process. The chapters explain the emergence of the production prac-tices associated with a particular type of media content; single and multi-camera production, headlines and "inverted pyramids", three-point lighting and gameplay animation. They also explain the emergence of different production roles – why we have directors, producers, reporters, correspondents etc. The chapters also describe the changes in these production practices and in the relationships between production roles, as media organisations use new technologies and production pro-cesses to try to achieve efficiencies, reducing costs and increasing profits.

As the chapters progress they begin to compare the production processes of the different types of content. They highlight the elements which make each of these types of production distinct, asking: how is filming a documentary or factual for-mat different from filming a feature film or a sitcom? How is the written structure of a news report different from the structure of a filmed drama series? The chap-ters show how these different forms of media production have coevolved, with new forms of production drawing inspiration from and, commercially impacting, existing forms.

Each chapter also focuses on both the US and UK. This is because, as Hilmes (2012:3) has argued "we cannot understand the cultural history of either the United States or Great Britain without taking into account the continuous flow of mutual influence circulating between them". Many of the media forms we study here first became industrialised in the US and then transferred to the UK (feature film, filmed series). Some emerged at around the same time in both countries (news reports, TV and radio studio shows) and some involved interaction between the two right from the start (entertainment formats and letsplay videos).

Finally, the comparative approach allows the book to present a transnational history of the media industries. After Chapter 1 explains the theory, Chapter 2, on film, covers the 1890s–1940s. Chapter 3, on live broadcast studio shows, focuses on the 1920s–1950s and Chapter 4, on filmed TV series, on the 1960s–1970s. Chapter 5, on news reports, breaks this pattern, reaching back to the nineteenth century before taking us through to the emergence of electronic newsgathering in the 1970s. Chapter 6, on entertainment formats, takes us from the emergence of cable in the 1980s to the height of the format boom in the mid-2000s. Chapter 7, on letsplay videos, takes us from the emergence of the internet to YouTube's 2018 response to the previous year's "adpocalypse".

1

A THEORY OF MEDIA PRODUCTION

An outline of the theory

The basic framework for the theory of media production outlined below is derived from economics. The reason for starting with economics is not based on a belief that economics *determines* what happens in the media industries, but that economic factors – markets, prices, sales, economies of scale etc. – strongly influence which media activities continue and which fall by the wayside. Neoclassical economic theory is derived from the idea of scarcity. It attempts to explain how societies choose to use the scarce resources they have. Its conception of resources reflects its origins in an era when economies were largely agrarian. Production is explained in terms of three resources – land, labour and capital. This leads to a second key concept – substitution. If a resource, like labour, becomes scarce, and so costs more, producers will make a substitution, replacing their workers with machines or technology.

It is important to emphasise that neither technology nor economics *determines* how media industries develop and change. Technologies create possibilities and economics influences which activities succeed or fail, but it is culture which influences the ideas we have about how to use technologies, the knowledge we develop to do this, and the responses we receive from others. Evolutionary economics explicitly identifies the role of social, cultural and political institutions (governments, regulators, public opinion) in influencing which types of economic activities, particularly in their early stages, are accepted as legitimate, and which are regulated, constrained or prohibited. The other chapters of this book use this approach to explain why particular types of media production emerge, continue, change or decline.

Production as inputs of labour and technology

Neoclassical economists understand production in terms of a simple model, the production function, which describes the quantity of outputs (products or services for a market) which can be produced from a combination of inputs (labour and technology). If the price of a production input increases (for example, if it becomes scarce) businesses will change their production processes by substituting cheaper inputs for the expensive one. If camera operators were in short supply, they might be able to charge higher rates of pay. To try to maintain profits or efficiency, businesses might respond by substituting camera operators with cheaper fixed rig cameras. But economists recognise the limits to the substitution of inputs. For example, if production workers have specialist skills in writing stories or creating images or sounds, it may be difficult to substitute them with lower paid workers or automated production equipment. Economists would explain the generally labour-intensive nature of much media production as resulting from this "inelasticity of substitution" of specialist media labour.

As already noted, a number of amendments to the above conception will be needed to develop a theory of media production. Some of these are already common within conventional economics. So, the production function model assumes companies respond to changes in prices of inputs (or demand for products), and individual businesses cannot themselves influence these prices. However, some "industrial" economists suggest that if firms achieve sufficient size and/or share of the market, they may achieve economies of *scale*, enabling them to pay less for labour or technology. So, a large media company may be able to reduce its costs by negotiating volume discounts with suppliers (for example, paper, ink, film, video etc.) or distributors (news agents, cinemas, broadcasters, web hosting companies). A second method of achieving these economies of scale is through *vertical integration*: integrating the supply of production inputs, the actual production process and the distribution of final products or services, within a single company. This enables businesses to be independent of suppliers or distributors and so plan their production processes to operate at the optimum scale. This achieves efficiencies because it means people and machines are working at maximum capacity, without any "idle time", waiting for deliveries of supplies or for the arrival of distributors (Moroni, 1992).

In addition to the limits of its conception of production, neoclassical economics has a limited conception of a product – assuming all the businesses in a sector produce homogeneous products. These products are "rival". If I buy a smartphone it is not available to other interested consumers who must buy an identical copy from the producer. Products are also tangible and private – they are used up (eventually) in consumption. Consumers demand products because they are useful or satisfying, and so when a product is used up, consumers may repeat purchase them. Businesses will keep expanding production as long as they make a profit on each product they sell. These assumptions help economists develop an understanding of an industry based on businesses producing similar products, competing with each other largely on the basis of differing prices.

Again, industrial economists like Porter (1985) noted some important strategies individual companies may use to protect themselves from competition. Some businesses may be able to exercise market control by having lower costs. Vertical integration, because it can deliver economies of scale, may enable them to offer their products at lower prices and so achieve a dominant market position, creating *barriers to entry* for new competitors. Alternatively, if a company can produce a product with higher quality or better functions, and so differentiate their products from their competitors' ("vertical differentiation"), consumers may be willing to pay higher prices for the product, in preference to a lower priced, lower quality product. Finally, if a company identifies a range of products, all relying on similar technology or knowledge, they may decide to integrate these similar businesses ("*horizontal integration*") either by buying their competitors or by launching new products themselves. This can deliver *economies of scope* giving them cost or other advantages over competitors who are only producing one product in the range. Rather than engage in damaging competition, we should expect media organisations to use these strategies (economies of scale and scope, vertical and horizontal integration etc.) to try to exercise some degree of *market control*, by achieving a dominant market share or by making it uneconomic for new competitors to enter the market ("barriers to entry").

However, the fundamental neoclassical model of competition, based largely on manufactured products, does not accurately describe the markets for cultural products like media content. Media products (especially live broadcasting) are less like tangible manufactured products, and more like services. The demand for a service is usually for something intangible (Rathmell, 1966). So, in services like hairdressing or healthcare, consumers do not value the actual performance of the service (the haircut or the operation) but its intangible content (the appearance or health benefits following the performance of the service). The demand for media products is similar; audiences do not value the physical form (the printed paper, DVD etc.) of the media product but its content – "the information or the message" (Doyle, 2002:12).

However, media organisations can achieve greater economies of scale in distribution than can services. A live musical or drama performance might reach hundreds or thousands of people in a theatre, auditorium or stadium. But to reach a larger number of consumers the performance must be repeated, often involving transporting a large number of people to deliver the performance locally to audiences. If the same performance were recorded onto a storage medium (film, tape, print or disc) it gains a greater degree of tangibility which means it can be stored, transported and traded. This process of converting services into tradeable forms is known as servitisation (Harjo et al., 2016) and has been especially important in the development of TV formats (see Chapter 6). Rather than moving the live performers, the use of storage media (including digital files) generates important economies of scale in media distribution. Rather than repeating the live performance, the use of storage media means that once a song or story has been performed (once the *first copy* has been produced) a media organisation can satisfy an infinite number of consumers without having to reproduce the performance. Although the first copy costs of media production are generally high, the costs of subsequent (recorded) copies are extremely low. This aspect of media products works spectacularly to the advantage of media businesses. The combination of high first copy cost and low-to-zero cost of subsequent copies enables media products to be distributed (via print, broadcast, internet, record/CD/video/DVD) to large numbers of people at very low cost (Doyle, 2002).

Where neoclassical economics assumes goods are rival and exclusive – consumption of a good prevents another person consuming the same good – this was not true of radio and TV for many years. Until the emergence of cable and satellite pay-TV, TV was a "public" good, distributed "free to air" without a means to charge audiences for content. The nature of broadcasting technology meant consumption of a programme by one person did not prevent consumption of the same product by another person. On the face of it, this would seem to make radio and TV programming a ubiquitous rather than a scarce resource, and would suggest that conventional economic concepts of demand, prices and markets would be useless in explaining its production.

However, while neoclassical economics leads us to think about resources for production in terms of land, and thus about production knowledge and technology in terms of farming or mining this resource, for the media industries, we can think of audience *attention*, the leisure time we have available for culture, as a scarce resource whose allocation can be explained in economic terms. "Attention economics" (Lanham, 2006) leads us to think about the knowledge required to attract and hold the attention of an audience; knowledge which originated in ancient Greece, in the art of rhetoric.

Thus, from the audience's perspective, a broadcast programme is not scarce or rival, and so they do not pay for it. But from the point of view of the broadcast network, and even more so, the advertiser, the relevant scarce resource is the time and attention of the audience. Advertisers' demand for audience attention is based on utility – it enables them to sell more products. Audiences supply this attention through the process of listening to or watching a programme. This creates a market in attention, with advertisers willing to pay higher prices to media organisations whose products attract the attention of a large or a particularly desirable audience (Falkinger, 2008). These "attention markets" are open to media organisations whose products are more private and rival (there is a scarcity of cinema seats or newspaper copies) as well as new media like the internet. This in turn means, as we shall see below, that creating value from media production depends on the core knowledge and skills required to attract the attention of the desired audience, in the right time and place, and ideally in the right frame of mind (Lanham, 2006).

Porter's (1985) idea of product differentiation, although a useful amendment to neoclassical theory, cannot capture the sheer extent of the differentiation of media products. As noted above, demand for many products is based on replacement purchases. When a product is consumed (a bag of coffee runs out or a toothbrush needs replacing) people may buy another from the same company because they want precisely the same utility (taste, functionality etc.) they received from the previous product. Demand for media products does not work in the same way because, once the original has been consumed, audiences demand new products (new stories, new information etc.) rather than an identical replacement. The demand for media products can thus be described as predicated on the assumption that media goods are *individually differenti-ated* (Rosse and Dertouzos, 1978). This characteristic of media products fundamentally alters the economics of their production; "since media products are necessarily dif-ferentiated and distinct, as viewed by audiences, media markets do not fit easily into traditional economic . . . analyses" (op. cit.:41).

To the audience, every media product is like a completely new innovation – the only way of knowing if the product would deliver the required utility (humour, suspense, relevant information) is to actually experience it (they are *experience* goods). For the same reason, it is difficult to judge if one media product is a good substitute for another or to make price comparisons. Thus, an important feature of attention markets is that, even though a media product may be "free" to the audi-ence (a broadcast programme or a free newspaper), audiences incur costs, first in giving their attention to the media product they consume, but additionally in the time they spend searching for a product they believe will deliver the desired expe-rience. Because of the difficulties in judging this utility before actually incurring the costs of consumption, these *search costs* are likely to be higher than in markets for conventional products.

We can now return to the original concept of the production function. Imagine a media company, a feature film producer deciding how much to spend on production – and so how many people to employee, facilities or equipment to buy or hire, marketing budget etc. In the real world, "management makes the produc-tion function decision on a yearly basis", having forecast projected demand for a company's outputs (Van de Ven, 1976:66). For a farming or manufacturing com-pany, this forecast may fairly closely resemble the previous year – a certain number of people buying replacement products, some new customers and the loss of some existing customers to competitors. Our feature film producer, however, will find it much more difficult to make this forecast accurately. There will be no replace-ment purchases, because each film is individually differentiated, and so a new film is not a replacement for a previous film. There are no "existing customers" because each new film is essentially a new product that customers have never experienced before – every customer is a new customer. But media products are not simply individually differentiated, they are also intangible, experience goods. Our film studio has very limited ability to communicate to potential audiences what the experience of its new film may be. This is not simply a conceptual problem. It fundamentally influences the effectiveness of markets in media products. The matching of sellers (our studio film) and buyers (audiences buying a ticket) in the film business is extremely wasteful and inefficient. For our feature film producer, the likelihood of failure (of not selling enough cinema tickets) is very high – studies suggest only one in ten feature films released will make a profit (de Vany, 2004). But this high failure rate is combined with a production process which makes the costs of feature production (the first copy costs) extremely high. Thus, our film studio making its production function decision is taking a much greater financial risk (of losing the money) than producers in most industries.

This is why market control strategies are extremely important for media producers, because they help to reduce the risks of failure. One important strategy is to try to increase the number of familiar elements so that individually differentiated media products acquire some of the characteristics of conventional products. While there is no "replacement" consumption, audiences do, at times, engage in *habitual* consumption. This is because, although media products are individually differentiated, the degree of differentiation varies. Comparing the production processes of media products, reveals the extent to which they vary in their proportions of new and familiar elements. As we will see, feature films tend to be the most individually differentiated (although movie franchises are increasingly common) with the greatest number of new and the smallest number of familiar elements, filmed series and studio shows are less individually differentiated, news reports and letsplay videos are least differentiated. Berlyne (1974) suggests that demand for experience goods (which don't have a knowable and predictable "utility") follows an inverted U-shape. Consumers gain lowest satisfaction from products which are either very novel or very familiar. They gain the highest satisfaction from new products with familiar elements. The "sweet spot" for media producers is, therefore, to achieve the optimum combination of new and familiar elements. As the subsequent chapters show, this prediction does appear to be supported by the development of *dominant designs* in different media industries. During the periods following the development of the dominant designs of the newspaper report, the feature, and the radio and TV series, these industries achieved their most significant habitual consumption; newspapers (1920s–1950s), cinema (1920s–1950s), radio (1920s–1950s) and free-to-air TV (1950s–1980s). But even at these times of habitual consumption, each differentiated media product (such as an individual TV show or a new series) remains, essentially, a new innovation leading to failure rates for TV series which are similarly high to feature films (Bielby and Bielby, 1994).

Media industries also adopt the strategies of other high-risk industries, for example following the portfolio strategy common in pharmaceuticals. Our film studio might therefore decide to produce a range of types of film to try to spread the financial risks of production, in case of a downturn in demand for a particular genre. Similarly, radio and TV channels may produce a range of programming genres, newspapers a range of subjects for news reports etc. This approach becomes a more significant market control strategy when media organisations try to spread the risk through horizontal integration. If our film producer was able to buy a TV network, this would spread the overall risk of production over two markets. Further, horizontal integration may help reduce competition by removing a competitor (the recent purchases of Instagram and Vine by Facebook and Twitter are examples of this strategy).

However, while the risks are great, so are the potential rewards. Media products do have an advantage over conventional products and services, because they are intangible, non-rival products which can be recorded onto inexpensive media (paper, film, tape, digital files) and distributed at low-to-zero marginal cost (via DVD, broadcast, cable or mobile network, or internet) – the costs of reaching a million consumers are not massively greater than the costs of reaching a thousand. This means that a "hit" feature or TV show can be hugely profitable. Media companies which develop a portfolio of products hope that the one-in-ten successful features or TV series they create may be profitable enough to more than cover the losses of the nine failures.

An alternative to the portfolio approach tries to exploit the *hit* characteristics of media markets. This suggests that success in the market is skewed towards a small number of "blockbuster" successes: 10% of the top 200 films typically account for 50% of industry revenue (Picard, 2005:67). Media businesses may try to implement Porter's *vertical differentiation* strategy (1985) to increase the chances that their product will be one of these blockbuster successes. This represents a significant difference in the way these media businesses take the production function decision. The production function suggests that if labour or technology become scarce and expensive, businesses will substitute one for the other to reduce costs. Attempting to create a blockbuster media product may involve deliberately seeking out scarce resources in order to differentiate the final product from competitors. This is particularly true of the decision to employ "talent" – famous actors, presenters, writers etc. Because every media production is essentially a "new" innovation, consumers face the same potential risk as producers – i.e. that they will invest (either money or their scarce attention time) in a product which does not deliver the desired experience. One way to reduce this risk for consumers is to try to reduce their "search" time, the time it takes them to identify a potentially rewarding product. As noted above, this may involve including familiar elements along with the novel elements of the product. But for these familiar elements to produce a blockbuster, they need to attract the attention of a very large number of people. Further, as Adler (2006) shows, this talent needs to have acquired their own, personal "consumption capital". Large numbers of people must have experienced his or her work before and have developed a special trust in that individual that they will deliver a similarly reliable experience in a new production.

Media organisations who cannot afford such scarce talent, may try to reduce the audience's search costs by finding other ways to communicate the probable quality of the experience of consuming the product. The "talent" strategy is, in fact, a subset of this "word of mouth" strategy; "when the artist is popular, it is easier to find discussants who are familiar with her or to find media coverage about her. This is why consumers prefer to consume what others also consume" (Adler, 2006:898). A study by Bughin et al. (2010:113) suggested "word of mouth is the primary factor behind 20 to 50 percent of all purchasing decisions" but noted that the percentage was highest "when consumers are buying a product for the first time". Because media products are both "experience" goods and differentiated "first time" purchases, this role of word of mouth has always been important in audience decisions.

These strategies of talent and word of mouth (or *influencer*) marketing have always played a major role in cultural industries but this has become ever more important as new channels and platforms have emerged. As first print and broadcast, then cable, satellite and digital platforms have emerged, so has the number of organisations seeking talent which can reliably attract consumers to devote scarce income (for features, newspapers and subscription TV and video on demand) or attention to "individually differentiated" products. Talent and word of mouth strategies seek to exploit the broader phenomenon of *network effects*; "an individual consumer maximizes its marginal utility by joining the majority and following the same artist. The more members the network has, the higher is the probability of finding suitable conversation partners" (Budzinski and Gaenssle, 2018:5).

The emergence of digital and social media has hugely extended the potential for network effects. This has informed a further strategy, known as *aggregation* which effectively enables digital companies like Amazon, Netflix, Facebook, Google and YouTube to become preferred distributors for a huge variety of products and so enables them to attract huge, global audiences and use technological leadership to "lock in" these audiences to the platform. Aggregation of content reduces the search costs for audiences in a number of ways. First, in presenting such a mass of content, these platforms can become a "one stop shop" for audiences wanting to find news, TV series, features, online video etc. This in turn lowers the search costs of advertisers wanting to reach global audiences. The revenue generated gives digital media companies huge resources to invest in improving their systems enabling audiences to search for content or providing audiences with recommendations of relevant content. Finally, the aggregated audience becomes a word of mouth network, further supporting audience decisions;

> social networks are a valuable adaptive mechanism for dealing with uncertainty, risk, and novelty at the macro-scale of populations, even while they are driven by micro-scale individual choices . . . just as individual consumers decide on this basis what to do, wear – or even be – so producers respond to the choices of others in deciding where to invest.
>
> *Hartley, 2007:21–2*

Production as a system of transactions

While these strategies may increase the profitability of a "hit", studies suggest that attempts to produce a predictable hit or blockbuster have little effect on the likelihood of success (see De Vany, 2004). Instead, media producers appear to face irreducible uncertainty about the relationship between the features of a media product (stars, stories or styles) and its likely appeal to an audience. This statistical evidence appears to confirm the findings of production studies and even some "how-to" books (see Introduction) that "nobody knows" how to produce a successful media product.

The uncertainty of media product markets has caused some economists to draw on an approach known as transaction cost economics (TCE) which rejects neoclassical economics' assumption that businesses and consumers have "perfect knowledge" (about the utility of goods or even their prices) (Slater and Spencer, 2000:65). Here, it is important to describe how TCE deals with production. As

Moroni (2014:11) notes, the neoclassical production function approach assumes that "knowledge is homogeneous, full and free, i.e. that production techniques are readily available to all firms". However, TCE proponents point out that production choices are more complex than simply substituting between labour and capital on the basis of price. Instead, businesses face uncertainty about the productivity of an input (a worker or machine, when employed, may not be as productive as expected; a supplier may not deliver as agreed).

Instead of thinking in terms of prices, TCE conceptualises production as (a series of) transactions. A newsroom, for example, could be reimagined as a series of transactions between workers at various stages of the process – reporting, subediting, editing, layout, publishing etc. In many cases these transactions are internal to the company, but TCE contends that this is not inevitably the case. In fact, to the contrary, we should assume that market transactions would be the most efficient way of allocating resources, and so we need to explain why organisations would choose to organise production themselves, when in theory it would be more cost effective to make these transactions on the market (Williamson, 1985). The reason, TCE contends, is that, businesses often have limited knowledge about a supplier (and so face the risk that they may not deliver as expected) or about a complex production process. In the latter case it may be difficult to differentiate between what the supplier must provide and what the company is, itself, responsible for. In this situation of "incomplete contracting" (op. cit.:89), the company may reduce its risks by having these transactions (production activities) conducted "in-house", by production staff whose work can be supervised and managed. TCE theorists thus offer a radically different explanation for "vertical integration" of production. Rather than being a strategy for achieving economies of scale to try to ensure market share, it may be driven by a desire to reduce uncertainties and risks in the production process. Thus, if a media producer faced difficulties in defining in a contract the performance they can expect from suppliers (e.g. intellectual property rights or levels of technical or creative quality) TCE would predict the media producer would vertically integrate production, as a lower cost method of reducing risks than using markets and contracts. Bringing the work "in-house" might involve buying a supplier company or employing workers on long-term contracts. By contrast, when producers know a great deal about both the production process and about suppliers, the risks involved may be limited and it may be easy to specify the production input in a contract with a supplier. In these circumstances businesses may decide production can be safely contracted (*outsourced*) to a supplier. The business will then follow a production function approach – buying production inputs on the basis of price.

Caves (2000) makes a distinction in creative production between simple creativity (a single author or artist) and complex creativity (produced by specialist teams). When an author approaches a publisher with a completed work, their commercial relationship may be captured in a relatively simple royalty contract. Another reason why media businesses may choose to contract with talent, rather than bring this part of production "in house" was suggested above: the ability of talent to generate word of mouth and network effects to increase audiences for a hit product.

This helps explain why, even when vertical integration offers economies of scale, market share or reduced risks, companies may choose to disintegrate and outsource aspects of production. Caves (2000) and Deakin et al. (2004) have drawn on TCE in their explanations of decisions to disintegrate US feature film and UK TV production to independent production companies (see Chapters 2 and 6). However, most elements of film and TV production are, in Caves's terms, "complex creativity", and so an additional element of explanation is needed for these decisions. The main theory which has attempted to do this is *flexible specialisation*, which is outlined below. However, this theory is dependent on a pre-existing theory of mass production which is described next.

Production as division of labour

While economists have compared media products with consumer durables, and noted their differentiation, media researchers have compared media products with an ideal of boundless creativity and innovation or political or sociocultural representation (such as Habermas's (1989) "public sphere") – and noted their homogeneity. The emergence of mass consumption of commercially produced media and cultural goods newspapers, commercial books, live entertainment film and radio was viewed by critics like the Frankfurt School writers (see Adorno, 2001), as the birth of a homogeneous "mass culture". Where "high culture" or traditional folk culture might facilitate freedom and creativity, mass culture recycled formulaic and sensational forms (dime store novels to Wild West, minstrel and freak shows, sentimental musicals).

The Frankfurt writers identified the rise of "cultural industries", in place of craft production, as the cause of these standardised, formulaic cultural products. This thinking starts from a further model of the production process – the division of labour. Adam Smith (1776) first illustrated how manufacturers use this technique to achieve *economies of specialisation*. Division of labour begins with *task decomposition* – an analysis of the overall task (such as manufacturing a product) and then decomposing this into smaller subtasks. The next step is to organise these tasks into a production process, a fixed set of relationships between workers, machines and materials. The logic of the division of labour technique is to continue specialisation by reducing the range of tasks each worker performs until they perform a single, narrowly defined task. This can increase efficiency (more output per worker) because workers develop specialist knowledge – they then learn to perform the task at optimum efficiency. The efficiency gains of specialisation may also be applied to technology, often referred to as mechanisation (or, if it enables complete substitution of labour, automation). This model of production, specialisation through extensive division of labour, was championed by Frederick Taylor (1914) whose aim was to replace custom and practice, rule-of-thumb ("heuristic") production practices with the so-called "scientific" management of production. This method of task decomposition (often termed "Taylorism") – the creation of highly specialised, standardised repetitive tasks – enabled substitution of skilled workers with lower paid unskilled workers or specialist machines. Taylor's model was then the basis for the mass production system developed by Henry Ford ("Fordism") which used moving conveyor belts (assembly lines) and other specialist machines to reduce the time taken (and thus cost) to assemble a Model T car from 106 to six hours between 1912–14 (Wilson and Mckinlay, 2010). This model reveals a further element of the economics of production which is not apparent in the production function. Businesses which implement a successful division of labour are effectively "shifting" the production function for their industry, by enabling a given level of input to produce a disproportionate increase in output (doubling spending on labour and technology results in more than a doubling of units of output).

However, following Marx's critique of Adam Smith, Braverman (1974) argued that task decomposition was not driven by a search for efficiency, but followed a specifically political agenda. Taylorism, he argued, decomposed skilled craft production tasks (controlled by workers) into their conceptual, cognitive elements (which could then be controlled by managers) and the execution of simple tasks (which could be allocated to unskilled workers). The capitalist's dependence on skilled labour was replaced by managers' ability to supervise worker performance more easily, intensifying exploitation by disciplining or dismissing those who failed to achieve the maximum possible output. There is some support for Braverman's argument; Ford himself claimed his system ensured managers exercised control over production and substituted higher waged craft workers with lower waged unskilled workers (Chinoy, 1982). However, there are many problems with Braverman's account as a general theory of the capitalist *mode of production* (see Dwyer, 2015b for a review).

The importance of this model is in Smith's account of specialisation and Braverman's analysis of the potential of this approach to benefit managers or corporations at the expense of some groups of workers. However, many accounts of "mass production" in media organisations (especially Staiger, 1985) propose that media organisations, fairly straightforwardly, implemented a Taylorist/ Fordist "mode of production". Janet Staiger's work (Staiger, 1979, 1985) is the most detailed attempt to argue that media production is based on standardised productions and routinised production tasks, permitting little scope for creativity and innovation. Many writers have argued that media production has indeed followed the principles of "mass production" of news (see Cottle, 2007), feature films (Schatz, 2012), filmed TV series (Anderson, 1994) and soap operas (Allen, 1985) etc.

Studies of the "production of culture" found similar *homogeneity* of media products (lack of diversity, marginalisation of non-mainstream political views, cultural forms etc.) in news (Gans, 1979, Tuchman, 1973) and TV drama (Gitlin, 1983). Rather than mass production, these authors saw oligopolistic market structures and in particular bureaucratic organisation as constraining the freedom of media producers, and requiring *routines* and sometimes *routinisation* of media production. Thus Mosco (2011:360) described news production, for example, as a "potentially open-ended process" which is homogenised by "bureaucratic controls . . . and . . . simplifying routines". Hirsch (1972:649) found that editors and executives acted as "institutional regulators of innovation" requiring creative workers to deliver homogeneous, predictable products.

Flexible production of innovative products

Having outlined the theory of mass production, we are now able to return to the question of vertical disintegration of media production, and the account offered by theories of "flexible specialisation". TCE explained vertical integration of production through the attempt to reduce risk. The implication of TCE was that companies would disintegrate or outsource production of simple tasks which could be defined in a contract. Mass production suggested that vertical integration (the classic being Ford's Highland Park Plant, with its assembly line) delivered economies of scale and enabled maximum productivity by permitting management to closely supervise worker performance of simple, specialised tasks.

Flexible specialisation (FS) theory suggests that vertical disintegration has occurred as part of an historic transition, a change in the capitalist mode of production (see Piore and Sabel, 1984). Across countries and industries, it is argued, there has been a shift from mass production by large integrated corporations to disintegrated businesses flexibly using production inputs from specialist suppliers. This theory accepts the strengths of the Fordist mode of production, outlined above, but argues it was eventually undermined by its weaknesses – particularly its *rigidity*, its dependence on standardised products and its inability to innovate new products to adapt to changes in demand or to meet "niche" demands. FS suggests that new digital technologies helped reduce the uncertainty and risk ("incomplete contracting" and transaction costs) associated with buying production inputs on the market. Disintegrating production in this way enabled large businesses to respond more rapidly to changes in tastes. By choosing, flexibly, from a wider range of specialist production inputs than could be generated "in-house", these companies could now achieve rapid product innovation. This *functional flexibility* retained some of the efficiencies of specialisation, enabling companies to *vary* worker specialisation – either because they could perform a broad range of tasks as efficiently as a single specialised task, or because they could change task completely without compromising productivity.

A number of writers have argued that media production has transformed FS (Storper, 1993, Caves, 2000, Starkey, 2004, Karlson and Picard, 2011). Starkey et al. (2000:303) explains the advantages of functional flexibility in TV; "the ability to reconvene a successful production team in a fluid environment where the majority of workers are essentially 'nomadic' is key to firms seeking advantage from innovative programming". Tempest (2003:191) suggests "flexible production in the television industry provides opportunities for managers, internal staff and freelance workers to learn across firm divides, from each other".

Critics of FS theory have argued that it exaggerates the extent to which disintegration of production has been driven by a need to transform the rigid specialisms of Taylorist or Fordist mass production to achieve product innovation (Arnold and Bongiovi, 2013). They argue that, in practice, worker specialisms have largely remained and "functional flexibility" ("internal labour market flexibility") has been limited. Nor has outsourcing, generally, been driven by a search for innovation by finding novel inputs from supplier firms. Instead, as Barrera (2014) argues, businesses faced with conditions of *urgency* in completing tasks or producing outputs, will tend to integrate production and employ workers "in house" on permanent contracts. An increase in competition (or other changes) which reduces the urgency of demand creates uncertainty about the necessary level of permanent staff. Disintegration allows businesses to pass on the financial risks of uncertainty to supplier firms or freelance or casualised labour. In this reading, vertical disintegration achieves only *numerical flexibility* (or "external labour market flexibility"), allowing companies to reduce their fixed costs by reducing their permanent workforce (often deunionising at the same time) and outsourcing production to freelancers or subcontractors, The high failure rate of products in media industries makes this numerical flexibility very valuable to businesses who can take on workers for production of a pilot product and, if the product fails, "let them go" without the costs of redundancies etc. Some FS theorists have been clear about the use of disintegration as "a means to reduce fixed costs [. . .] as components of the network ceasing to have a function are disbanded rather than becoming a burden on the whole" (Barnatt and Starkey, 1997:273). Even on this reading, however, the implication of the theory is that the resulting precarity of employment in the media industries is the price to be paid for the greater innovation produced (Arnold and Bongiovi, 2013).

The emergence of the internet has brought a further iteration of this flexible model of production and innovation. Von Hippel (2005) has proposed a model of open innovation which argues that digital technology has so reduced transaction costs that businesses can disintegrate production tasks to a vast market of freelancers or 'users'. Writers like Tapscott and Williams (2008) and Leadbeater (2009) argue that a "new economy" has emerged which again favours disintegration, flexibility and specialist independent producers. Haefliger et al. (2010:1198) summarise this argument:

> usually embedded in a community of users with similar needs, user entrepreneurs operate under favorable conditions: the community plays a vital role in diffusing new designs while user entrepreneurs are granted early access to feedback and information relevant to commercialization prior to firm foundation.

Anderson (2007) has argued that the internet has inverted the traditional economics of the blockbuster, enabling small producers to compete by finding audiences for the "long tail" of content which had previously constituted the failed products obscured by the successes of the blockbusters.

Production in industry evolution

We have noted that the production function model makes assumptions about businesses' ability to substitute labour for capital, which are not borne out empirically. For much of its history, media production used technologies (print, film, audio and video tape) which could not easily be substituted with labour. This approach also assumed businesses have "perfect knowledge". The TCE approach addressed this issue, but, as with the mass production and FS approaches, tended to assume that businesses were relatively free to develop the division of labour which is most efficient or posed lowest risk. However, there is evidence that actual production technologies impose limits on the freedom to decompose tasks. For example, in media production recording has to happen before editing. The nature of the technology requires production tasks to take place in a particular sequence (it establishes *interdependencies* between tasks) which limits the decomposition of those tasks into subtasks and (therefore) limits the extent to which they can be disintegrated and outsourced.

This suggests that technology and knowledge may affect the operation of economic forces – like markets and prices. To account for this, researchers like Nelson and Winter (1982) developed an approach known as *evolutionary economics*. This proposes a fundamentally important role for knowledge in economics; "where neoclassical economics assumes agents make substitutions in markets (i.e., a reorganization of who has what), evolutionary economics assumes agents make connections . . . the dynamic is change in the knowledge connections within the system" (Dopfer and Potts, 2008). This suggests a final model of production, based on businesses solving problems using specific types of knowledge.

Evolutionary economists do not return to the idea of "perfect knowledge" however. Instead, they assume businesses are continually looking for ways (new knowledge) to make money. However, because businesses have limited time to search out, process and evaluate all the relevant information about potential solutions (they have "bounded rationality", see Simon and March, 1976), even when production is based on the physical sciences, they do not find the perfect solution to problems. Instead production knowledge reflects a simplified model of reality; "human beings never depict reality in a one-to-one map, but need to economize on scarce cognitive resources by throwing a net of simplified models over a complex reality" (Dopfer and Potts, 2008). These conceptual models have been described as *cognitive schema* (Simon and March, 1975), routines (Nelson and Winter, 1982) or rules (Dopfer and Potts, 2008).

Although these mental models are "bounded" by the limits of the information available to businesses, they are not arbitrary. Instead they derive from the particular field of knowledge in which the business operates (e.g. recording sound or images, printing, digital or analogue communication etc.). Each field develops a legitimate pattern ("paradigm") of "normal problem solving activity" (Dosi, 1982:155). The internal logic ("path dependence") of this trajectory helps businesses identify new products or processes (positive heuristics or rules-of-thumb) as well as those to avoid. Technological trajectories are not simply based on underlying scientific principles but also reflect "conventional wisdom". Evolutionary economics is important because its focus on technology and knowledge helps establish the links between the structural levels of the market, the organisational level of the business and the shop floor or workplace level of production. This is achieved through the concept of an *industry life cycle* (ILC). The rest of this section outlines the phases of the ILC model and illustrates how they can be adapted to be applied to media production.

An ILC begins when new knowledge discovery creates a new conceptual schema or paradigm, a new technological trajectory or a radical variant of an existing technology. These new *technological discontinuities* provide opportunities for entrepreneurs to launch new products or production processes which may then create a new industry (Schumpeter, 1942). At its simplest, the argument is that media industries only exist because of the discovery and development of materials and techniques. The evolution of the media industries began in the nineteenth century when a range of technological discontinuities (especially film and radio) emerged at the same time as some related existing industries (live entertainment, newspapers etc.) were beginning to reach mass markets. These two developments in turn articulated with an advertising industry emerging to promote the growing mass markets for consumer goods.

In contrast to neoclassical economics, evolutionary economics suggests that industries do not reach a stable equilibrium. Instead, the ILC is a continual process through which existing industries are disrupted by new technological discontinuities. This can lead to industry decline, or more commonly to *coevolution*. The next chapters in this book illustrate how existing live entertainment industries were disrupted by, and coevolved with, the film industry. The film industry was then disrupted by, and coevolved with, TV, which had itself already disrupted radio broadcasting and, to an extent, newspapers. Broadcast TV was then disrupted by, and coevolved with, cable, satellite and digital TV. Finally, all these industries were disrupted by and forced to coevolve with the internet and the smartphone.

ILC theory suggests that immediately following a technological discontinuity – when the technology is still in a "fluid" phase – businesses are uncertain about the future direction both of the technology and of consumer demand (see Klepper, 1997). At this stage, the barriers to entry to this emerging industry are low and there is an opportunity for businesses to enter the industry ("new entrants"). This is a phase of *experimenting* with the technology. In response to the new paradigm, a pioneer firm may develop a working prototype (a newspaper, film projector, radio broadcast station or an internet-enabled phone). If there is evidence of some demand for these new products, other businesses (either industry incumbents or other new entrants) may explore the technology and launch a range of alternative designs (for example, when radio broadcasters began developing TV, the Hollywood studios experimented with using broadcasting to distribute films to cinemas). Eventually, a business releases a first commercial design, often targeted at a niche market of high income "early adopters" (an upmarket newspaper, a metropolitan cinema, a broadcast network, an internet-enabled phone for business users). This creates a particularly intense form of market competition because, "product markets are ill-defined, products are unstandardised, processes are uncoordinated and user–supplier interactions shape the pattern of innovation" (Hobday, 1998:699).

In contrast to conventional economics or TCE, the market pressures at this stage are understood to be social and cultural, as much as they are economic. Evolutionary theory suggests both sets of market participants are looking for ways to end this period of extreme uncertainty, to their own advantage. Before consumers can respond to price information, or the differing technical features of alternative designs, they need the knowledge and conceptual framework to understand the purpose of these novel products, and accept their *legitimacy* (the launch of media products, is often accompanied by forms of "moral panic" about their impact on society, children etc.). Businesses need to engage in extensive (and expensive) marketing and communication to help overcome this "experience good" problem. Governments and regulators are often important in resolving this uncertainty. This may be because they have to give their assent before businesses can begin commercial sales of a new product (licensing a new broadcast radio station for example) or to make a decision about a technical standard to be adopted. Or it may be because they have to issue *regulations* to quell public disquiet about an industry. Societal debates and political or regulatory decisions about the legitimacy of media products – whether reflecting concerns about the "effects" of media content on morality and behaviour, particularly of children, or the role of news in the democratic process – have been particularly important in the development of the media industries and the operation of media markets. Regulatory decisions may also influence the adoption of technological standards which may in turn advantage some designs over others. These high-profile decisions about *regulation* may be what ultimately establishes, or undermines, public acceptance and understanding of the legitimacy of a new product or service.

Industry evolution reaches maturity when the initial range of competing product designs gives way to widespread acceptance of a *dominant design*. All companies are incentivised to adopt the dominant design (even if, like VHS, it is technically inferior to competing designs), including the companies whose alternative designs fail to gain acceptance. This is because a dominant design resolves the uncertainty caused by intense competition and permits the broad spread of relevant knowledge through the dispersal of templates – *conventions, codes, rules* etc. (Beckert, 2010). The acceptance of the dominant design causes a move in the industry from variety and diversity towards greater standardisation. This dominant design element of the life cycle approach poses the greatest challenge in adapting evolutionary economics to the analysis of media industries. Thus far, the authors who have applied this approach to the media industries (van Kranenberg and Hogenbirk, 2006, Tschmuck, 2006, Küng, 2008, Funk, 2012) have focused on the technological delivery systems for media (the technology of broadcasting or satellite TV) rather than the core intangible media product which is the basis of consumers' demand for the tangible carrier (such as the radio or TV set).

However, evolutionary economics does present an opportunity to take this theoretical step. For example, Garud et al. (2013:791) note that "an industry that emerges around an innovation develops a distinct identity and incorporates a particular *style* or recipe for operation" (my emphasis). Developing this idea of styles requires greater attention to the role of culture than is currently featured in either neoclassical or evolutionary economics. We have noted that the media industries produce "experience goods" for "attention markets". The core knowledge required, therefore, is not the technological knowledge of recording or distributing text, images or sound but the cultural knowledge of gaining and holding audience atten- tion. As Lanham (2006) notes, this knowledge originated (in written form at least) in ancient Greece with the art of rhetoric. Literary, linguistic and cultural theories describe a range of techniques for gaining and holding audience attention, and for enabling emotional and aesthetic audience experiences. These stylistic techniques are variously referred to as conventions, devices, "discourse strategies" etc. *Rhetorical text type* theories (such as Fludernik, 2000), for example, describe the genres of non-fiction and interpersonal communication, as well as fiction and drama. This allows us to distinguish between the core methods used to gain audience attention in different types of media production. First, we can distinguish between fiction and non-fiction. Non-fiction ("expository") genres include reports (used extensively in news), description and explanation. Fictional genres come under the heading of narrative. Second, we can identify a range of methods of organising information to try to make it coherent for an audience, and so to hold their attention. As Ytreberg (2001:359) notes, some of these "coherence conventions" are relatively simple, linking the information together using a single principle. Information linked using time creates a chronology; using space might create the layout of a page; using a category generates a catalogue or a list. Other methods are more complex. Thus, information can be made coherent when structured as a story (narrative) or as an argument (rhetoric). Feature films and novels combine two systems, structuring the information both as a story and according to a grammar or syntax (whether the structure of a sentence or the "grammar" of film editing).

Narrative text types are common in media production and communicate by showing an audience the cause and effect relationships between people and objects. These can be relationships of similarity (metaphors) or of context (metonyms). Many media narratives (fictional and non-fiction) are metonymic, following the design of "realistic literature"; "such literature represents actions as based on cause and effect and as contiguous in time and space. Whilst metonymy is associated with realism, metaphor is associated with poetry, romanticism and surrealism" (Chandler, 2007:157). As Chapter 3 describes, a central element of the dominant design of the feature film was a system of coherence – the "continuity system" – for showing the relationships between actors as continuous in time and space.

In narratives, cause and effect is largely shown through conflict between charac- ters (heroes and villains). Echoing Lanham's (2006) argument, these techniques of gaining audience attention originated in the design principles of the Greek myths and tragedies and of fairy tales. These conflicts do not simply occur at random, instead the narrative is usually structure as a "focused chain" (such as a quest or a journey) of conflict events (Ytreberg, 2001). And this structure has to be *motivated*, the hero does not simply decide to go on a quest or journey, instead she is faced with a problem and motivated by an inciting incident which necessitates the jour- ney. It is the need to solve the problem which creates conflict with antagonists, leading to a climax of the narrative when the hero and villain are "transformed", and the conflict resolved, leading to a satisfactory end of the story (ibid.).

The different genres of story largely reflect the different ways the conflict is resolved and the different experience the audience is expected to have. Crudely, if the hero wins we may have a drama/action story, if she loses we have a tragedy, and if he falls over or gets married we have a (romantic) comedy. Narrative media designs tend to include more than one story, and in this case these stories are described as "plots" each with its own structure, type of conflict and transformation (Newman, 2006). Usually, one plot is the central story and the others are sub-plots. Thus, an action story may might be combined with a sub-plot where the heroine discovers love (a romance sub-plot), or undergoes a deeper personal transformation (an education sub-plot). The use of sub-plots has been common in series and serial fiction since the nineteenth century. Chapter 4 outlines the use of sub-plots to retain audience attention across a TV series.

Both narrative and non-narrative designs may use a range of techniques – *coherence structures* or "discourse strategies" – to present information and try to achieve the desired effect on the audience. These techniques exist independently of the genre designs. The same coherence convention (such as the shot-reverse-shot filming technique described in Chapter 2) may be used to achieve different effects in drama and in news (Redfern, 2014). A "conversation" in a factual studio show or an online forum would become a piece of "dialogue" in a scripted drama.

The next step, therefore, is to explore how far these cultural theories of style (and associated concepts of conventions, "text types" and "discourse strategies") can be used to develop and enrich the concept of industry styles used in ILC theories. Here, the key link is the ILC concept of a "dominant design". The theory advanced here proposes that, after a period of technological discontinuity and experimentation, the media industries developed a number of dominant designs: the feature film, the studio show, the filmed series, the news report, the entertainment format, and the letsplay video. This does not exhaust the range of content designs across media industries, but these are selected as key designs used within the media industries.

However, we must make clear distinctions between these cultural designs, and the dominant designs developed in the manufacturing industries which were the sources of data for the ILC model. The dominant designs of manufacturing industry – such as the iPhone for example – represent a basis for mass production of identical goods. The dominant designs discussed in this book represent a combination of elements (conventions, coherence structures, discourse strategies etc.) which can be flexibly used to create goods which are both recognisable examples of a text type and also individually differentiated, "experience" goods. The periods of experimentation during which these designs were established drew on preexisting cultural forms (such as live drama) which are of ancient origin. Despite the economies of scale which drive media organisations to maximise occasional "hit" products through global distribution, media products are always, to an extent, culturally specific. More than, for example, the iPhone, a media product produced in one culture will tend, when distributed to audiences in another culture, to incur a "cultural discount", a reduction in the audience attention it can attract or a reduction in willingness to pay for the content (Hoskins and Mirus, 1988).

The ILC approach suggests that designs become "dominant designs" through a social process. This "stabilisation of conventions" and routines occurs via "industry-wide narratives" and an industry-wide discourse, originating and circulating through many different sources – trade media, trade shows and events and company brochures – where market actors enact a collective agenda, an industry-wide technological and conceptual schema (Garud et al., 2013:790). The adoption of these dominant designs (and the associated knowledge templates and conventions) is referred to in the literature as *industry isomorphism* (Beckert, 2010). This knowledge is often institutionalised through the formation of specific professions, occupations, crafts or "fields". These "are born of the concerted efforts of collective actors to fashion a stable consensus regarding rules of conduct and membership criteria that routinize action in pursuit of collective interests" (Fligstein and McAdam, 2012:92). This social process of developing common conventions is close to Neale's concept of genres as a sociological concept; "as systems of orientations, expectations and conventions that circulate between industry, text and subject". (Neale, 1980:19). As Lowrey (2012:226) notes: "the shared understanding about the media's practices, processes, and form spreads, and this increases legitimacy to the point that the media entity becomes naturalized and taken for granted". Sarrina Li and Lee (2010:368) also argue,

> the phenomenon of mimetic isomorphism has been more pervasive in the mass media industry than in other industries . . . media producers frequently adopt strategies or models that have proved successful within the industry in order to make their work more manageable.

ILC theorists also note that, once they adopt this knowledge, industry associations, professions, trade unions, craft associations may use it to their advantage, which can make this conventional wisdom resistant to change (Fligstein and McAdam, 2012).

Media workers have, at certain points in the ILC, developed significant *occupational control* of production either through professionalisation or through the formation of trade/craft unions. Particularly in journalism and public service broadcasting, media occupations have been able to present their professional/craft autonomy as a guarantor of the legitimacy of media content against commercial or political/ideological pressures. Media researchers have subjected this same autonomy, genre conventions, professional values, craft norms and routines to critique, holding them responsible for producing cultural or political homogeneity of media content (Shoemaker and Reece, 1996). Similarly, while the deployment of these routines achieves efficiencies, the same processes can be subjected to critique as the causes of rigidities and resistance to change.

This process of resisting change also operates at the level of the market as those companies which emerge successful in the battle to produce the dominant design begin to develop economies of scale which create barriers to entry. They are also likely to exploit the strategies of vertical integration, described above, to achieve market control. As these companies exercise market control, new businesses face barriers to entry and there is a *shake out* of smaller competitors, which are either forced out of business or acquired, leading to market consolidation (Klepper, 1997). Studies of media markets have highlighted their tendency for market share to be concentrated among a small group of large companies (Murdock, 1982). Despite constant technological disruptions, large organisations like 21st Century Fox, Comcast, Disney, Viacom etc. have used a range of strategies to retain control of significant shares of global media markets (Albarran, 2016). However, dominant designs in media industries exercise a much less strong homogenising force than in manufacturing, for example. The high failure rate and "experience good" nature of media products create the potential for small producers to achieve unexpected "hits". This limits the "shakeout" of small media businesses, creating a tendency for media markets to become segmented between a small group of large businesses (often called *majors*) supplying some versions of the dominant design and a larger number of smaller businesses (*independents*) supplying specialist market niches with alternative versions.

The final stage of the ILC enables us to understand major changes in production. As an industry matures around a dominant design produced by a group of major producers, businesses are able to "learn by doing", solving problems in production of the dominant design and achieve efficiencies through *process innovations*. Rather than a "scientific" process of task decomposition via Taylorist principles; "problem-solving by boundedly rational agents must necessarily proceed by decomposing any large, complex and intractable problem into smaller sub-problems that can be solved independently" (Marengo and Dosi, 2005). The knowledge created through this process may be embodied in routines, but as Feldman and Pentland (2003) note, these are routines not in the sense of fixed programmes or rules (the "routinisation" entailed in Taylorism) but in the sense of patterns of action, sets of practices which form a coherent system. The enactment of these routines, their application to any practical problem, is always open to interpretation and debate.

The achievement of production efficiencies is importantly related to two factors; *task variability* and *task analysability* (Thompson, 1967). Crucially the latter is dependent on the former. If their central task varies too much, businesses are unable to develop detailed analyses of the most efficient ways of completing tasks. ILC suggests that it is only when an industry has accepted a dominant design that task variability reduces. Businesses, especially those with a large market share, are then able to devote resources to process innovation by decomposing this design into the most efficient subtasks. This explanation of changes in production provides an alternative to those which suggest changes in production must reflect the implementation of an historic "mode of production" (such as the sequential assembly line, or a transition to "functional flexibility"). In place of this deterministic explanation (Taylor's idea of "one best way"), ILC suggests businesses do not possess sufficient knowledge to simply rationalise production (because they have "bounded rationality") but face dilemmas in finding the optimum arrangement of production tasks. Rather than Taylor's and Adam Smith's sequential division of tasks, they may arrange tasks in parallel, reciprocally or even independently of one another. These decisions may not simply be influenced by a desire to simplify tasks and so speed up execution of individual tasks. Instead businesses may attempt to minimise the *cycle time*, the time it takes to complete the whole production process. Alternatively, they may attempt to maximise "throughput", the flow of materials through the process. Achieving these efficiencies may involve "balancing" the activities of workers and machines, minimising *set-up* and *idle* times of machines or tasks, reducing waste of resources or decreasing the distances travelled by workers, machines or products (Morroni, 1996).

Rather than assuming a sequential assembly line division of labour will always be imposed, evolutionary theorists suggest specific technologies may impose certain task interdependencies. ILC thus provides an alternative to the TCE explanation of decisions either to vertically integrate or to disintegrate stages of production (or production and distribution). While TCE explains these decisions in terms of attempts to reduce uncertainty and risk, ILC suggests these decisions may reflect the technical characteristics of producing the dominant design at different stages of the life cycle; "most technologies and industries are born with a highly vertically integrated structure, undergo a process of disintegration as the industry grows in the expansion phase and then re-integrate in the maturity phase" (Marengo and Dosi, 2005:305).

ILC suggests that the adoption of a dominant design and the exercise of market control enables businesses and workers to engage in task decomposition and so produce detailed knowledge, including how to achieve efficiencies in producing this design. This attempt to achieve process efficiencies follows the logic of specialisation and division of labour outlined by Adam Smith, in minimising the need for workers to make "ad hoc" decisions individually or in communication with colleagues, so they can maximise the time they spend on a specialist task or tasks. However, the outcomes may be very different from Frederick Taylor's prescription for work organisation or Ford's assembly line. This approach suggests that the extent of division of labour or rationalisation of the production process is limited both by the degree of task variability and by the nature of task interdependencies. These in turn relate to the degree of flexibility within the dominant design and the nature (or "affordances") of the specific materials and technologies used in an industry.

Evolutionary theory suggests there is then a further social process by which knowledge may be codified into general rules or routines, specified as formal instructions (listing the steps or rules production workers should follow in executing tasks), embedded in the design of specialised production software or hardware, or embodied in the physical layout and structure of the workplace or factory (mechanisation or automation). Again, the greater the degree of task variability, the less this knowledge can be codified and specified in this way and the more the knowledge will remain tacit, and the technologies and workspaces flexible and open to change.

However, we have already noted that, as cultural artefacts, media text types do not function – economically or technically – in the same way as manufactured products. In particular, since media products are individually differentiated, their dominant designs constitute a much more limited degree of product standardisation than in manufactured goods. Thus, media production must have a high degree of task variability compared to other industries. Since no tasks are exactly repeated – no journalist or screenwriter rewrites exactly the same story, no TV or film actor speaks exactly the same lines, no camera operator shoots the same scene – it is not possible to decompose these tasks into simple, predictable subtasks which can be summarised in standard operating procedures or embedded into machine programming. However, different media products have different levels of individual differentiation and so different degrees of task variability. Where a Hollywood feature film might represent the highest degree of task variability, TV series and formats may involve less variability, and 24-hour news services (on TV or online) least variability.

For some researchers (and some practitioners) this degree of task variability makes media production a craft rather than an industrial process (see Banks, 2010, Hirsch, 1972). However, media businesses achieve efficiencies through "economies of repetition" where production knowledge relevant to one production, remains relevant, even if differently applied, to the next production. And, as Perrow (1967) makes clear, the characteristic of craft production is that while the task is variable, production knowledge is analysable. Task analysability is not simply a reflection of variability, but also relates to the type of knowledge and technology used in production. When task analysability is limited, formal task decomposition may be less efficient than giving workers discretion to analyse tasks on an "ad hoc" basis. ILC theory suggests all businesses develop routines and cognitive schema, which may not be explicit in formal rules, and may be sufficiently flexible to allow for task variation, but which enable efficient problem-solving: "the term 'routine' connotes, deliberately, behavior that is conducted without much thinking about it, as like habits or customs . . . routines can be understood as the behaviors deemed appropriate and effective in the settings in which they are invoked" (Nelson, 1995:68). Together these routines form a "grammar" – a set of practices, processes and behaviours.

The high failure rate of media products demonstrates that following examples of previous successes does not ensure the commercial performance of new features. This indicates that analysability of media production tasks is very limited. This partly relates to variables in the product market (including the "experience good" nature of media products), but also reflects the nature of genre and discourse strategies as sources of knowledge to guide production. There are very few formal rules (excepting legal and regulatory constraints) about how to produce media content. Instead there are routines (cognitive schemas, beliefs, principles, heuristics); "patterned, routinized, repeated practices and forms that media workers use to do their jobs" (Shoemaker and Reese, 1996:105). As sociological "production studies" have demonstrated, the presence of these types of routines is common across media sectors (Tuchman, 1973, Gitlin, 1983).

Media products are able to combine both individual differentiation and routine problem-solving work patterns, because the dominant media designs (features, studio shows etc.) constitute very "open" architectures rather than detailed blueprints.

Knowledge of the broad outlines of the dominant design, or the relevant genre conventions and discourse strategies, provides only a very basic guide to producing desired effects for an audience (comedy, tragedy, news etc.) for each new production. To this extent, it is true that "nobody knows". But what this means in practice is that a media product design is never completed, even at the stage of a detailed continuity script for a feature. Instead, the design continues to be developed throughout the production process. Media producers are continually applying their knowledge of genre and discourse strategies (and relevant technical knowledge of recording/editing etc.) to interpret and develop the original design, through the production of subgenres; treatments, script drafts, page layouts, storyboards, rough edits etc.

Media product design is thus a collective process of trial-and-error where production workers show colleagues early drafts, rehearsals and other pilot versions of the final product. While this process of interpretation gives workers some autonomy to make design decisions at their stage of production, it also creates reciprocal interdependencies between tasks, as workers at one stage of production have to check the impact of their decisions on work done at earlier stages, and vice versa.

Thompson (1967) argues that in processes involving "reciprocal interdependence", workers have to coordinate task completion between themselves, using informal communication ("mutual adjustment"). This takes place through explicit *discourse* (Saferstein, 1992) but also through a normative division of labour. Each of the dominant designs of media production has become associated with an informal role structure, a set of production roles (sound recordist, reporter, graphics, producer etc.) which can be adapted to changing needs. Bechky (2006) showed how informal coordination and verbal and non-verbal communication, relying on these shared normative rules, values, identities and behaviours, enabled workers to know, more or less exactly, what to expect of each other.

This chapter has suggested that evolutionary economics, and in particular the ILC model of production, adapted to the specific characteristics of media products, may provide a means of relating levels of analysis to explain changes in production which is superior to the other models reviewed. In particular, the chapter has argued that this model, rooted in theories of economics and innovation, provides an explanation of why these designs emerged, why they have survived a range of disruptive technological discontinuities, and how their production processes have changed. The following chapters test the ability of the theory to provide satisfactory explanations of the emergence of the selected media products.

2

PRODUCING FEATURE FILMS

Technological discontinuity

In the late nineteenth century, the development of technologies for film – using photographic images in rapid sequence to give the illusion of continuous "moving pictures" – encouraged entrepreneurs to experiment with commercialisation. The inventors and first manufacturers of film cameras and projectors, companies such as Edison and Biograph, saw film content not as the major product in itself, but as the means to sell equipment for production and viewing (like the broadcast pioneers, see Chapter 3). The Lumières' Cinématographe, for example, like home video cameras and cameras in phones later, was aimed at amateur film-makers; "in the evening, you can show the developed pictures moving as in real life" (cited in Albera, 2012:123). Beginning in 1889 Edison began to use its Kinetograph camera to produce short (30-second) films which paying customers could watch, as individuals using Kinetoscope "Peep Show" slot machines in amusement arcades. Finally, the Lumières and others established public projection, showing films to an audience in theatres, as the dominant consumption model of the film industry.

Around 1906, film producers introduced electric lighting to replace shooting with natural light (which was affected by weather, the seasons etc.) (Balshofer and Miller, 1967). This enabled the refined control of light, in studio filming. The emergence of sound recording, in the 1920s (see Chapter 3), brought further experimentation, the conversion of studios to "soundstages" and sound filming on location. In the 1950s–60s, technological changes, particularly to cameras, made location shooting much less expensive, reducing the requirement for studio filming, dramatically lowering the costs of feature production. This lowered the barriers to entry to film production enabling "independent" producers to enter the market

Dominant design

This section describes three stages in the evolution of the dominant design – the one-reeler, the feature film and the blockbuster. The evolution of the feature film involved changes along four dimensions; the length of the film (changing from 30 seconds to feature length), its text type (drama replacing other genres), visual techniques (shot sizes and lengths) and additional effects (from the addition of sound to CGI).

In the earliest films, drawing on the text types of variety theatre, Edison had recorded the acts of acrobats, dancers, even Buffalo Bill's Wild West show. Much like individual online viewing today, there were comedy films of animals (*Professor Wilton's Boxing Cats*) and male-oriented "adult" content – women performing burlesque routines e.g. *Birth of a Pearl* (1901) and *From Showgirl to Burlesque Queen* (1903) (Jacobson, 2011). The move to public projection brought film into direct competition with live entertainment, and in response, vaudeville theatres began to include films in their variety bills. The approach adopted bore many similarities to early TV (see Chapter 3). Film was used to record "star" acts (comedy, dance, sports) "as live" in a continuous process and as single shots. Then several short films would be put together to form around 20 minutes of a variety theatre programme, lasting a few hours, which might also include a "presenter", a cinema showman, who would directly address the audience (Gunning, 1994).

The development of the narrative structure for film also began during this period. Film was used to record the short dramas (playlets, melodramas, historical vignettes, pantomimes) performed in variety theatres, to enable them to be shown in other theatres. These films naturally followed the theatrical conventions used in the playlet. The front of the stage (or proscenium) acted as the "fourth wall" of a room, so actors would not directly address the audience (Figure 2.1). To ensure all audience members had an unobstructed view, the important narrative action was "framed" within this proscenium. The action was filmed "as live" in a continuous process, in a single shot.

To reproduce the live theatrical experience on film, film-makers directed action to occur within this visual frame – the "proscenium shot" – from a single stationary camera. This established a central position for the camera and an invisible "line" of action (the proscenium line) in front of it. "The foot of the camera was connected with the edges of the set with cords or wooden laths, establishing parameters that were the equivalent of proscenium boundaries on a stage" (Tibbetts, 1985:13). Film actors followed theatrical conventions, largely restricting their movement to the centre line and entering either from the wings or from traps in the floor (ibid.). Since the camera could not move, and these films were limited to a single shot, the only need to edit the film was to join complete scenes together.

As film companies began to produce dramas specifically for theatres and nickelodeons, these filming conventions were transferred from the theatre to film studios (see Process innovation, this volume, p. 54) using natural light. The results compared poorly with the experience audiences were used to from

The Proscenium Arch Theatre

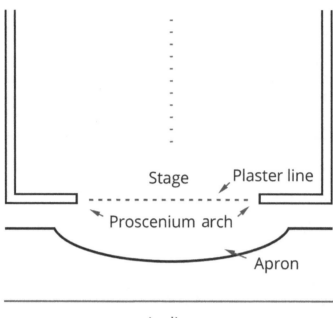

FIGURE 2.1 Diagram: proscenium theatre layout

Credit: Maggie Evans.

gas-lit live theatres, leading film-makers to prefer to set scenes on location. Directors, like D. W. Griffith, transferred filming discipline from stage and studio to locations. The camera "was not only never to be moved, but . . . was sometimes even anchored to the floor with strong lash-line secured by a stage screw" (Griffith's cameraman Karl Brown cited in Tibbetts, 1985:16). However, without the constraints of the proscenium, stage actors "were constantly moving outside camera range to deliver their most telling effects" (ibid.). Griffith's solution was to:

> "put down the lines", white cord stretched between pegs, creating a "proscenium" frame showing actors and crew the height and width dimensions of the shot. Actors would then walk carelessly down toward the camera, secure in the knowledge that as long as they stayed inside that white cord, their feet would not be cut off . . . They could move . . . freely so long as they stayed within the lines.
>
> *Ibid.*

FIGURE 2.2 Establisher shot from *Pirates of the Caribbean*

Credit: Pirates of the Caribbean: The Curse of the Black Pearl, Walt Disney Pictures, 2003.

This technique for filming proscenium shots on location created the first "establishing shots", still a core element of the feature film. Figure 2.2 shows how, in an establisher, from *Pirates of The Caribbean: The Curse of The Black Pearl*, a single wide shot can "cover" all the main action in a scene. Actors and objects can move within frame.

Chapter 1 argued that industries evolve through a period of experimentation, followed by more general adoption of the dominant design ("mimetic isomorphism"). As Smith (2012:7) makes clear, the dominant design of the feature film followed just such a process, emerging "through trial-and-error, self-experimentation by filmmakers, experimentation on audiences with box office as the dependent measure, and the rapid transmission between filmmakers and across countries and the globe".

Chapter 1 also suggested that dominant designs in media represented the combination of existing "text types" to produce new ones. The crucial first experiment, which effectively turned film into a new text type (different from recording of live theatre), was the decision to move the camera. This enabled film-makers to use a variety of shots to show the audience aspects of dramatic action from a range of perspectives and angles, and to show them details by radically altering the size of their viewing frame. Film could now take audiences beyond the experience they could gain from theatre's central (proscenium) position. In abandoning the coherence structure of drama, film lacked its own rules for establishing coherence for the audience. This is because, at this point in their evolution, although film cameras could move, they could not move *while recording*, and so films could not include "developing" shots, which would show audiences how the camera movement changed relationships between people and objects. Instead, linking together two shots from different places would break the unities of space and time which had governed drama since Aristotle's *Poetics* (Bordwell et al., 1985). Edwin Porter who directed the first successful multishot movie, *The Great Train Robbery* (1903), feared that these discontinuities would make the film incoherent to the viewer – giving audiences "a dizzying experience" (Musser, 1994). Rather than better attracting their attention, Porter feared audiences would become so aware of shot changes, their attention would focus on this aspect and disengage from the story. Thus, *Robbery* was (by modern standards) extremely conservative in its use of shot changes. It was largely filmed in a series of wide shots (but contained 13 others, including a pan and tilt) most of which lasted the duration of the scene, so the change of scene disguised the change of shot (op. cit.). However, famously, it included a dramatic medium close-up shot – the robber shooting directly at the camera. The commercial success of *Robbery* demonstrated the advantages multishot films could have over live theatre and single shot films in gaining audience attention. From this point on, for example, close-ups were increasingly used to enable audiences to correctly identify characters – a key dramatic problem with single shot films (op. cit.). Figure 2.7 illustrates a common use of a close-up.

Film-makers wanting to use shot changes more extensively than Porter began looking to develop systems of coherence to resolve the problem of the space and time discontinuities created by camera movement. In doing so, they drew on techniques used in another text type, the magic lantern shows. Similar to traditional magic shows, the lantern shows focused on creating optical "tricks" and illusions. Using slide projectors, they developed techniques for using the eye's persistence of vision effect to help disguise a transition between two different images and perspectives. Using two or three lanterns allowed one slide to be superimposed over another, disguising the discontinuity between the two images (a transition which would later become the "dissolve" in film). A change of perspective could also be disguised by pulling a long slide slowly through the lantern (a technique which would develop into the panning shot). Discontinuous transitions between scenes and characters could be softened and signalled by using shutters and blinds to brighten or dim lights (which became the fade up or down to black). Some early directors, like George Albert Smith and George Melies, who had worked on magic lantern shows before entering the film industry, began to apply these coherence structures to retain audience attention through discontinuities between shots. While most film-makers had, like Porter, reserved editing for transitions between scenes, Smith was one of the first film-makers to edit *within a scene*, to transition between the standard proscenium wide shot and some closer shots (including early point-of-view shots) (Bordwell et al., 1985). Melies developed the use of split-screens and (in particular) straight "cuts". As audiences became familiar with the conventions of shot changes, this simple straight "cut" technique would begin to replace transitions like the dissolve and the wipe.

Melies was famous for introducing magic lantern "optical tricks" like superimposition and stop-frame animation, to make people and objects appear, disappear or change shape. The adoption of these "special effects" techniques further influenced the change of film production from filming a scene "as live", continuously in a single

FIGURE 2.3   Special effects shot: Captain Jack Sparrow

Credit: Pirates of the Caribbean: The Curse of the Black Pearl, Walt Disney Pictures, 2003.

shot, to filming scenes in a range of individual shots, in discontinuous, stop-start process. By stopping the recording for an actor to leave the scene, for example, special effects could be invisible – an object or actor could disappear, or their appearance (costume or make-up) change dramatically. Figure 2.3 shows how CGI has enhanced these special effects, combining the filmed shot of the eyes of the actor (Johnny Depp as Captain Jack Sparrow) with the computer-animated footage of the skeleton.

Film-makers like D. W. Griffith and his contemporaries began to develop the conventions for coherence in multishot films. They discovered that audiences interpreted very minor movements of the camera, not as a deliberate change in perspective, but as an accidental discontinuity, an unintended break in the continuous representation of a character or object (a "jump cut"). This led to establishing the convention of the "30° rule", which held that, for audiences to understand that a transition between two different shots of the same character was a deliberate change of perspective, the camera must move at least 30° from its original position.

A second coherence principle emerged from the theatrical convention of arranging action along the "proscenium line" across the stage. Because audiences already understood this convention, directors would place actors and objects along this line to establish their locations (for the audience) at the beginning of a scene (hence the term "establishing" shot). In the establisher, then, the proscenium line is at right angles to the audience. Directors found that moving the camera beyond this invisible line – to the equivalent of the upstage area (see Figure 2.1) – had a surprising effect. Rather than breaking the audience's illusion of a "fourth wall", and losing the "suspension of disbelief" which was essential to their attention, audiences assumed that their own perspective (the camera) had remained stationary, and the characters had swapped sides of the invisible line. Similar shot changes of moving characters or (on location) vehicles would be understood as sudden moves in the opposite direction. This discovery resulted in a convention governing the upper limit of camera movement, the so-called 180° rule. In this coherence convention, the camera can move, but it is bounded by the theatrical convention of the "proscenium line". As long as the camera does not "cross the line", audiences are not confused about the locations or movements of people or objects.

A third convention showed a further departure from live theatre. In theatre, an actor or object leaving the stage in one direction would re-enter from the same side. Implementing this convention in films with shot changes again caused confusion, this time about direction. If an actor or vehicle left the frame moving to the right of the screen, and then re-entered from the same side, the audience would understand this as a reversal in direction. The coherence convention of screen direction, therefore, held that an actor or vehicle exiting a shot to the right would enter the following shot from the left, to ensure audiences understood they were continuing to move left to right along the proscenium 180° line.

However, experiments in developing coherence conventions did not simply focus on coherence in space and time. They also explored methods of achieving narrative coherence, using film as a text type – as a means for telling dramatic stories. Bordwell et al. (1985) show that film-makers drew on narrative conventions from three popular contemporary text types; the short story, the novel and the "well-made play". However, the essential coherence principle for all three:

> boiled down to a similar notion. The artwork was to be organised around a single central factor—an intended impression, a theme. No unrelated elements were admissible, and the elements that were present should be motivated . . . directing spectator attention away from the actual system of narration and towards the story itself . . . encouraging viewers to believe they are seeing everything in a direct, unmediated way.
>
> *Bordwell et al., 1985:158*

In the terms of Chapter 1, Griffith, in particular, began to use this key technique for narrative coherence, to guide the process of decomposing the task of presenting the story action in a scene. This involved decomposition of the proscenium shot, into a *sequence* of smaller shots. According to this convention, each new piece of visual information (each new shot) should be *motivated* (made "legitimate") by the need to give the audience new story information. The resulting conventions of filming sequences would become the central means of organising coherence in feature films; "it was through this alternation of long shot and close up that . . . cinema was to attain maximum effect" (Burch, 1979:88).

Thus, the conventions for entering and exiting shot, primarily developed to inform the audience about the direction of movement of characters, developed into general principles for narratively motivating shot changes by "*matching*" (or accurately repeating) visual information across several shots. "Matching on action" involved ensuring that actions and movements of characters and objects in the proscenium "establishing" shot were accurately repeated in the recording of smaller shots. This helped establish coherence for the audience who now understood the narrative *reason* for the discontinuity, the change of shot, as their need to "follow" the continuing action of the character. Thus, an actor might leave screen, motivating a transition to a shot revealing why and where they were moving (a "match on exit"). In close-up shots, which included no information about the location of other characters, directors would use an "eyeline" match, ensuring that the direction an actor was looking was closely matched by another actor looking in the opposite direction in the next close-up. In Figures 2.4 and 2.5, covering a piece of dialogue, the eyeline of Geoffrey Rush's character, Barbossa, looks screen right to motivate the cut to Sparrow whose eyeline looking screen left "matches" Barbossa's.

The key component part of the feature film, therefore, is the sequence, typically constructed around a series of shot changes (Gunning, 1994). The coherence of the sequence is narratively motivated, with the shots moving progressively closer to the centre of the action. The sequence thus follows a classic narrative structure with a climax, where the most important story information – action and dialogue – is covered in close shots. This structure is illustrated in the sequence of shots from *Pirates*, beginning with the original theatrical proscenium – "wide", "establishing" or "master" – shot (Figure 2.6). This shot also illustrates how the use of conflict, as a cause and effect mechanism (see Chapter 1) is used to motivate the structure of the film sequence. It further illustrates the role of the quest or journey for the same purpose. The shot includes the most important location and story information about Sparrow's antagonists (Barbossa and his pirates) and the nature of their conflict and his quest; Barbossa must kill Will Turner (Orlando Bloom) to lift the curse, while

FIGURE 2.4 Eyeline shot: Captain Barbossa

Credit: Pirates of the Caribbean: The Curse of the Black Pearl, Walt Disney Pictures, 2003.

FIGURE 2.5 "Matching" eyeline shot: Captain Jack Sparrow

Credit: Pirates of the Caribbean: The Curse of the Black Pearl, Walt Disney Pictures, 2003.

Sparrow must free Turner and take some of the gold to be able to reclaim his ship, *The Black Pearl*.

This sequence also uses another Griffith coherence mechanism, "parallel editing". The sequence cuts away from Barbossa and Turner in the cave, to a shot outside, where Sparrow is with Norrington (Jack Davenport) and his redcoats in a small landing boat discussing Sparrow's plan to free Turner. This allows the director Gore Verbinski to build up the drama of the sequence by "cross cutting" between

FIGURE 2.6 Wide shot: antagonists and Will Turner

Credit: Pirates of the Caribbean: The Curse of the Black Pearl, Walt Disney Pictures, 2003.

the parallel story action on Norrington's ships (imprisoning Kiera Knightley's character, Elizabeth Swann, and preparing the ambush for Barbossa) and the threat to Turner inside the cave. Once this causal relationship is established, a transition shot, from behind Sparrow, as his rowing boat enters the cave, shows the spatial relationships between Barbossa's pirates and Norrington's soldiers.

The advent of sound enabled film-makers to use on and off-screen sounds, such as sound effects and music, and verbal cues in dialogue, as additional technical and narrative motivations for shot changes (because sounds attract our attention). Thus, the next shot (Figure 2.7) a medium close-up, follows the narrative coherence method of progressing the story by moving from wider to increasingly closer shots, closing in on the main characters, enabling them to communicate their dramatic dialogue and interaction. A sound, Sparrow's line of dialogue, rises above the sound of the pirates' chanting, interrupting Barbossa's ritual murder of Turner and motivating the medium shot of him discovering Sparrow's presence in the cave. These two shots set up a new 180° "proscenium" line, this time between protagonist and antagonist.

The arrival of the talkies saw the refinement of the sequence with the addition of a coherence mechanism, pioneered by Griffith, known as the "shot-reverse-shot" or "reverse angle" technique. As with the match on action, shot changes were motivated by the need to "follow" story action – in this case the "turn taking" in dialogue, with the camera cutting to show, in close-up, which character is speaking and to whom. In Figure 2.8, a close-up of Sparrow sets up the central interaction (action and/or dialogue) to come, between the two central characters. Sparrow's line of dialogue, revealing the plan for the ambush, establishes that he intends to trick Barbossa into giving up Turner by appearing to double-cross Norrington.

FIGURE 2.7   Medium close-up: Barbossa

Credit: Pirates of the Caribbean: The Curse of the Black Pearl, Walt Disney Pictures, 2003.

FIGURE 2.8 Close-up: Captain Jack Sparrow

Credit: Pirates of the Caribbean: The Curse of the Black Pearl, Walt Disney Pictures, 2003.

This allows further narrative complication, with a cut back to the parallel action of Norrington, outside the cave, revealing to his soldiers that he intends to double-cross Sparrow!

As Sparrow moves towards Barbossa, the shot-reverse-shot technique is used to cover this dialogue and story information in close-up (a single). In Figure 2.9, the

FIGURE 2.9 Close-up: Captain Barbossa

Credit: Pirates of the Caribbean: The Curse of the Black Pearl, Walt Disney Pictures, 2003.

shot of Barbossa threatening to continue with the murder of Turner, is taken from a camera which remains, as with the previous shot, the same side of the 180° line between the two characters.

As sequences became longer and more complicated, conventions about the narrative motivation of shot changes were moderated by the need to reinforce spatial coherence. Sequences might return to the wide shot, delivering information which might be narratively "redundant", but may be necessary, if significant movement had taken place, to show the audience the new locations of people and objects in the layout of the scene. As feature films began to include expensive sets and special effects, particularly in the era of the blockbuster, directors sought ways to extend important dramatic sequences. In the "shot-reverse-shot" structure, retaining the 180° and 30° conventions clearly limited the number of camera angles available to film action. To extend sequences, increasingly, directors wanted to use the full 360° of camera movement. To do this, whilst maintaining coherence, required the construction of a literal "fourth wall" on set, in the space where the original camera set-up had been. The beginning of the sequence would be filmed as shot-reverse-shot, along the 180° axis, but would include an action or line of dialogue to motivate a shot change, to a position across this line. The camera would then be moved across the line (upstage on Figure 2.1, the proscenium theatre diagram) and the area where the camera and crew had been would be dressed to create a setting for this part of the sequence.

In the close-up shot (Figure 2.10), Barbossa (Geoffrey Rush) is now framed towards the centre of the screen. The shot is used to motivate the camera movement

FIGURE 2.10 "Crossing the line" shot: Captain Barbossa

Credit: Pirates of the Caribbean: The Curse of the Black Pearl, Walt Disney Pictures, 2003.

across the 180° line. Thus, his action is a "look" to his left (screen right) and his line of dialogue ("I suppose in exchange you're wanting me not to kill the whelp?") motivates a shot of Turner. This is followed by the camera move, across the line, to film a new section of the sequence. By "crossing the line" in this way Verbinski is able to extend this dramatic sequence by beginning another shot-reverse-shot sequence, from the opposite side of the 180° line. This follows the conventional sequence structure, beginning with a "re-establishing" shot, showing the lay out of the characters on a new proscenium line at 90° to the audience. Although narratively redundant, this information is necessary to establish how the positions of the characters have changed (relative to the audience) from their earlier close-up shots (Figures 2.7 and 2.8). In Figure 2.11, Sparrow has moved to the left of the screen, in contrast to the previous establisher, Figure 2.2, showing him on the right. Barbossa remains in the centre of the screen where he was framed in his previous shot, while Turner (and his pirate captor) now occupies the right of screen.

The next shot (Figure 2.12), a closer shot of Sparrow, follows the conventional structure of the shot-reverse-shot sequence. However, Verbinski uses a further coherence technique, the over-the-shoulder shot, to reinforce the audience's comprehension of these new positions. The shot does this by including narratively "redundant" information – the side of Barbossa's head and shoulder. Although Barbossa's shoulder is in the foreground of the shot, it is defocused, to motivate the audience to expect Sparrow's line of dialogue to be the next important piece of story information.

FIGURE 2.11 Re-establishing shot

Credit: Pirates of the Caribbean: The Curse of the Black Pearl, Walt Disney Pictures, 2003.

FIGURE 2.12 Over-the-shoulder shot: Captain Jack Sparrow

Credit: Pirates of the Caribbean: The Curse of the Black Pearl, Walt Disney Pictures, 2003.

Legitimacy and regulation

Chapter 1 suggested that the adoption of dominant designs occurs partly through a social process of imitation ("isomorphism"). This is not to say that Hollywood's dominant design has not been subject to continual critique of its legitimacy. In the 1960s, film-makers of the New Wave began to critique the methods of "covering" action described above; for their "formulaic" nature and their high level of narrative redundancy (Geuens, 2000). These critics proposed alternative methods of covering action, which they argued were more creative (and even politically radical) – such as "decoupage" and "the long take" (Ulrich, 2016). However, as Chapter 1 noted, the widespread adoption of a dominant design builds in both economic and cultural reasons for resisting such alternatives. Partly, this relates to the "network effects" generated by widespread audience acceptance of these conventions as legitimate coherence techniques.

As noted above, the film industry went through two industry life cycles. Both were disrupted by legitimacy problems and subsequent regulatory action to undermine the market control techniques of the incumbent oligopolists. The nickelodeon industry encountered "legitimacy" problems which came to the attention of regulators. Newspaper reports of fires and injuries brought criticism of their health and safety records, while others worried about the effect of films dealing with crime or adultery on the moral well-being of their patrons. Some local authorities managed to force the nickelodeons to close on Sundays and prohibited admission of unaccompanied children. The oligopoly controlling the industry, the Motion Picture Patents Company (MPPC), responded by supporting reforms which by 1913 led to a New York City ordinance setting standards for nickelodeons (Mezias and Boyle, 2002).

Partly to boost the legitimacy of the industry, film-makers moved from filming variety acts to filming vaudeville playlets – successful plays, novels, popular stories and historical incidents, edited or excerpted into highlights to fit the standard (15–20-minute) length of the vaudeville turn. Vaudeville entrepreneurs, particularly in New York, sought to compete by hiring stars from "legitimate" theatre in dramas like Edwin Porter's *The Night before Christmas* (1905).

The nickelodeon's dominant design, the one-reeler, faced competition from a new, popular product which had legitimacy with middle-class audiences and regulators. The "feature" film (the name came from the vaudeville term for the main attraction) borrowed from the extravagantly staged epics of contemporary legitimate theatre. Alongside the new product, feature producers sought to attract urban middle-class audiences through the transformation of the morally questionable nickelodeon venues into something closer to "legitimate" theatres. America's largest cities gained the first "movie palaces", with up to 3,000 seats, orchestras and ornate architecture (Pearson, 1996).

The final blow to the nickelodeon industry was the attack, from competitors and regulators, on the legitimacy of the practices of the short film producers' cartel the MPPC. In 1912, the US Justice Department began an anti-trust action against the MPPC's use of its patents and, following conviction for restraint of trade, the cartel was wound up (Mezias and Boyle, 2002).

The oligopoly of the MPPC was replaced by the oligopoly of the feature producers of the Motion Picture Producers and Distributors of America (MPPDA). These companies achieved stability and dominance of the market through the "studio system" based on vertical integration. However, the studios relied on control of a large and expanding market to cover the high fixed costs of feature production and the large debts they had taken on to build their cinema chains. The Depression sent a "shock" through this system. Between 1930 and 1932, weekly cinema attendances fell from 80 million to 55 million, studio revenues from $730 million to $480 million, and the studios' $52 million profit turned into a $55 million loss (Bakker, 2005). The 1933 National Industrial Recovery Act (NIRA) saved major US industries by legitimising a range of oligopolistic industrial practices and, through the National Labor Relations Board, protected employment by authorising widespread trade union representation. Thus, the studios were allowed to engage in anti-competitive practices (such as block booking and blind bidding) for which the MPPC had been attacked (Bakker, 2012a). Similarly, regulation led to union control of stable, salaried production jobs for off-screen workers.

Once the Depression had passed, however, regulators began to question the protection of the studios. The "studio system" then experienced the same legitimation crisis as had the MPPC three decades earlier. Oligopolistic control was now declared illegitimate – anti-competitive for consumers and a barrier to entry by the new independent producers and distributors. The *U.S. v. Paramount Pictures* 334 U.S. 131 (1948) judgement broke up the vertically integrated "big five" studios, forcing them to sell their cinema chains (Storper, 1989).

An unrelated regulatory change incentivised the entry of independent producers to the market in the 1950s. Increases in taxes on salaries, but not on profits, made it much more tax efficient for star actors and directors to form companies and sell their services on the open market. Similarly, regulation made market entry to this business easier for talent agencies than for production companies. As noted below, FS accounts have emphasised the distinction between permanent "in-house" employment of actors, in the studio era, and outsourcing and "flexible" employment afterwards. However, Kemper (2010) shows talent agencies were an active part of the most vertically integrated period of the studio system. Just as agents were complaining that the studios used their oligopsonistic control of the labour market to impose unfair contracts on actors and other talent, so those same agencies reached agreements with Hollywood guilds and academies (especially the Screen Actors Guild) on legitimate codes of practice and the licensing of agents. However, while talent "agents" were prevented from also acting as producers, the role of talent managers was less defined. Screen Actors Guild regulations prevented the studios from entering the talent agency industry, but talent managers could enter film production (the impact on these changes in US TV is outlined in Chapter 3).

Market control

This section first outlines how the early film industry coevolved with live entertainment. It then describes how changes in the market structure interacted with the periods of design experimentation and regulatory changes detailed above, enabling the feature to become the dominant design. Chapter 1 noted how the process of recording performances on storage media (film, tape and digital file) created by technological discontinuities disrupted the live entertainment industry by enabling the creation of products (films, TV shows etc.) which could substitute for live entertainment. The chapter noted that where live entertainment needed the same high cost inputs for every output produced, film required these inputs only for the "first copy". Both industries thus tended to follow a "hit model" approach – a successful product could more than recoup production costs through mass sales. But the ability to record a performance gave film economies of scale which were not available to live entertainment. Because production and consumption could be separated, film could be used to transmit hit performances to new national and international audiences. This gave film product characteristics which also aided mass distribution: where live entertainment is rival (the number of consumers is limited by the size of the theatre), films are non-rival and so a single performance or production could be consumed by an almost infinite number of consumers. As Bakker (2012b:1036) noted, "In 1905 the eight-year-old Charlie Chaplin performed in three large music halls an evening . . . in 1915, each night he could be seen in thousands of halls across the world".

While this gave the film industry a competitive advantage over live entertainment, there was no inevitability the feature would be adopted as the dominant design. Edison's success with the peep show design and Kinetoscope parlours meant he initially ruled out film projection. However, the Lumières' 1895 use of a mass public projection system to show a 30-minute programme of short films to a paying audience demonstrated the demand to watch films in public theatres. By 1897 films were considered a form of public, rather than private or domestic, entertainment. In 1918 Edison ended production for the "peep show" market (Pearson, 1996).

Porter's *Great Train Robbery* (1903) established the mass US market for one-reel drama films, attracting two million people a day (Gunning, 1994). This encouraged entry by entrepreneurs to establish the first permanent cinemas – the nickelodeons (named after their five cent ticket price). The continuing popularity of one-reel films initiated a "nickelodeon boom", the numbers growing from 3,000 to 10,000 between 1908 and 1910, attracting 26 million customers a week (Merritt, 2002). However, the legitimacy issues described above limited the market mainly to working-class audiences, keeping entry prices low. Further, the nickelodeons themselves were small (most had fewer than 200 seats to avoid having to pay for a theatre licence) limiting the potential revenue from each screening. To maximise profits, the owners needed to "turnover" the paying audience rapidly, with most programming 12–18 performances a day, seven days a week (Bakker, 2012a). This, in turn, meant nickelodeon owners preferred to rent rather than buy films from producers. The one-reel drama became established as the dominant design because it suited the audience sizes, programmes (and projectors) of the nickelodeons' "programme-based" pattern of exhibition (retailing); "short films (one reel in length) were the industry standard between the industry's founding in 1896 and 1912" (Boyle, 2003:808).

In 1908 Edison, Biograph and Eastman Kodak established the MPPC to use their ownership of patents to control the market (and thus prices) of the 35mm film, cameras and projectors they produced. Nine other companies agreed exclusive licences and joined the cartel. The cartel then moved to control film distribution, ending its practice of selling licences to "exchanges" and establishing its own distributor (the General Film Company or GFC) with the monopoly in renting MPPC films to nickelodeons. This forced most of the 150 existing film exchanges to sell their businesses to the GFC (Mezias and Boyle, 2002). The GFC was then able to use its "supplier power" to force the nickelodeons to accept "block booking" – hiring only MPPC films, in volume, at MPPC prices. Although anti-competitive, as Fell (1983) notes, this strategy was common in contemporary industries (including legitimate theatre). Quinn (2001:41) observes, "these practices were considered dramatic improvements over the haphazard distribution and exhibition practices of the previous decade".

However, a weakness in the MPPC model was that it failed to capitalise on a fundamental economic advantage of recorded media. Chapter 1 noted that there are incentives for media producers to invest in high quality productions, because if they create a "hit" the marginal costs of mass distribution of this first copy are very low. But, because the MPPC rented its films to nickelodeons for a fixed ("per reel") fee, they had little incentive to produce higher quality films since, if the film was a hit, the nickelodeon owners benefited. Once they had covered their rental fee, the nickelodeons received all the additional ticket sales income generated by a hit film.

This weakness was exposed, and the MPPC's market control undermined, when new entrants to the US market introduced the multi-reel "feature" film. Italian companies produced features which provided a full evening's entertainment; *Quo Vadis?* (1913) lasted more than two hours, employed star stage actors and introduced the techniques of camera movement and lighting described above. Features were immediately successful. While an MPPC short might run in a nickelodeon for two days before sales declined, *Dante's Inferno* (1911) ran for two weeks (Bakker, 2005). This demonstrated that existing film audiences would substitute features for the one-reelers, and that middle-class audiences would substitute features for legitimate theatre. Both groups showed they were willing to pay higher prices for features (25 cents–75 cents) than one-reelers (5 cents–10 cents) (ibid.).

This success attracted American companies to produce features. However, those MPPC companies who invested in feature production – Vitagraph's *The Life of Moses* (1909) was the first American-made multi-reeler – discovered a further weakness of the cartel's business model. The nickelodeons attracted audiences with a "programme" of short films (Quinn, 2001). For this reason, the GFC "advertised and distributed its product by the [company] brand – exhibitors, exchanges, and the public were expected to request films by company names" (Mezias and Kuperman, 2001:217). The new multi-reelers differentiated a single film by its title and star "talent", undermining the attraction of the nickelodeon's core "programme" product (ibid.). Replacing a short film "programme" with a single long film reduced the nickelodeons' turnover. A second problem concerned the limited revenues nickelodeons were able to make (because of their limited size and the admission prices they could charge). The MPPC's customers were thus either unable or unwilling to pay higher rental prices required for features.

The MPPC's key weapon, in protecting its market from the new feature producers, was its monopoly over distribution through its control of the GFC. The GFC, therefore, refused to distribute whole features and the nickelodeons insisted on showing them one reel at a time, sometimes weeks apart (Musser, 1994). But this simply created an opportunity for new entrants to the distribution market, to supply the unmet demand for features. Independent distributors rented the films from European producers and bypassed the MPPC and the nickelodeons, showing features in rented theatres, town halls and public spaces (Mezias and Kuperman, 2001). Crucially, they replaced the practice of a flat rental fee to theatre owners, by a fee which increased in proportion to box office receipts. This enabled these independent distributors to capitalise on the potential of a hit in a way the MPPC could not.

In 1915 *Birth of a Nation* established the feature as film's dominant design. The film opened at $2 a seat (equivalent to a Broadway play) and ran for 40 weeks (Staiger, 1985). In the same year "a cinema showing average features that changed each day had daily sales of $300 and a [profit] margin of 42% ($125)" (Bakker,

2005:323–4). By 1919 the "revenue per meter" of feature films was 67% higher than for all other types of films combined (ibid.).

> By the mid-teens, the feature had established its dominance over the one-reelers, and production, distribution, and exhibition practices standardized the product's design and marketing . . . each movie became a unique product, heavily advertised, feature-length photoplay . . . [with] unique production qualities and star appeal that differentiated features and multi-reels from shorts.
>
> *Staiger, 1985:231*

By 1914, US demand for features reached around 45 million weekly admissions, rising to stabilise at 80–90 million throughout the 1930s to 1940s. This success attracted more new entrants; the number of companies producing features increased from one to 114 between 1912 and 1914 (American Film Institute, 1988). But this period of a large number of suppliers and intense competition in the market was brief. The new "independent" producers – Carl Laemmle, William Fox, Louis B. Mayer, the Warner Brothers and particularly Adolph Zukor – soon began to establish oligopolistic market control. "These "independents" succeeded at what the well-financed members of the [MPPC] Trust had failed to accomplish – control of the production, distribution, and exhibition of movies" (Gomery, 1996:45). They approached the industry from a knowledge, not of the technical or creative process, but of the market:

> most of (these) entrepreneurs . . . began as investors in real estate, and in the early 1900s were pioneers in the Nickelodeons . . . This in contrast to the members of the MPPC, which mostly started as manufacturers of equipment and film, and then by necessity had to branch out into film production.
>
> *Bakker, 2005:310–51*

Where the MPPC had vertically integrated equipment manufacture, film production and distribution, Zukor focused on integrating production, distribution and exhibition. Zukor's move into feature production was inspired by his experience of exhibition, when he showed Pathé's three reel, *Passion Play* (1903):

> We stayed on with that picture for months and did a land office business . . . it occurred to me that if we could take a novel or a play and put it on the screen, the people would be interested (. . .) I did approach all the producers . . . (but) they did not believe that people would sit through pictures that ran three, four, five reels . . . I made up my mind definitively to take big plays and celebrities of the stage and put them on the screen.
>
> *Cited in Bakker, 2012a:32*

He imported the four-reel French feature, *Les Amours de la Reine Elizabeth* (1911) starring Sarah Bernhardt, and when the MPPC refused to give it a licence, released it through a chain of vaudeville theatres, premiering at New York's Lyceum.

With the profits from the film, he established his production company, Famous
Players, to make features of classic stories with "star" stage actors. Where the MPPC
had tried to encourage habitual audience consumption through the traditional use
of company brand, Zukor saw the potential to create hits by branding individual
films through their story titles and star names. As noted in Chapter 1, star names
(and "talent") have remained a central means for producers to reduce the inherent
uncertainty which the individual differentiation of media products creates for audiences. The studios developed strategies of "promoting careers through the subtle
gradation and renewal of type that kept (a star) reassuringly familiar yet refreshingly
surprising" (Mordden, 1988:46). Zukor's first star, Mary Pickford, increased her
weekly salary from $100 in 1909 to $10,000 by 1917. By the same year, 95% of US
features included a star actor (Koszarski, 1994).

Zukor's next focus was exhibition. By 1913 he had formed the Paramount
Pictures chain of cinemas, focused on the most profitable markets – the major US
cities. By the following year, he had built his own nationwide network, Paramount
Pictures Corporation, to distribute films. The next step was to begin vertical integration of production and distribution. Famous Players signed a 25-year contract to
supply Paramount with features. With this stability of demand, Zukor could plan
a "season" of films for his cinemas in the way broadcast networks (see Chapter 3)
would programme their channels. Each cinema showed a regular weekly programme of five or six new feature releases. This vertical integration of production
and distribution gave Zukor huge "supplier power" over independent cinema
owners – in 1914 and 1915, Paramount was "the only company that could provide cinemas with a full year's supply of features" (Bakker, 2012a:34). Paramount's
increasing ownership of its own cinemas weakened the cinemas' own "buyer
power". This enabled Zukor to impose further control over the market. Cinemas
wanting to buy the new Mary Pickford film had to "block book" a "bundle" of
other Paramount features with lesser actors and smaller budgets. Paramount also
imposed "blind bidding" – cinemas would have to buy the bundle of films knowing very little about them, before they had even been produced. The impact of
Paramount's market power was almost immediate; it quickly gained the largest
share of the market and increased its gross income from $10.3 million in 1917
to $17.3 million in 1918 (ibid.). By 1923, Famous Players films were regularly
screened in a quarter of US cinemas:

> As the silent era drew to a close, it was Zukor and Paramount who had
> the top stars, the most world-wide distribution, and the most extensive and
> prestigious theatre chain – the very model of the integrated business through
> which Hollywood's power was asserted.
>
> *Gomery, 1997:51*

The success of Zukor's strategy brought rapid "isomorphism" across the
industry, "Practically all principal manufacturers concluded to adopt Zukor's
compromise – pay large prices, if need be, to directors, novelists, dramatists and

continuity writers, hoping thereby to find something novel and startling to attract the crowds to their own photoplays" (Hampton, cited in Bakker, 2012a:34). Paramount's vertical integration strategy was followed by Metro-Goldywn-Mayer (1924), Fox (1925) and Warner Brothers (1926). This in turn brought oligopolistic control of the market. In 1922, the studios formed the Motion Pictures Producers and Distributors of America (MPPDA) which effectively replaced the MPPC. By 1923 80% of US film production came from six vertically integrated producer-distributors. By the early 1930s, the studios controlled around a sixth of all cinemas (Miller and Shamsie, 1996). By the 1940s eight companies made 75% of all features and captured 90% of US box office receipts (Gomery, 1997).

The block booking approach informed the response to the fall in demand during the Depression. The studios offered audiences a "double feature", two movies for the price of one. While the expensive, "prestige" A-movies (forerunners of the "blockbuster") were distributed on the percentage basis to reward "hits", B-movies reverted to the flat rental fee of the nickelodeon era. Because they were "block booked" with the A-features, the studios calculated they could ensure B-movies would return a predictable profit and by the 1940s B-features represented 50% or more of the output of the major studios.

The final element of the studios' market control consisted of the formidable barriers to new competitors in that market. The studios had seen off the main competitor to their product – by 1920, 90% of nickelodeon firms had ceased trading (Bakker, 2005). The economies of scale they achieved saw off competition from independent producers and deterred new entrants. In 1919, Mary Pickford, Charlie Chaplin, Douglas Fairbanks and D. W. Griffith created United Artists (UA). Although cinema owners were attracted by the films with such stars, independents were unable to supply the "seasons" of features – three films, per star, per year – the chains now required. New technologies, particularly sound recording, increased the fixed costs of production. Variable costs, like advertising, increased from $5 million in 1913 to $67 million by 1925. Unable to compete, the independent sector saw a "shake-out" with many companies being bought by the major studios (Mordden, 1988). "In 1905 entrepreneurs . . . could enter the motion picture exhibition business with a few hundred dollars. In 1925 . . . (it) became part of the Pantheon of American big business business" (Gomery, 1997:43).

This section has used the theory proposed in Chapter 1 to show how the industry vertically integrated production after the feature had replaced its rivals as the dominant design. The final step is to account for the disintegration of production represented by the break-up of the studio system and the outsourcing of production to independent companies.

Chapter 1 explained that the break-up of this studio system has formed the evidential basis for a debate about the economics of media production. Two theories were outlined. Flexible specialisation (FS) suggested that the studios had mass produced standardised features, and that the break-up resulted from the lack of quality and variety of these films. To produce the variety and quality of films needed to attract audiences, the studios were forced to end mass production, disintegrate the production process and outsource to independent production companies providing specialist services or whole films (see for example Storper, 1993, Scott, 2004). The alternative approach, transaction cost theory (TCE), explained the break-up in terms of a transition from a high cost, integrated mass production to a lower cost "spot production" (Caves, 2000).

Theorists of mass production, FS and TCE agree that the immediate cause of the break-up was a change in regulation: the Paramount verdict forced the studios to sell off their cinema chains (Schatz, 2012, Storper, 1993, Caves, 2000). The initial result, as intended, was to inhibit the studios' control over cinema booking (through "blind booking" etc.) and open up this market to competition, including from independent producers. However, as Aksoy and Robins (1992) showed, the high costs of international sales offices and the studios' large feature catalogues created economies of scale which preserved the barriers to entry to feature distribution. The studios thus retained control of the growing market for international distribution of films.

In the TCE and FS accounts, the disintegration of cinema exhibition represents a "disturbance" (Caves, 2000) or an "external shock" (Storper, 1993) to the studio system. Further, the studios' retention of control over distribution was an element of continuity rather than change in the system. For both theories, the key element in the break-up is the transformation of production, and here both agree that the central cause was the emergence of competition from the live production and distribution of TV shows (see Chapter 3). Quite separate from their loss of control over cinema booking, the whole industry contracted. Demand for feature films declined and between 1945 and 1950 cinema attendances fell from 90 million to 50 million. In the 1930s, around 65% of the US population attended the cinema. By 1964 this had fallen to around 10%, a proportion which has remained relatively constant to date (Pautz, 2002). It is important to note that this decline began *before* the widespread purchase of TV sets (Dwyer, 2015b). Rather than simply the impact of a competitive product, the decline in cinema attendance appears to have been a result of broader societal changes, including suburbanisation (ibid.).

One of the studios' key responses to this reduction in demand was a reduction in the volume of their output, almost by half, between 1940 and 1956 (Caves, 2000). At first sight, this would seem to support a TCE explanation of the decision to outsource to independents. The reduction in output volume undermined the studios' economies of scale, making some of their fixed costs (particularly soundstages) unsustainable. The studios thus sold off facilities, shed staff or sought independent producers who could hire their soundstages. By contrast, Caves (2000:94) suggests, "around 1950, independent producers' costs were 30 percent lower than the studios". This would suggest a straightforward explanation for a transition from expensive, fixed cost, in-house production to inexpensive, variable cost, independent production. However, Caves notes that such comparisons are "hazardous" and Robins' (1993:112) study of Warner Brothers found that "the shift to independent production did not provide a means for Warner to reduce production budgets".

Furthermore, as shown below, the move to focus on production of "blockbusters" dramatically *increased* the costs of feature production in the post-studio era.

FS proposes that the studios' outsourcing to independents was driven by a search, not to reduce costs, but to increase quality, innovation and product variety. TV impacted demand for the studios' standardised mass produced features. To increase product variety, the studios transformed production from high volume assembly lines, using dedicated, "in-house" inputs of technology, labour or expertise to "functional flexibility", using specialised inputs, for varied, "one-off" projects. Here, Storper (1989) cites the studios' early moves to CinemaScope, colour film and 3D. However, the evidence does not appear to support this explanation. First, the independents do not appear to have supplied the specialist inputs the theory would suggest. The experiments Storper referred to largely failed and film production reverted to 2D (and much even to black and white) (Mordden, 1988). Rather than providing functional flexibility, these companies appear to have provided numerical flexibility, allowing studios to reduce their overhead costs – the number of soundstages and post-production facilities they operated – and contract these additional facilities as needed (Dwyer, 2015b).

Second, Balio (1990) finds little evidence that independent producers provided specialist inputs to the studios. Although some developed niche products (such as Cubby Broccoli's *James Bond* franchise) most independents continued the studios' approach of spreading risk across a portfolio of genres (Dwyer, 2015b). In fact, Balio argues, independents saw specialisation as a weakness; "by placing all his eggs in a single basket . . . an independent placed himself at a disadvantage if his particular brand of pictures had limited appeal" (op. cit.:174).

If we reject the TCE and FS explanations, we need an alternative. Doing this requires a more detailed examination of the dominant design and the impact of the fall in demand for features. Since their days of "bundling" films, the studios had produced three classes of feature; "programmers" (shorter, lower budget films, with minor stars), "specials" (combined well-known stars and standard running times to deliver on predictable budgets) and super-specials or "prestige" features (with the top stars, long running times and, consequentially, much bigger budgets). During the Depression, they added the B-movie (low cost and often series-based) which was initially the most affected by the fall in demand. Robins (1993) shows that pre-war, almost all completed features covered their costs, but post-war, "B"-movie revenues collapsed. Contrary to FS theory, the studios' response to the fall in demand for movies does *not* appear to have been to engage in a search for radical product innovation or variety. Instead, they severely reduced their output of B-movies and focused on refining the competitive advantages of their A-movies by focusing on the top-of-the-range or "prestige" features – later known as "blockbusters". Christensen (1997) observes this as classic strategic response to competition across a range of industries.

As a result (as shown in more detail below), the end of the studio system did not result in a radical transformation of feature production to achieve product variety or innovation. First, studios did not abandon in-house production, but continued to produce around 30–40% of US features themselves. Second, as Chapter 4 shows, much of the studios' lost B-movie production was converted, without major transformation, to the production of filmed TV series. Third, rather than increasing product variety, the studios search for "blockbuster" features appears to have restricted innovation; "because production financing became riskier than ever. The majors were not about to venture from the tried and true" (Balio, 1993:67).

The decision to outsource production to independent film producers, in large part, reflected the studios' continuing reliance on the central element of Zukor's original conception of this "tried and true" formula – the star brand. Many accounts drawing on theories of mass production, TCE and FS (especially Caves, 2000), have emphasised the contrast between the famous seven-year option contracts, with which the studios retained stars for their in-house productions, and the "per-film" contracts which replaced them. The evidence cited is usually the dramatic reduction in the number of performers under long-term contract to the studios – from 742 to 229 between 1947 and 1956 (Mordden, 1988). However, as noted above, the continual negotiation, renegotiation and amendment of these long-term contracts (as well as the common practice of studios loaning their in-house stars to other studios) had been the basis for the significant role played by talent agents from the early years of the studio system (Kemper, 2010). In the 1950s, regulatory changes increased the power of actors and their agents and reduced the oligopsonistic power of the studios in the labour market. Changes in tax regulations (see Chapter 3) made it much more profitable for actors to be self-employed than to be employees, encouraging them to end long-term contracts and set up their own independent companies, working for the studios on "per-film" contracts. However, the regulatory regime, described above, prevented the studios from vertically integrating these independent talent companies into their business. The same regulations allowed major talent agencies like William Morris and Lew Wasserman's Music Corporation of America (MCA) to forwards integrate into film production. This combination presented talent agencies with the opportunity to facilitate the movement of the star actors they represented out of long-term contracts with studios and into independent companies, often set up and managed by the agency (op. cit.). Studio outsourcing to independents was crucially influenced by their continuing requirement for star actors within the original dominant design of the feature. A similar process influenced the US networks' decision to outsource TV production decades earlier than in the UK (see Chapters 3 and 6).

Contrary to the FS account, these independent companies were not, largely, independent film *producers*. As Balio notes, of all the types of independent companies in the post-studio era, "the packager was the most typical . . . [these companies] assembled the ingredients of a picture, but . . . typically took *a secondary position in the production*. More often than not, the packager was also a talent agent" (Balio, 1990:173, my emphasis). Rather than seeking to increase innovation and product variety by outsourcing to new independent producers, the studios were continuing their traditional relationship with "bankable" stars. "Stars, in fact, became more important than ever; in this era of retrenchment financing a picture of any consequence without a name of proven box office worth would have been unthinkable" (Balio, 1990:10). Chapter 3 takes up this analysis of the talent agencies' role in independent production for TV.

Process innovation

So far, this chapter has attempted to show how, as outlined in Chapter 1, the adoption of a dominant design, was followed by attempts to control the product market through the vertical integration of production, distribution and cinema exhibition. We have also seen how and why production was outsourced after this market control mechanism broke down. This section examines documented changes in the process of producing individual films. This analysis of changes in production compares the explanations offered by FS and other approaches with those outlined in Chapter 1 concerning the relationship between the adoption of a dominant design and the decomposition of this design into production tasks, which achieve process efficiencies through the development of knowledge, routines and discourse that facilitate the reduction of idle time, waste etc.

As shown above, the early years of film were characterised by a range of experimental product designs. The unscripted "design" of factual short films ("scenics" and "topicals") created a high level of task variability. This limited the extent to which this task could be decomposed, in advance of shooting, to enable planning of production. Instead, most production decisions had to be taken on the spot, during shooting, generally by the camera operator who attempted to "capture" the action, "ad hoc"; "the cameraman was little more than a janitor of light. He had not art to make but a job to do: catching the action" (Mordden, 1988:4–5). This process of "catching the action" would become typical of the filming of observational documentaries in the 1960s to 1970s (see Chapter 6).

This task variability was compounded by the technical limitations of early cameras (less than a minute for a film reel, no possibility to move the camera, poor responsiveness to light etc.) and the inherent uncertainties of location filming; "even when an event did occur, the success of the film might depend on uncontrollable factors such as the weather: if the film jammed or was inadequately exposed, news events did not repeat themselves for retakes" (Staiger, 1985:204). To control these environmental influences, particularly light, the first film studio, Edison's Black Maria, was designed as "a means for maintaining strict regulation of sunlight, the only illumination source powerful enough to allow him to rapidly expose film at the intensity necessary to legibly capture successive stages of motion" (Jacobson, 2011:235). This era of studio design owed much to photography studios, the flat black backdrop providing maximum contrast to the lit area. The alternative design, the "single shot" one-reel drama, influenced studio designers to adopt a more theatrical stage model, incorporating a conventional stage with painted backdrops and scenery. However, filming scenes in evenly distributed, natural light with few shadows, emphasised the shallowness of the stage and the flatness of the backdrop, scenery and props. The introduction of electric lighting, with tungsten spotlights which could be focused (and brightened or dimmed) on people, objects and sets, enabled the development of "triple" (three-point) lighting techniques, creating a better simulation of a 3D scene on a 2D screen. Balshofer and Miller (1967) show how this also enabled directors to re-create lighting effects used in theatres to cue audience attention via genre references (horror, noir, musicals etc.).

The success of *The Great Train Robbery* (1903) inaugurated a boom in demand, leading production companies to try to increase output (Musser, 1994). However, Porter epitomised Staiger's idea of the "artisan-cameraman", controlling every aspect of production; "Porter didn't choose to specialise in any one branch of picture making, be it director, cameraman or producer. He felt he had to be involved in every part of it" (Balshofer and Miller, 1967:51). As the MPPC companies attempted to increase output, they encountered strict labour market constraints – there was a limited supply of "cameramen so skilled in a variety of work processes" (Staiger, 1985:204). Further, as changes in camera technology made operation more complex, camera operators developed a range of specialised and exclusive knowledge; "generally, the knowledge of this technology was outside the province of the director, whose major photographic criterion at that time was visibility of action" (Staiger, 1985:206). This left responsibility for decisions concerning the technical and aesthetic quality of a shot largely to camera operators. The increase in production was thus achieved by decomposition of the task of drama production. Rather than originating a production system from first principles, the industry adopted knowledge, routines and a division of labour from the theatre. In the nineteenth century the growth in demand for theatre led the newly commercial theatre companies to increase both the number of performances and their complexity through a division of the original actor-manager role, and the emergence of a new specialist creative project management role – the director (Lehner, 2009). As Staiger (1985:206) notes: "the day of specialisation had arrived . . . after 1907, it became atypical in fictional narrative production, for the work functions of director and cameraman to be combined".

In addition to this division of functions, film-makers like D. W. Griffith adopted the theatre's decomposition of the task of drama production, which he had learned as a theatre actor, into a series of sequential activities; identifying a story outline, casting actors, designing scenery and costumes, and rehearsing to refine actor movement and dialogue (ibid.). The coevolution of film with theatre meant that as demand for films grew, demand for theatre tickets fell, causing theatres to shed experienced workers many of whom were then recruited into the film industry. The results of these process innovations were rapid – by 1908 Griffith's single unit was producing two reels a week, the same output of several units at Porter's company. Across the industry, US annual output increased from 605 to 2,825 films between 1906 and 1909 (op. cit.).

The adoption of the feature film provided the opportunity to achieve further process efficiencies in film production. The increasing demand for features brought a search for methods to increase output. In 1913 Biograph contracted to provide its

exhibitors with two features a week. Balio refers to the huge increase in output during this period as "feeding the maw of exhibition" (Balio, 1993:73). The revolution
in film production required to meet this demand was pioneered by Thomas Ince, a
production assistant-turned-director who in 1913 gave up directing to become the
first modern film producer. His transformation of this process focused on three elements; the redesign of the film studio, the adoption of the organisational structure
of the modern corporation and the development of the continuity script.

Ince (famously) consulted the designers of Ford's recently opened Highland
Park factory to guide development of his purpose-built facility, Inceville, in 1911.
To cut down on costs and "waiting times" he vertically integrated all production
inputs by having his own timberland, sawmill and steamers to transport wood to
the site and his own emergency services and utilities on site. To economise on
transport to filming locations he developed the concept of the studio "backlot" –
an area with a variety of large, complex permanent sets, appropriate to the product
genre range (a Western town, a frontier fort, a New York street, a ship etc.). To
reduce problems of quality and set-up times the studios included stages with a
range of lighting systems (open to natural light, glass-enclosed and "dark"), while
the backlot sets linked rooms together to increase the number of available angles
and ease camera movement and transitions between interior and exterior shots.
The backlot also enabled economies of repetition (as the same sets were continually
reused) (Staiger, 1985).

As well as permanent facilities, vertical integration involved having a permanent workforce. Through the nickelodeon era, the industry had depended on
freelancers; "actors, technicians, and directors moved between production companies frequently" (Mezias and Boyle, 2002:128). But the level of demand for
features, and the level of output planned, enabled Ince to keep labour employed
at optimum levels, moving straight from one film to another, with no idle time in
between. He replaced freelance actors and musicians with an in-house company
and an in-house orchestra. Freelance production staff were replaced by permanent
departments for finance, scenarios, directing, arts (sets), costumes and cameras.
Although some reflected the departments of a traditional theatre company (art
direction, properties and wardrobes) others incorporated film specialisations (story
selection and screenwriting, casting, direction, scene docks and set construction,
laboratory processing, cinematography) (Lehner, 2009). The scale of the operation was also new, with whole buildings devoted to departments which in theatres
might have comprised one or two people.

Despite his focus on the script and the establishment of a specialist writing
department (a staff of six scenario writers) Inceville could not keep pace with the
demand for films; "it was seen that the studio force could not produce each week a
sufficiently strong story, and outside writers were invited to contribute suggestions,
for which they were paid from five to fifteen dollars" (Townsend, 1909, cited in
Staiger, 1985:206). Production of story ideas, therefore, was never fully integrated
and Ince had to continue the practice of "outsourcing" this aspect of production to the market for story outlines. Gradually the studios developed large story

departments systematically searching the global literary and stage marketplaces for adaptable novels, plays, short stories and original film ideas.

However, Ince's radical process innovation was his decision to use the potential of film's recording process. As in the factory system, Ince was able to decompose the tasks of live drama production by *decoupling* the sequential dependencies between its tasks. In planning how to *reintegrate* these tasks, a crucial difference between theatre and film was that in "live" theatre, production and reception occured simultaneously. This established a set of tightly coupled, sequential dependencies, which requires that many production tasks are performed in the same sequence as the story itself. Single shot films were also made in this largely "as live" manner, filming action in story sequence. The short length and the pace of one-reel production had limited the extent of design or planning. Most MPPC directors worked either with very brief descriptions of scenarios or more detailed descriptions of plot, characters and stage directions, but limited dialogue (Staiger, 1979). Directors, production workers and actors used their tacit skills to make decisions on the spot.

The dominant design of the feature, however, had already begun to require greater planning. Features involved large casts and elaborate set designs, and this complexity created a technical impetus towards planning; "as feature films became longer, stories became more complicated, requiring more complex shooting scripts" (Gomery, 1997:46). Ince began to analyse the waste and delays caused by the still common practice of shooting from scenarios. A director would "get the germ idea of a plot, assemble a cast, go out on location and start to shoot, having only a hazy idea of what he was going to do" (Ince, cited in Regev, 2016:597). By leaving these decisions to be taken on the spot, rather than planned in advance, expensive resources were left standing idle, while the director made production decisions (settings, props, costumes, shots, sequences etc.) often in discussion with crew members (op. cit.). As well as "idle time" this process could generate unintended consequences which could lead to wasted resources. As each decision was taken, the crew would record it in notebooks and sketch pads; "records made on the spot without consideration of potential difficulties in the next set-ups" (Staiger, 1985:227). Poor decisions or problems in communicating these decisions might lead to failure to follow conventions (like the 180° rule) through a sequence of separate shots, creating problems in editing. Correcting mistakes required additional use of expensive inputs (cast, crew and sets) to reshoot sequences. If errors were not identified until editing, all the inputs might have to be reassembled and the whole scene reshot from scratch. Ince's consultants understood that planning could cut waste and improve quality;

> as the scientific management expert pointed out, a paper plan and record was a lot more reliable and predictable than an individual's memory, in recalling . . . staging entrances and exits, matching movements to adjacent spaces while maintaining conventions of screen direction, and correlating crosscutting.
>
> *Staiger, 1985:227*

But Ince saw that because recording technology required production to be performed well in advance of, and separately from, reception, it opened up options for separation of the existing task interdependencies and a radical re-engineering of feature production. The development of the multishot film, with multiple camera movements, had already transformed film from the "as live" continuous recording of scenes, to a discontinuous process of recording shots. Each *shot* was staged and recorded (often several times) before the camera was moved, so the next shot could be set, staged and recorded. This process also helped reduce the risks created by the method of filming from scenarios. Studios developed the "coverage" system of shooting action several times from different angles. If an editor discovered a problem with a shot (overexposure, poor framing etc.) it could be resolved in the editing process by using a transition shot, either a "cutaway" (from the action to a matching shot such as a reaction from the reverse angle) or a wide shot of the same action. Whilst this avoided complete reshoots at the edit stage, the "coverage" system involved considerable redundancy in creating shots, many of which would not be used. Ince's innovation was to see that this discontinuous process of production could be organised, not in terms of narrative comprehension, but in terms of achieving the most efficient use of expensive production inputs. Recording enabled production to be planned in the sequence which made the most economic sense – to make most efficient use of star actors or studio sets, by planning to shoot all the scenes which used these resources at the same time.

Achieving this required a written plan. First, Ince ended the use of scenarios and reduced task variability by ensuring films were produced from detailed screenplays which described each scene, its location and the basic actions of each character. Second he established a process of decomposing this script into a written plan – a series of production tasks, with directions on how they were to be performed – known as a continuity script (Staiger, 1979). The continuity detailed all the scenes and their titles and (in place of dialogue) their intertitles. A location plot planned out movements between interior and exterior sets, and to any external filming locations. All shots were listed and numbered and then each scene outlined showing which (numbered) shots were needed to produce the scene. The actual production was monitored against the continuity script by the creation of a new role, the "continuity clerk", who checked the completion of shots and script pages against the planned production schedule, so that delays could be identified immediately. By listing locations, sets, actors and shooting days the continuity script could be used, along with conventional accounting techniques, to break down the predicted costs (labour, film footage etc.) of the film (Taves, 2012).

This planning process immediately reduced the delays and set-up times (i.e. idle time) associated with the method of shooting from scenarios, reducing use of the most expensive inputs of film stock, cameras, sets, lighting, labour and stars (i.e. very highly paid labour). Staiger cites a contemporary witness;

> We failed to see actors made up and dressed for their various roles, loafing about the stages or on locations; perturbed directors running here and there attempting to bring order out of chaos, while locations waited and cameramen idly smoked their cigarettes, waiting for the next scene.
>
> *Staiger, 1979:19*

The continuity script also improved efficiency in post-production or editing. Rather than relying on notes made (or not made) during shooting, the continuities provided directors and editors with a comprehensive guide as to how the elements created in the sequence of production would be reordered back into the narrative sequence of the original story. This process innovation enabled Ince to keep track of all the current productions at Inceville. Each script was given a unique number (in case of changes in title), the dates when filming started and finished, when the final print was sent to the distributor and even the release date. The continuity script thus provided Ince with detailed management information, enabling him to plan a product portfolio (by genre) and an annual production schedule.

Many actors found (and sometimes still find) this process impacted on the quality of their performance, echoing Myrna Loy's complaint; "You shoot all the scenes that happen to be on that set . . . the set is what rules you" (cited in Regev, 2016:600). But Ince achieved the efficiencies and the increase in output he had intended. Films were written, produced, cut, assembled and delivered within a week at Inceville. The studio began, in 1911, producing one two-reel picture a week. In 1913, it produced 150 two-reeler movies (Staiger, 1985).

Ince's success made Inceville a model for other studios. The proess of "isomorphism" followed, with a "massive" growth of studio construction in the early 1910s, as MPPC companies, like Edison, Biograph, Vitagraph, Gaumont and Pathé designed purpose-built film studios to meet demand (Jacobson, 2011). Similarly, Ince's format for the continuity script had, by 1914, become generally adopted across the industry.

Ince also began the process of adapting the coordination and control mechanisms of the twentieth-century corporation to the task of film production. He introduced a clearer hierarchy, headed by a classic chief executive ("studio head") to select ("greenlight") films to produce; the producer, to budget and schedule production and recruit staff (writers, art directors, directors etc.) from the production departments; heads of these departments, responsible for decisions within their specialism area (so casting directors would recruit actors); and the director (filming the script and editing the film). The hierarchical management of film production was then developed by Irving Thalberg, who realised that in his role as "central producer" at MGM he could not control costs and coordinate the specialist departments across the 40–50 features that studio produced each year (Lampel et al., 2006). Thalberg developed the role of film producer to resemble its current function, a project manager coordinating the work of the specialist departments and individuals, to bring a project to completion. A further degree of specialisation led to the creation of assistant producer roles, specialising in the range of genres produced by the studio, supervising a handful of features each year (op. cit.).

The fall in demand and financial constraints of the Depression led the studios to focus on increasing the output and reducing the costs of their B-movie product. These achieved economies of repetition, and reduced task variability, by effectively becoming drama series. Using a model similar to that already adopted in radio soap operas (see Chapter 3), scriptwriting costs were reduced by acquiring series properties at low cost – "comic strips, radio shows, dime store fiction" (Henderson, 2017:24). Productivity was maximised by working studio assets "at optimum capacity" (Balio, 1993) by "recycling" scripts, in-house actors and stock footage. This reduced the "cycle" time for a B-movie to a 15–25 day production schedule. Warner produced its so-called "factory Westerns" at under $50,000 each while, by 1940, B-features produced 50% of the output volume of Warner, Fox, Paramount and MGM. As Chapter 4 notes, this B-movie series production process became the basis of the filmed TV series of the 1960s and 1970s (Henderson, 2017).

In the product market of the post-studio era, without the market control of the past, the studios lacked the ability to plan a programme of features for a year, cover their fixed costs and bring in a profit. The new system of outsourcing offered them the ability to approve films on a project-by-project basis without incurring costs until they were convinced the film represented a good risk.

Staiger, Musser and many others explain these changes in film production, from the original "artisanal" cameraman form of production, as a classic Taylorist separation of conception and execution. This separation "destroys an ideal of the whole person, both the creator and the producer of one's ideas" (Staiger, 1979:18). Chisholm (1993:147) suggests that in "1908, movies were produced factory style". Staiger (1985:207) argues of Inceville:

> it is not unimportant that this system of production centralized its work processes in the studio/ factory. This allowed an ease in controlling labor time, eliminating irregularity of production, and permitting detailed division of labor as well as reducing material and labor cost.

Inceville, she argues, was "the model based on a well-organized factory". This view has continued to be the orthodox description of film production in this period; "Ince took assembly-line techniques, perfected by manufacturing giants like Henry Ford, and applied them to the movie industry" (Norman, cited in Conor, 2014). Other writers argue that the B-movie era was the height of mass production when, "not only the casting but the sets, props, music, even the story formula itself could be standardized, rendering what was already a low-budget enterprise that much more efficient and economical" (Schatz, 1996:257).

Others have emphasised the importance of increasing management and corporate control over film production. Staiger argues that the management hierarchies began to appear in 1907, while later innovations "introduced a new set of top managers – producers such as Thomas Ince and later Irving Thalberg who meticulously controlled the making of their firm's films" (Staiger, 1985:224). Lampel notes that Thalberg was the first Hollywood producer to fire a director (Eric Von Stroheim) for failing to observe the budget and production schedule, and "then used his acquired reputation as tough manager to cut budgets and enforce schedules" (Lampel, 2011: 456).

In considering this argument, it is important to note that even some of the proponents of mass production theory recognise that feature production did not follow the pattern of factories, blueprints and close management supervision. In fact, "under the right circumstances and given adequate resources, unit production proved to be remarkably flexible, and quite responsive to changes in both audience tastes and studio personnel" (Schatz, 2012:173). Others, like Mezias and Boyle (2002:123), describe this era of production as "an administrative innovation system (which) treated each film as a unique product, allowing for enhanced creative quality, but also monitored costs, controlling the financial threat posed by the greater capital expenditures required in the production of features".

Second, despite the many process and design innovations of film, drama production still retained a core similarity with theatre. At every stage of production, a script contained "a high degree of 'equivocality'" with "multiple, mutually conflicting interpretations" (Lehner, 2009:201). This created an irreducible level of task variability which severely limited the extent to which studio heads could decompose production tasks into standard routines with simple unvarying steps to achieve a Taylorist or Fordist mass production process. Staiger takes Ince's famous line on his scripts – "shoot as written" – as evidence he saw continuity as a manufacturing blueprint so that "the written instructions organized the assembly of the film throughout the various separate phases and places of its creation" (Staiger, 1985:227). However, in practice this was not possible. Whatever a producer like Ince might say, as 20th Century Fox's Darryl Zanuck admitted, "on the set the director has 90 percent control. You may be able to persuade him to do this or that, but only within 10 percent. The rest of it, he's going to do it" (cited in Regev, 2016:609). This means that "the script may conjure images of Niagara Falls, but the Director may only be planning a tight shot of a rocky ledge" (Maier, 2013:83).

Third, film production never achieved the predictability or efficiencies claimed. As a Warner's production assistant noted during the production of *King's Row*, as late as 1941: ". . . This will be 23 days over the schedule and very considerably over the budget. Considering the broken manner in which this show has been shot as regarding sets, cast, etc., I only hope it fits together right" (cited in Regev, 2016:608). Further, it was not rational for studio heads like Ince to try to control production in a Taylorist or Fordist manner. As Chapter 1 noted, the economics of media markets make investments in quality, to achieve a possible hit, at least as rational as tight control of costs. Thalberg championed screen testing of features; "if audiences did not like something or failed to respond in the appropriate way, he did not hesitate to have parts of the picture reshot" (Balio, 1993:75). As he famously stated, "movies aren't made, they're remade" (cited in Lampel et al., 2006:51).

Chapter 1 suggested an alternative explanation for changes in production. With this view, the emergence of a dominant design (the one-reeler and the feature) enables process efficiencies to be achieved through refining industry, or even company specific knowledge and "cognitive schemas", into working practices and "routines" which are adapted through discourse and mutual adjustment between production workers. Such routines are not the specified rules of Taylorist routinisation, but patterns of action which are always open to interpretation. It is this need for interpretation in the application of routines which produces discourse and "mutual adjustment" in resolving the continuing task uncertainty. As Chapter 1 argued, this means that the "design" of media products and the planning of production tasks continue throughout the production process.

Individual differentiation and task variability reduce the potential for decomposition of the task into simplified discrete steps. Technology complicates this by creating a number of tight interdependencies between tasks, with jobs like camera operator and grip using the same equipment. Together, these limits on planning mean that each individual shot is a bespoke act, involving more or less interpretation. Complex moving shots may involve the actions of several people, all engaged in "mutual adjustment" to try to achieve the end result. But this makes the process fragile: "a mistimed/missed beat by one individual or group affects the rest – 'It's a house of cards, if one department completely falls over, we all go out!'" (Maier, 2013:89).

Over time, production workers develop routines to try to manage these interdependencies. In ancient Greece, actors rehearsed intensively for months to plan the *reciprocal interdependencies* between the individual's *performance* of her tasks (action and dialogue) and the similarly individual performances of other actors and crew. This process involved planning physical and temporal interdependencies – the timings and physical locations of actions and dialogue – as well as creative ones. Individual performances of actions and dialogue, and the interaction between them, could alter the meaning and effects of those actions for the audience. For each production, and each scene directors (and often others) attempt to plan the movement of actors, crew and equipment to achieve the highest quality footage in the least time possible (Lehner, 2009).

Nineteenth century theatre developed the technique of "blocking" actor movements against lighting and other equipment (the British operetta writer W. S. Gilbert has been credited with developing the technique, using blocks to plan the movements of actors across sources of light) (Stedman, 1996). However, movement in theatre was restricted by the need to accommodate the proscenium view and so the blocking process was required only to plan lateral movements largely across the front "apron" of the theatre. In early films, actors' uncertainty around camera framing tended to reproduce this lateral movement across the set, rather than using the depth of the studio. Sophisticated set design, electric lighting in studios, more mobile cameras and directional microphones all enabled more complex movement of actors and cameras in depth as well as laterally.

This openness to interpretation and task variability means there is always potential for discourse about the best way to apply this knowledge and these routines to any given task; "film sets are characterized by an atmosphere of continual communication, in which people update one another and provide information over a variety of technologies such as walkie-talkies, cellular phones, and megaphones" (Bechky, 2006:10). This is not a democratic discourse. Even in small independent production companies "strong vertical economic ties among director, producer and distributor positively impact the execution of routine tasks" (Hadida, 2009:314). Such productions also reflect the industry's established differentials in autonomy between "creative" and "craft" skills, "the behavioral latitude granted a producer or director does not extend down the crew hierarchy to the grips and the electricians" (Bechky, 2006:16)

Despite this hierarchy, the continuing task variability presents ongoing limits to management control. Directors and producers have to lead, guide and moderate this collaborative discourse to arrive at a shared interpretation of the script and a shared understanding of the production process necessary to achieve it. A description of an interaction between an Assistant Director (AD) and crew members illustrates this: "The AD will walk through everything [in the script]. 'Scene 1: Interior restaurant – *Café Diplomatica*: Day 2. A couple set in front of two half-eaten meals; blah, blah, blah . . .' And then they'll say, 'Whoa! Okay, wait a second, what are they eating exactly here? Does it matter?' (Writer 4)" (cited in Maier, 2013:114). This discourse helps allocate tasks to particular skilled groups or individuals "that is not always clear – that weird in-between grey area, where you don't quite know whether it is a prop or costumes or a set thing" (ibid.).

This section has argued that feature production was never remotely similar to mass production (see also Dwyer, 2015b). FS theory (see Storper, 1993) accepts the claims about mass production and goes on to argue that the post-studio era was driven by an attempt to overcome the limitations of the standardised, mass produced feature films of the studio era, and achieve the "functional flexibility", combining skills, technology and tasks in new ways, to produce a wider variety of more innovative products. However, even if we accept that the studio system did not involve mass production, an alternative version of FS theory focuses on the conservatism of occupational groups in resisting change to production practices. Two FS theorists, Storper and Christopherson (1987), show that the unions and guilds established for different specialist trades introduced protection of their occupations, enabling them to resist changes which challenged these protected roles. And as noted above, the regulations of the NIRA had supported the restriction of competition in both product and labour markets. The National Labor Relations Board effectively authorised trade union control of entry to stable salaried employment in the studios. Furthermore, Caves (2006: 551) shows that vertical disintegration did undermine this union control of the labour market; "the craft unions that had long siphoned substantial rents from the major movie studios found themselves unable to control access to competitive supplies of skilled labor". However, the question remains whether this change was really driven by a need for "functional flexibility" in production. Another interpretation is that this change was largely driven by a search for "numerical" flexibility. This relates, not to a need for innovation in the development of new products, but to a need to reduce fixed costs in order to cope with a fall in demand for output. As noted above, the post-studio era saw a change in habits of cinema attendance and the studios responded by reducing production of B-movies, to supply the double features which had been necessary to generate demand in the Depression. At this point, much film production changed from a salaried career to a pattern of casual, freelance employment. This gave the studios (and the new independent producers) the "numerical flexibility", to take on costs only when a film started production. However, it is hard to see how this would support an FS explanation. Although there clearly were increases in functional flexibility following the end of the studio era, the essential hierarchical and lateral functional specialisations of feature production remained. Again, contra FS theory, the evidence does not suggest that the studios needed to produce more innovative products to compete with TV. As Chapter 3 demonstrates, by the early 1950s Hollywood had returned to the B-movie production system in supplying filmed series to the TV networks. Rather than a need for innovation, the changes in production following the disintegration of the studios seem clearly linked to the change in cinema attendance and the reduction in the urgency of demand for studio output. In the new era, the studios relied on the existence of "latent organisations" – "below the line" staff and small companies supplying technical inputs (soundstage rental, production equipment and post-production facilities) – to enable them to cope with fluctuating levels of output (Starkey et al., 2000).

3

PRODUCING STUDIO SHOWS

Some writers have suggested that studio TV production is an inherently inferior form (compared with features and filmed series) exhibiting a "zero-degree" or "styleless" style (Butler, 2007, Caldwell, 1995). Caldwell describes *I Love Lucy* (*ILL*); "a monotonous, flat and generic lighting style . . . block-ing and directing were nondescript . . . frame it wide; cut it to thirty or sixty minutes and deliver to the networks" (Caldwell, 1995:52). Others, by con-trast, see studio production at the top of the aesthetic hierarchy. For Kompare (2006:22) studio TV's "liveness" reflects a "rhetoric of high-class aesthetics", an attempt by the TV networks to ape the elite culture of live theatre rather than the popular culture of film. In this account, studio production techniques are explained as the result of an "ideology of liveness", an ideological commit-ment to prefer live production over recording (see also Feuer, 1983). A third school of thought understands studio production as the application of "mass production" techniques to radio and TV. Meyers (1997:124) describes the "assembly line" methods and Cox (1999:19) the "sweatshop conditions" of radio soap opera writing. Allen (1985:47) sees soap operas as "a mass produced narrative form" each "script outline (is) . . . a blueprint on the basis of which the final product is assembled" (op. cit.:54). Levine (2001) references "assem-bly line" processes and routinisation in the production of *General Hospital* (*GH*) while Bakewell and Garnham (1970:14) trace "the economic develop-ment of the programme factory".

This chapter presents an alternative account, explaining the evolution of stu-dio production, in the terms of Chapter 1, as the development of a dominant design (the studio show) within the constraints of early (live) broadcasting, which included pressures for cost-effectiveness. As Chapters 5 and 6 show, studio pro-duction has been used for many unscripted TV text types; news and sports, music and game shows. This chapter focuses on the dominant scripted text types used in studio production – the soap opera, the sitcom and the variety talk show. Rather than assuming the inferiority of studio production, we might note that, despite much speculation about the role of original filmed TV drama series in driving use of new subscription services, the most popular content on Netflix in the UK in 2018, beating recently produced big budget dramas like *The Crown* and *Stranger Things*, was the US network studio sitcom *Friends*, which began transmission in 1994 (Ofcom, 2018a).

Technological discontinuity

Compared to recording sound or images on film, TV and radio broadcasting, like the telegraph and telephone, have always involved live, simultaneous communication of sound and images. Early electromechanical systems included Marconi's 1906 transmission of speech and recorded music, and experimental broadcasts of images – NBC's Felix the Cat doll in 1928 and the BBC's 1929 transmission of a black and white image (Briggs, 1965).

Later electronic TV systems involved an electronic camera lens reflecting light energy from a scene, focusing it on a photoelectric surface, in turn transforming it into electric pulses constituting an electronic analogue of the scene. The camera first "scanned" these charges (like reading a page) in order, enabling them to be reassembled in the same order, and then amplified them, transmitting the charge first to a transmitter and then receiver (Eddy, 1945).

Dominant design

This section analyses an episode of the dominant design, the sitcom *Friends*, for comparison with the sequence from *Pirates of The Caribbean* analysed in Chapter 2. *Friends* has become a TV phenomenon. For a decade, it established the primacy of NBC's Thursday night schedule over other networks and more recently it has become the foundation of Netflix's success in the UK (Ofcom, 2018a). The sitcom was produced by Bright/Kauffman/Crane and largely shot in studio 24 of Warner Brothers Television's Burbank Studios (Eng, 2018). Built in 1935, this studio had been used for features until the '50s when it was converted for Warner's production of filmed series (including *Wonder Woman*) before being converted to sitcom production, with seating for a studio audience (for *Full House*, *Friends* and then *Two and a Half Men*). This section focuses on an episode, "The One with the Embryos" (first broadcast on January 15, 1998, in season four), which used only two sets; the apartment and the hospital radiology room. Like many other sitcoms, each season of *Friends* included one, cheaper to make, "bottle" episode (see Process innovation, this volume, p. 88) using a limited number of permanent sets and only the core cast (no guest stars). This simply accentuates one element of the studio show dominant design; they are largely set indoors and even many "exteriors" (like the street outside the Central Perk coffee shop) are studio interiors, without location sound.

FIGURE 3.1   Establisher shot from *Friends*.

Credit: "The One with the Embryos", *Friends*, Bright/Kauffman/Crane Productions/Warner Brothers Television, 1998.

The establishing shot (Figure 3.1) illustrates many of the elements of multi-camera studio production. There is less sense of depth, of distance between Chandler (Matt Perry) in the foreground and Monica (Courtney Cox) in the background. This is partly a result of the size of the set and partly of the overhead "high key" lighting, which provides even lighting throughout the set, rather than using the three-point technique to light individual shots. As explained (see Process innovation, this volume, p. 88) below, this is to enable the "as live" process of shooting continuous scenes. This same constraint explains the way group shots are filmed (whether at the table, in a restaurant or on the sofa in Central Perk) with a space at the front. In a feature, this scene might be shot with Monica moving to the empty chair at the table. Her lines would be covered by moving the camera "across the line", as explained in Chapter 2. In the multi-camera sitcom system, it is not possible to cross the line without showing the studio audience, and halting the continuous filming of the scene.

The dialogue sets up the dramatic questions driving the two plots of this episode. The comedy is generated by the attempts to discuss seriously the question of whether Phoebe (Lisa Kudrow) will become pregnant through the IVF process, before the characters instantly get distracted by the question of who will win their quiz.

The B-plot was necessitated by Lisa Kudrow's pregnancy. The producers felt that to have another parent in the series (as well as Ross/David Schwimmer) would have begun to undermine the core concept of the series – the dramatic questions many people face in the period between childhood and a settled career or family. "We didn't want to do another TV show where you had a woman carrying packages in front of her for nine months and in big coats. We wanted to find a way to actually incorporate it into the story" (Eng, 2018). The surrogacy story became the "arc"

FIGURE 3.2 Single shot: Phoebe

Credit: "The One with the Embryos", *Friends*, Bright/Kauffman/Crane Productions/Warner Brothers Television, 1998.

for the character of Phoebe for season four (see Chapter 4). The shot (Figure 3.2) illustrates how sitcoms can combine comedy with drama, as Phoebe delivers a heartfelt "pep talk" to the embryos. Conveying this drama influences the filming and editing decisions, as Bright recalled: "I didn't want a cut. If we had a cut, it would've kind of spoiled it . . . It probably took two takes" (ibid.).

The dramatic and comedic climax of the quiz plot is the quiz itself and the "lightning round" tiebreaker. Producing this scene illustrates the importance of the live studio audience (a major difference from studio soap operas) to sitcom production;

FIGURE 3.3 "Action" shot: coin toss

Credit: "The One with the Embryos", *Friends*, Bright/Kauffman/Crane Productions/Warner Brothers Television, 1998.

"Doing the contest over and over and that level of investment . . . You'll do a take and if a joke doesn't get enough of a response, the writers would huddle and try to beat it" (ibid.).

This scene also included one of the two pieces of action in the episode (tossing a coin to decide who goes first, Figure 3.3) and illustrates why sitcom producers prefer continuous filming of the scene over including action which might interrupt the comedy;

> I think actually during the show the coin toss also landed perfectly the first time on the table, but in rehearsal it went off. We were afraid it was going to be one of those things that held us up.
>
> *Ibid.*

The central A-plot question – will they *really* give up their apartment? – is built up in conflict over whether the bet should be taken seriously and, between Rachel (Jennifer Aniston) and Monica, over who is responsible for the problem. Even in such a classic two-person dialogue scene, studio shows have a much more limited *variety* of shots than features or filmed series. In a feature, like *Pirates of The Caribbean*, this would have been covered in a shot-reverse-shot structure moving in from mid shots to close-ups. Here the two cameras remain in mid shot so the scene can be recorded "as-live", without breaking to set up the different shot sizes or obscuring the studio audience's view of the action.

Figures 3.4 and 3.5 show limited implementation of continuity editing principles, with Monica's eyeline matching Rachel's (from the previous shot) and spatial continuity shown by filming "over-the-shoulder" of Rachel. However, as the shot change is achieved using live vision mixing, rather than editing film or tape, the effect is more of "switching" between viewpoints rather than a sequence moving in a grammatical logic from shot to shot.

The next shot (Figure 3.6) resolves the A-plot as Chandler and Joey (Matt Le Blanc) move in, riding the dog statue. This shot also covers the most significant

FIGURE 3.4 Mid shot: Rachel in dialogue with Monica

Credit: "The One with the Embryos", *Friends*, Bright/Kauffman/Crane Productions/Warner Brothers Television, 1998.

FIGURE 3.5 Over-the-shoulder shot: Monica in dialogue with Rachel

Credit: "The One with the Embryos", *Friends*, Bright/Kauffman/Crane Productions/Warner Brothers Television, 1998.

"action" of actor and object movement in the episode. Compared to a feature or the wide shots from *Game of Thrones* in Chapter 4, this is a very limited piece of action and again this reflects the limits of continuous multi-camera filming compared to the discontinuous process of features or filmed series. Rather than covering the action in a sequence of shots, the whole movement is covered in the single wide shot, with the camera stationary. As Executive Producer Kevin Bright noted;

FIGURE 3.6 Action shot: Joey and Chandler riding dog statue

Credit: "The One with the Embryos", *Friends*, Bright/Kauffman/Crane Productions/Warner Brothers Television, 1998.

The guys coming in on Pat the Dog was something that was a little hard to control, but fortunately in front of the audience it worked perfectly. Every time you pushed it, the wheels weren't locked, so you never knew where it was going to go. So sometimes in rehearsal it went right off the set into the cameras.

Eng, 2018

The two plots are brought together in the final scene as the fight over the apartments is interrupted by Phoebe's announcement that she is pregnant. The other characters reverse their previous mistake, forgetting about the quiz and the apartments, and forming a group hug to celebrate the news (Figure 3.7).

This model of studio production was developed, as much as anywhere, by *Friends'* home network, NBC. But as NBC President, Sylvester Weaver, made clear in 1950 – this was a process of experimentation; "in the development of any new form of communications . . . there must be an exploratory period in which procedures are laid down and patterns are set, before the successful use of the medium can be developed" (cited in Baughman, 1997:719). This section describes how radio producers in the US established the dominant designs which remain the basis of much contemporary studio production. Hilmes (2012) argues convincingly that the radio era provided the opportunity for much of the experimentation which enabled the emergence of the studio model. Rather than a single dominant design, like the feature film, broadcasting's scheduling or programming model of content distribution (see Market control, this volume, p. 80) meant that the networks developed a portfolio approach, a product range or a variety of text types. For this, the broadcasters drew on many existing text types; US radio stations were owned by magazines,

FIGURE 3.7 Wide shot: group hug

Credit: "The One with the Embryos", *Friends*, Bright/Kauffman/Crane Productions/Warner Brothers Television, 1998.

newspapers and theatres and the BBC quickly began to develop programmes around the national diary of important (religious, political, sporting etc.) events.

However, as shown below, under market pressures the variety show, hosted by established vaudeville/music hall talent, evolved into a range of dominant designs for studio production – the variety or talk show, the soap opera and the sitcom – of (generally) weekly, hour-long series. Comedians like Eddie Cantor hosted variety shows before a live studio audience, introduced so stage comedians could continue to base their timing and delivery on audience reactions. The BBC's variety shows represented an "isomorphic" adoption of this dominant design:

> U.S. broadcasting increasingly appeared to the B.B.C variety staff as a fruitful source of inspiration . . . Americans were invited to England to offer their services, but variety producers on the verge of a crisis of creativity were encouraged to go to the States
>
> *Camporesi, 1989:151*

This accelerated with the introduction of commercial competition in 1955. Spurred by ITV's imitations of US variety shows – like *Sunday Night at the London Palladium* – the following year the BBC increased its light entertainment output by 89 hours (compared to a six hour increase in drama) (op. cit.).

The development of the sitcom began in the mid 1930s as comedians experimented with serial narrative structures as an alternative to the variety show structure of comedy routines. These sitcom series were influenced by earlier serial comedy text types including newspaper comic strips and Hollywood sitcoms, which began around 1910, such as *John Bunny* (Vitagraph) and *Mr and Mrs Jones* (Biograph). NBC's *Amos 'n' Andy* played a key role in developing design elements including casting the comedian(s) as a character whose personal and professional life involved regular comic situations with a recurring cast of comedians and actors (McLeod, 2005). The combination of comic routines and narrative tended to allow for a smaller number of plots than in soap opera but the presence of two interlinking (A and B) plots continued in *Newhart* in the 1980s (Mayerle, 1989) and was illustrated (above) in *Friends*. When *Amos 'n' Andy* began attracting a weekly audience of 40 million, the sitcom became the dominant design for light entertainment. The show later transferred to TV and the process of isomorphism brought a range of similar shows (like *The Rise of the Goldbergs*) (op. cit.). The second step in the sitcom's rise to dominance was *ILL* in 1951 (also adapted from a radio show) which became the first TV programme regularly reaching two-thirds of US TV homes and established the sitcom's potential in TV syndication markets (Copeland, 2007).

Again, isomorphism brought similar developments at the BBC, whose most popular series in in the late '30s, *Band Waggon*, was a deliberate attempt to imitate a similarly titled US sitcom. As its star, Arthur Askey, noted: "the B.B.C. was thinking of doing what they did on radio in America: having big comedy shows at a certain time on a certain night of the week" (Camporesi, 1989:156). Similarly, *It's That Man Again* (1939) was designed to be an English version of the *Burns and Allen*

Show (Hilmes, 2012). The impact of *ILL* in establishing the sitcom text type was as formidable in the UK as in the US. While ITV bought *ILL*, the BBC imported *The Phil Silvers Show*. But rather than simply adopting these US forms, both channels began to develop their own sitcoms addressing local themes, like *Hancock's Half Hour* (BBC) and *The Army Game* (ITV).

As the broadcasters developed the range of dominant designs they needed for their schedules, the alternative to the sitcom became the soap opera. Early US radio stations had adapted newspaper serial stories into radio drama series – famously, Irma Phillips' *Painted Dreams* (Allen, 1985). Initially, believing the potential audiences were low, US networks had used the daytime parts of their schedules for low-cost "infomercials" designed to instruct female consumers in the use of cooking, cleaning and beauty products. The advertising agency BSH played a key role in convincing advertisers to pay the higher costs of producing radio serial dramas for broadcast during the daytime. BSH's radio producers, Frank and Ann Hummert, adapted their soap operas from existing popular series, including comic strips like *Superman* and *Tarzan*. Their range of soaps continued broadcasting for decades – like *Ma Perkins* (1933–60) and *The Romance of Helen Trent* (1933–60) (Meyers, 1997). By 1941 soaps had become the dominant design of daytime radio, in the US, and made up almost 90% of advertiser-funded shows. After an initial period when US TV focused on anthology dramas, this design transferred to US TV, the genre reaching its peak with 18 soaps on air in the US in 1969, and as soaps became longer, a peak of 168,000 minutes broadcast in 1981 (Harrington et al., 2015).

The design of these studio shows developed in the radio industry and then transferred and was adapted for TV studios. Thus, studio shows developed as a means of recreating the experience of a live drama using the affordances of the broadcast studio. The radio networks had begun by broadcasting live events. However, this faced the problem that unlike the human brain, electronic microphones picked up all sounds equally. The development of directional microphones mounted on "booms" (driven by the introduction of sound feature films) enabled better sound "coverage" – similar to camera coverage (see Chapter 2) – of moving actors. However, outside broadcasts still struggled to deal with the distortion effect of wind noise on microphones. To isolate the sound of the performers from these types of background, music producers and then radio networks began construction of specialist sound studios: "sound recordings are normally 'posed' and undertaken in special places to isolate sound sources from possible interference" (Voorhees, 1930:211). Radio studios still faced a problem in recreating the audience experience of hearing sounds live. Again, microphones were much less effective than the human brain in balancing the appropriate relative volumes of different sounds (voices, musical instruments, sound effects etc.). This was originally achieved via techniques for calculating the appropriate distances to place microphones in relation to sound sources (Hanson and Morris, 1931). Again, the solution was an innovation from the "talkies" – adopted in radio. At this point, sound for features was recorded on wax disks, which made sound editing very difficult. To resolve this, the Hollywood studios developed sound mixing desks, with "fader" controls, so that the relative volumes of different sound sources could be "balanced" and recorded, "as live" on set (Bordwell et al., 1985). By the late 1930s, specialist audio mixing consoles became standard in radio studios; the basis of sound "production".

As Hilmes (2012) and others note, early TV production involved adapting the dominant radio studio text types (soap operas, variety series and the emerging sitcom form) for TV. It is here that we can trace the next steps in the differences between feature sequences and the *Friends* sequence above. Early engineers noted that adapting radio series for TV involved an additional challenge: "in television production we have the timing of the stage with the complications of photographic technique" (cited in Barker, 1991:311). Studio TV production thus involved the coevolution of the "as live" production and distribution of radio (where production and consumption happened simultaneously) with the discontinuous recording process developed for feature production (where production and consumption were completely separated). Furthermore, the technology of electronic video cameras was, in many ways, more similar to that of the radio microphone than to the film camera. For many years, it was not possible to record and edit the electronic video signal created by the TV camera (op. cit.). Even the creation of a focused image required a stationary camera set at a fixed distance from the person or object to be filmed, prohibiting camera movement. This focusing problem prevented video cameras from showing a "depth of field" before or behind a person or object. Effectively, TV cameras could only provide close-ups. TV's tendency to shoot in close-up was also reinforced by the small size of the TV screens initially available to audiences. Unlike early film production, where the inability to change shot was simply accepted by the industry and its audiences, in the early days of TV both groups were accustomed to seeing cinema dramas filmed in sequences, using a wide variety of shots to cover actor movement and dialogue. By contrast, TV offered only close-up shots, severe limits on camera movement, no ability to record shots to enable shot changes, and thus very limited actor movement.

Although there are (by definition) no recordings of the early live TV studio productions, we can trace the separate development of the multi-camera studio show from accounts based on early production documents, like Barker's (1991) description of *The Man with a Flower in His Mouth* (BBC July, 1930) – the UK's first broadcast TV drama. The script was chosen because it could be produced even within the limits set by the technology – three characters, only speaking dialogue (i.e. no action) and with a single chair as the "set". Because any attempt to move the camera to set up a different shot would have revealed the discontinuous movement of both camera and actors, the producers experimented with ways of preserving the invisibility of technique to which audiences were accustomed. To achieve a transition between shots, they created an early equivalent of a live "fade"; "a large wooden board . . . was slowly slid in front of the character" until the second actor was in place (Barker, 1991:312). Again, influenced by the feature film, there was an attempt to provide a narrative motivation for these transitions, with actors looking left or right and attempting to create "eyeline matches" live. Just as the early film was a single wide shot, so the early TV programme was restricted to close-ups: "many early productions consisted of nothing but close-ups" (ibid.).

Producers experimented with ways of creating the equivalent of a feature film sequence using the live video camera. Since it was not possible to record shots, the only means of changing shot was to use two live video cameras. However, to achieve an "invisible" transition between shots where one of the actors moved significantly, or the camera moved from one set to another, required the equivalent of a feature film "cutaway". Again, since this could not be recorded on video (and the "fader" board was extremely visible), a third live video camera was required to provide a third shot which could be held while one or more of the other cameras moved. Barker (1991) describes this use of two cameras for close-ups of the (two) actors and one for close-up "cutaways" (of props or the actors' hands). TV engineers were clear that they were attempting to combine live studio production with feature production techniques: "to present the variety of close-ups and long shots and angles the movies have made desirable" (Barker, 1991:311).

The model of radio studio production provided the technology to transition between the shots provided by the three cameras; the live sound mixer (which enabled transitions between microphones and sound sources) was adapted for "vision mixing". The producers of *The Queen's Messenger* (1928) saw this as a natural evolution: "the idea of multiple video sources and a mixer seemed natural to engineers trained in radio" (ibid.). The drama was performed live with video cameras shooting continuously. In the studio gallery, the vision mixer transitioned from one camera to another by fading the first camera down to black whilst simultaneously fading up the image from the second camera. TV producers began to develop vison mixing methods of approximating the conventional shot transitions (cuts, dissolves, wipes, superimpositions etc.) of the feature film.

The difficulty of editing videotape meant that, even after the introduction of cameras which could move and methods of recording the camera output on tape, studio production changed only from live to recording performances "as live" on tape. This involved much greater variability of tasks than the discontinuous process of feature production. Where feature production used continuity to try to create a "live" performance from a series of recorded shots, studio production began with a continuous, live performance and attempted to generate the shots needed to tell this story visually, as it happened. Live, multi-camera, vision mixed, studio production faced significant problems in attempting to gain the attention of audiences accustomed to film. Because video cameras were not, for many years, camcorders, during shooting they had to be connected to the vision mixer by large electronic cables. To achieve the developing shots normal in features, for example, as the camera moved to follow an actor, in multi-camera production, could mean one camera moved into the shot of another camera, destroying the invisibility of technique (Eddy, 1945). Further, the number of "takes" of each shot was limited by the "live" (only one take) or "as live" (just a few) process. More complex camera movements – involving for example a change in focal length, in the height of the camera or the use of dollies, pans, tilts or zooms – had to be "right first time".

So, for example, a camera move towards a character, "motivated" by the need for the audience to see closer detail of an emerging dramatic reaction, would involve refocusing during the shot – something very difficult to achieve with early cameras. Particular problems were faced in attempting to replicate the shot-reverse-shot sequences standard in features. In a multi-camera studio set-up moving one camera, to provide a "reverse angle", would be very likely to reveal one of the other cameras or other aspects (lights, microphones, crew) of production.

Together, these restrictions have resulted in TV studio shows having a much more limited range of shots than features. The 180° rule has tended to be applied in a more conservative way, similar to the "proscenium" approach – with all three cameras remaining behind the "line". A centrally placed camera might take wider and establishing shots, one camera left and another right might move and resize to provide differ shot sizes and angles. The tendency to use relatively standard shot transitions in TV sequences was reinforced by the process of "vision mixing", calling these shots "live" rather than having the leisure to select shots in editing feature sequences. In the shooting of TV sequences, studio camera operators are often required to "offer" predictable (rehearsed or routine) transition points (for example a match on action) to enable vision mixers and directors to create a sequence "live".

The constraints of studio production also limited the extent to which three-point lighting (shadows and contrasts) techniques from features (see Chapter 2) could be adopted in TV sequences. First, the TV camera's requirement for a large amount of light to generate a clear image limited the range of low-lighting techniques possible and led to a preference for "high key" lighting (Caldwell, 1995). Second, using several cameras simultaneously required design of a single lighting set-up to provide satisfactory illumination for all three camera angles at once, usually including wider shots and close-ups (Eddy, 1945). Finally, the presence of three moving cameras on the studio floor virtually ruled out the floor-level lighting used in features. The solution – lighting TV studios from above – limited its use to create a 3D effect, further emphasising studio TV's "flat" look. Colour TV later required much more light than black and white and relied even more heavily on lighting from above and from the front (Copeland, 2007).

These limitations had caused multi-camera recording on film to be abandoned in feature production (Bordwell et al., 1985). However, when *Amos 'n' Andy* transferred to CBS TV it was recorded using multiple film cameras at the Hal Roach Studios and then the sitcom *ILL* established the multi-camera, "as live" recorded series as the dominant design for studio production of sitcoms and then soaps (Copeland, 2007). *ILL* was recorded on a Hollywood sound stage and could have been recorded with a single camera, except that the network, CBS, required that it become the first network TV series recorded (following the radio sitcom design) with a studio audience (see Process innovation, this volume, p. 88). *ILL* producers, Desilu, realised the stop-start, out-of-sequence process of feature production would inhibit audience engagement, and so the cast performed the story in the narrative order it would appear to TV viewers.

Regulation and legitimacy

More than in features, regulation played a key role in establishing the oligopolistic network structure of the US commercial broadcasting market, and the monopolistic structure of the public service, non-commercial BBC. In time, as technology permitted more channels, the UK moved to a similarly oligopolistic structure. These regulatory decisions were driven by contrasting arguments, from different lobbying interests, about the legitimacy of broadcasting. Although these were social and political processes, they were generally legitimised as technological choices.

Although the 1912 Radio Act enabled wartime nationalisation of Marconi radio stations, and a potential state monopoly, the idea of public broadcasting lacked legitimacy in the US, perceived as "a merger of state power and media as well as a violation of the First Amendment" (Meyers, 2011a). Initially, the market was extremely competitive – the technological simplicity and low cost of radio technology meant the only barrier to new entrants was created by the radio spectrum. In 1920, the Department of Commerce divided the country into hundreds of markets and issued broadcast licences to multiple businesses in each local market. But, the same year, the government also supported the radio manufacturers (GE, AT&T, Westinghouse and United Fruit) in forming the Radio Corporation of America (RCA) to develop the market for radio receivers. The boom in receiver sales meant that from 1921 to 1923 the radio manufacturers economically outperformed the US car industry (McChesney, 1995).

By 1923, 510 stations had begun broadcasting operated either by colleges and churches (providing public service programmes) or by retailers, manufacturers, newspapers and cinemas (promoting their businesses). But beneath this competition and variety, the manufacturers controlled two-thirds of the stations in operation (Leblebici et al., 1991). The opportunity for the manufacturers to develop their control of broadcast distribution came when a legal decision allowed 200 unlicensed stations to broadcast on the same wavelength. The ensuing technical chaos meant that by 1924 although 1,105 stations had been licensed, 572 had failed. The regulators eventually accepted the manufacturers' argument that, in threatening their ability to operate commercially, this crisis undermined the legitimacy of free competition in the market and demonstrated the case that a regulated market with 'nation-wide chains of broadcasting systems' would best provide quality, efficiency and serve the public interest (McChesney, 1995). In 1927 legislators created the Federal Radio Commission (FRC) to manage access to the radio spectrum by restricting the number of licences in each geographic market. RCA then successfully persuaded regulators to require AT&T to end its monopoly use of its cable network, opening it up for RCA's National Broadcasting Company (NBC) to distribute programmes to local stations across the US. Further networks, Columbia (CBS) (1929) and Mutual Broadcasting Systems (MBS) (1934), followed.

To legitimise their oligopolistic control of the receiver market, and network control of content distribution, the manufacturers had emphasised the importance of public service broadcasting. Regulators like Herbert Hoover, accepting this argument, believed "direct" advertising would be the "quickest way to kill broadcasting" because audiences would not accept it (Anello and Cahill, 1963:285). As late as 1926, advertising pioneer Frank A. Arnold believed: "neither my agency nor any other had a definite interest in radio . . . because there was no basis on which to interest the national advertiser" (cited in Camporesi, 1990:262). AT&T changed this approach in 1922 when its WEAF station began selling "indirect" advertising (without price or product details) via sponsored broadcasts. Advertisers would "create 'sponsor identification' in the minds of audiences who would buy a sponsor's products out of gratitude for free entertainment" (Meyers, 2011a:357). The Radio Act (1927) accepted this demonstration of the legitimacy of indirect advertising with audiences, and created a radio advertising market by licensing commercial stations.

US developments had a strong influence on UK broadcasting. US manufacturers, eager to create another market for receivers, pressured the British government to license radio stations (Briggs, 1965). It became apparent that in the US, "people were willing to buy their radio sets by the million . . . British entrepreneurs had learnt that broadcasting could be highly profitable, at least to set manufacturers" (Camporesi, 1990:262). However, the development of a successful US advertising market did not generate support for advertiser-funded broadcasting in the UK. The strong political influence of UK newspapers, protecting their control of the advertising market, was firmly against commercial broadcasting, while UK advertisers "did not play any significant role in the discussion on broadcasting policy in Britain" (ibid.). Instead, the regulatory "chaos" of early US broadcasting was again used to legitimise the creation of a regulated, public service network (ibid.). In 1922, faced with the prospects either of mass importation of US receivers or a monopoly for the UK manufacturer Marconi, the UK regulator, the Post Office, roughly followed the RCA model by establishing a consortium of manufacturers – the British Broadcasting Company (BBCo). The BBCo's revenue was guaranteed by providing protection from US receiver imports and a licence fee imposed on radio audiences in exchange for a commitment to establish a broadcast network. However, when this arrangement came up for renewal in 1925, the BBCo's problems of financing commercial broadcasting through receivers, along with broader debates about the legitimacy of commercial media, led the government to convert the BBCo into the BBC, a monopoly public corporation, tasked with public service broadcasting, and supported by the receiver licence fee (Crisell, 2002).

Some researchers have argued that both the UK and US networks subscribed to an "ideology of liveness". Kompare (2006:129) argues: "radio broadcasting was dominated by commercial and governmental interests who championed an ideal of live programming from the 1920s to 1940s . . . against the seemingly more practical principle of recording performances for later broadcasts". There clearly were forces advancing the superior legitimacy of live production. Since the late 1920s, the US regulators, the FRC and later the Federal Communications Commission (FCC) had attempted to protect expensive local production of original live programmes against competition from radio stations relying on records or TV stations reshowing Hollywood B-movies (Hilmes, 2012). Some advertisers believed "live" productions brought more prestige to their brands, and talent unions clearly favoured live production over recording, to guarantee continuing employment for creators. However, there were also interests in favour of recorded programming. Since the early 1930s independent producers of recorded (or "transcribed") audio programming had coevolved with the networks, solving the problem of broadcasting across US time zones by recording live programmes during transmission to distribute to stations across the country. These audio and later telefilm producers became suppliers (syndicators) of non-prime time recorded programmes, particularly to unaffiliated local stations (Kompare, 2006). This created the potential to undermine network control of the advertising market should their affiliate stations decide to deal directly with the independents. The independents might even develop a competitor network with an alternative advertising platform.

The decisions in favour of live programming in the early years of TV were partly technical. As noted, video signals could not be recorded, and so networks accustomed to live radio production were likely to carry at least some aspects of this model forward to the TV era. However, as the section below argues, live TV studio production, and the early attempts of networks like NBC to associate this with the high culture of Broadway drama and variety productions, were largely driven by an attempt to counter the broader critique of the legitimacy of commercial broadcasting which had been developing for the previous two decades. In the Depression years in the US, as advertising budgets had come under pressure, the networks began to allow programmes to include direct selling – explicit price and sales pitches. Radio audiences declined and listener complaints to the FRC and the networks soared – with public criticism of overcommercial programming often directed at the role of the sponsor. By 1932, a "radio reform" movement had formed, campaigning for regulation to counter sponsor influence, and protect the public interest, by placing control (and responsibility) over programming in the networks (Pickard, 2013).

The networks were restricted in their ability to respond to this critique because their "time franchise" business model discouraged, and to an extent prevented, them from exercising control over programme content. Rather than make changes in prime time, the networks began to use in-house producers to develop innovative "sustaining" programmes during daytime, which in turn became publicly associated with public service values. The FCC "Blue Book" "underscored the disparity between the mass appeal sponsored programs (soap operas and popular music) and the sustaining programs (drama, minority cultural programming, access for non-profit/civic organisations and experimental programs) of the radio networks" (Boddy, 1993:97).

When the networks moved into TV, they became determined to develop greater control over advertiser influence on programming. As the next section shows, this entailed moving to the "spot" market approach to advertising sales. At the same time, executives like Pat Weaver at NBC sought to differentiate the quality of the new TV product from the challenged legitimacy of commercial radio, through live programming produced in-house like the "public service"-sustaining programmes, and using Broadway talent.

Market control

Chapter 1 explained how, even with an apparently "free" product like broadcast TV, markets operate in allocating the scarce resource of audience "attention". This chapter has described how broadcasters developed the dominant design of the studio show as an effective means of attracting the attention of large audiences. This section explains how the networks developed strategies to try to control the market in selling audience attention to advertisers. It is often argued that the US networks developed a "radio model" which they carried on into the TV era. Hilmes (1999:49) argues that by 1927 "radio broadcasting had taken on most of the structural, economic and regulatory features that were to characterize the radio, and later television, industry for the next fifty years". However, while the dominant designs of radio were clearly the basis of the studio shows adopted by the TV networks (in both the UK and the US) this section argues that the market control techniques used in commercial TV (in both countries) were different from the radio model established by the US radio networks.

The section above noted that following the technological discontinuity of radio broadcasting, the US government enabled broad entry to the market, producing intense competition in the industry. However, the small scale of local advertising markets (often dominated by a local newspaper) made many of these new, small commercial stations unprofitable (McChesney, 1995). The technical problems of interfering radio signals led the regulators to begin to restrict market entry and support the development of broadcast networks owned by the radio manufacturers. The networks began to develop a national advertising market, working with the advertising agencies to create an audience rating system and thus a pricing mechanism (ratings points) for national radio advertising sales. This, in turn, gave the networks demand-based economies of scale compared to smaller stations. The networks could sell nationwide audience reach to national advertisers and could force local advertisers, wanting to advertise in particular cities, to buy time across the whole network – so-called "must buy" stations (Funk, 2012). The networks thus established control over the national market, acting as gatekeepers between corporations wanting access to US consumers and the chain of local stations whose airtime the networks sold. Recognising this control, the number of local stations affiliated to one of the networks increased from 6% to 97% over the next 20 years (ibid.).

Chapter 1 suggested that companies with significant market shares, gained through control of distribution, have strong incentives to consolidate market control through vertically integrating distribution and production. However, as the chapter also showed, the technical characteristics of broadcasting made it a non-rival, "public good", without an opportunity to recover the high "first copy" costs of live entertainment production through revenue from a paying public. Thus, rather than a scarcity of programming creating a market of consumers willing to pay, it was the scarce attention time of audiences which created a market in advertisers willing to pay to reach those consumers. AT&T, established the "dominant design" for selling advertising via time slots, "because selling airtime seemed exactly like selling telephone time" (Winston, 2002:80). The networks developed this business model, operating their stations like telephone booths, selling advertisers a "time franchise", a monopoly on a 15, 30 or 60 minute "segment" of the broadcast day. The low fees available from advertisers meant the networks saw programme production as a high risk, compared to their business in advertising sales and distribution. For the advertisers, major corporations concerned to protect their brands, the opportunities of reaching national audiences had to be balanced against the risks of association with poor programming in the experimental stage of a new medium. The corporations trusted their advertising agencies, more than the unproven broadcast networks, to produce programmes "allied with their selling thought" (Hilmes, 2007:17). Similarly, the advertising agencies saw the potential to earn commission fees (additional to those for buying airtime) by entering programme production to fill these time segments. Instead of the networks integrating programme production with distribution, therefore, the US corporations integrated production with their marketing departments.

This dominant design of advertising sales (a weekly time franchise, most often an hour) in turn encouraged the development of a dominant design for programming; the hour-long series, usually with the sponsor's name in the title, *The Eveready Hour* or *The Chase & Sanborn Hour* (ibid.). The focus on programming as a means of selling further undermined the legitimacy of public service broadcasting, as advertisers argued that the new medium should bring "the show world, to the world of commerce" (Meyers, 2011b:211). The commercial form of the hour-long series slot encouraged advertisers to experiment with serial and series text types, particularly in radio's daytime hours. The low daytime audiences discouraged advertiser investment and so networks sold 15-minute daytime segments at half the prime time price, offering "volume" discounts to advertisers buying several segments. A number of agencies, especially BSH, began to persuade advertisers that 15-minute serial dramas could attract a female audience and so promote soap powders, cereals and cosmetics. When Procter & Gamble developed a range of soap operas, each promoting a different P&G product, a new dominant text type was created. The commercial success of many radio soaps and comedy shows meant that the advertising agencies were the "true originators of most of the broadcast forms still with us" (Hilmes, 1999:81).

However, changes in the advertising market, particularly the Depression, put this system of outsourced production under pressure, first through profitability and then legitimacy. An executive noted:

> a $20,000 all-star program on a coast-to-coast network may get fine press notices and win the sympathetic applause of those self-appointed advertising critics who are working for high cultural standards – but it's a dead loss to the advertiser if it's all showmanship and no salesmanship.
>
> *Cited in Meyers, 2011a:361*

As noted above, the networks' decision to allow direct selling affected audiences and brought public criticism of the industry via a "radio reform" movement. This critique of the legitimacy of the US model of broadcasting was compounded by problems with its commercial operation. Despite initial fears, the radio advertising market escaped the overall drop in advertising spending during the Depression, growing from $18 million –to $165 million from 1929 to 1937 (op. cit.). However, the existing business model limited growth because new advertisers wanting to enter the market, found themselves excluded from those "time franchises" with the highest audience ratings. Further, advertisers who did "own" expensive franchises began to complain that the programmes immediately preceding or following theirs were inappropriate. Some agencies, like BSH, had attempted to solve this problem of adjacencies, and maintain audience attention from one programme to another, by "block booking" airtime across the broadcast day.

The catalyst for a change in the US model came with the introduction of TV. As they sought to respond to this new opportunity, both advertisers and networks began to identify a solution to these problems of the radio model – a return to the "print model" of advertising sales, where the "platform" owner took the editorial and programming risks, and advertisers could "participate" by associating themselves with successful titles and content. In the early 1950s, network heads like NBC's Sylvester "Pat" Weaver, a former radio advertising executive, developed this "magazine" approach to TV advertising, replacing the single sponsor, "owning" a programme/time slot, with several "participating" sponsors buying "insertions", without themselves being directly involved in production (Meyers, 2011a). The networks' experiments with "spot" advertising during daytime hours demonstrated that audiences could be attracted to remain with a network if the content was organised into a schedule, with appropriate types of content arranged in sequence. This "spot" model gained commercial legitimacy when advertising research revealed audiences could identify different products advertised within the same programme.

From the networks' perspective, their business model had changed from achieving the maximum price from the maximum sales of "time franchises" to attracting the largest number of participating sponsors for a TV series. This brought a change in strategy from a single focus on advertising sales towards greater concern to maximise audiences. This approach was influenced by a process of isomorphism, an adoption of an approach to content distribution which became dominant across the industry:

> studies of the United States' broadcasting oligopolies of the nineteen thirties and forties show that artists, directors and support staffs, irrespective as to whether they fell under the aegis of agencies or networks, pushed ahead with the filling-out of a "full line" of broadcasting programme formats.
>
> *Barnouw, 1968:74–5*

The basics of a model for network control of programming, in the public interest, existed in the UK. The BBC's creation of a network reaching a national audience was driven not by the need to create an advertising market, but by the need to provide universal public service to legitimise the licence fee. The demand for increased transmission hours came (initially) from the licence paying audience rather than advertisers. The BBC's Programme Board planned programming in a basic schedule ("the weekly programme sheet") eight weeks in advance. Initially, the BBC schedule did not have the "fixed points" of the US network "time franchises", with programmes at regular times. Instead, apart from news and religious series, many programmes "dodged about from week to week" (Crisell, 2002:53). Under pressure from commercial competition (from Radio Luxembourg) the BBC began to organise programming to provide variety across the day; "the idea of a 'programme series', pushed much farther . . . in 1934, owed something to the American idea of the So-and-So Hour" (Briggs, 1965:102).

But the origins of the scheduling model adopted across the broadcast industry lay further back in the history of popular live entertainment – especially variety theatre. In the UK, ATV's Lew Grade, who came from the music hall industry, drew an explicit parallel:

> when you put a variety bill together, you cannot please the whole audience with the whole programme . . . you need to have sufficient elements so that at least half the programme appeals to all the audience. I used the same tactics on television.
>
> *Turnock, 2007:67*

Vaudeville, music hall and nickelodeons had all organised entertainment into a "bill" of "acts" (or segments) of sufficient variety to retain audience interest across several hours' entertainment (see Chapter 2). The networks began to develop techniques to combine the magazine approach to advertising sales with maximising audiences through "scheduling" strategies; organising programmes into "blocks" of similar shows to build audience "flow" across successive programmes, sometimes moving programmes against the wishes of individual sponsors (Baughman, 2007). The reward for successful scheduling might be attracting the largest or most affluent audience, to encourage that audience to stay with the network, or to try to attract target audiences from a competitor.

We have already seen that, unlike the Hollywood majors and UK broadcast networks, the US radio networks had chosen to "outsource" production from the start. US radio production was largely outsourced to advertising agencies working for brands who paid the costs of production. Some advertising agencies, lacking skills in either show business or radio production techniques, turned to their existing (product endorsement) relationships with talent (performers and writers) to create programme "packages" (programme concepts, performing talent and scripts) to be produced by independent theatrical or musical producers, talent agencies and small companies producing and distributing recorded radio programmes ("syndicators" and "transcription" companies). Others developed their production capabilities through large-scale recruitment of skilled production staff from the networks. By the 1930s, however, this independent sector had largely been "shaken out" and production of most national sponsored radio programmes was vertically integrated; produced either by the radio departments of established agencies or by new entrants, advertising agencies specialising in radio advertising and production (Funk, 2012).

The legitimacy problems of the 1930s led some of the advertisers to reassess the risks of programme production by advertising agencies: "a failed program could create a negative association with their product as well as a successful one a positive association" (Meyers, 2011a:362). The emergence of TV caused advertisers to ask more profound questions about their involvement in programme production. Radio had originally appealed because it was cheaper to produce than newspapers and magazines (and achieved wider national distribution). However, as the radio networks had continued to increase transmission hours, advertisers faced opportunity costs (losing audience attention to competitors) if they did not increase the number of series they sponsored. The model of production finance, and outsourcing to agencies, also included a mechanism for increasing production costs. Because advertisers did not pay the full costs of production, only paying the agencies a commission on the costs of talent recruitment and purchasing airtime, the agencies had incentives to increase both programme quality and their commissions by paying high prices for talent (especially Hollywood stars). Early estimates suggested TV would cost ten times as much as radio, and so the advertisers began to identify a number of incentives to disintegrate their programme production activities. On the supplier side of the advertising market, the US broadcasters were keen that TV would provide the opportunity to re-establish the legitimacy of commercial broadcasting with audiences and regulators. The spot advertising model and the scheduling approach provided advertisers with an alternative to the radio model of buying a "time franchise" and paying for production of a whole series. Instead, they could simply pay for the airtime they wanted and leave the broadcasters to produce the programming (Baughman, 2007).

These early years of broadcast TV saw some moves by US networks to integrate production with their emerging control of distribution. As noted, some researchers have explained such moves as a reflection of an "ideology of liveness" subscribed to by the both UK and US networks. By contrast, this section follows the approach outlined in Chapter 1, where vertical integration of production was explained in terms of strategic moves towards market control. The clearest US network attempt to bring TV production "in-house" was during Weaver's early years at NBC (see Gomery, 2007). Weaver's role in developing the magazine approach to advertising led him to focus on a quality programme schedule as a key means of maximising audiences (and spot prices). As concerns had grown about overcommercialisation of radio, the networks had begun to use in-house producers to develop innovative "sustaining" programmes during daytime, which, in turn, became publicly associated with public service values. As noted, the FCC had identified the networks' sustaining programmes with the idea of public service. This perception of the quality of network produced content convinced Weaver that in-house, rather than agency, production would help TV avoid the legitimacy problems of the commercial radio model:

> I brought in some of the top ad agency programming men to help me . . . and
> I told them, 'Look we ruined radio. Let's not let it happen to television. Let's
> stage our own programs and just sell advertising time to the agencies'.
>
> *Cited in McCormack, 2017*

In addition to these issues of legitimacy, Weaver believed the security of the net-work's control over the advertising market rested in its ability to supply advertisers, audiences and affiliates with dominant text types that the independent syndicators or Hollywood studios could not match. To enable advertisers to purchase the TV equivalent of space in print magazines, Weaver created some live magazine-style TV formats by combining radio's daytime talk format with elements of the variety show (Gomery, 2007). Some of these in-house productions (*Today* and *Tonight*) remain core to the NBC schedule. However, the flagships of his approach were prime time, spec-tacular, in-house, live studio variety and comedy shows – like Milton Berle's *Texaco Star Theater*, Sid Caesar's *Your Show of Shows* (*YSS*) and Donald O'Connor's *Colgate Comedy Hour*. Rather than an "ideology of liveness", this can be understood as an attempt to compete by differentiating the dominant text type of TV from that of the feature film. Weaver saw TV as the next stage in the coevolution of broadcasting and live entertainment, bringing top Broadway talent to national audiences. "Television is not movies", he argued "it is show business in the living room" (Baugham, 1997:718).

Vertical integration of TV production faced a number of key challenges. Unlike Hollywood, the requirements of a full programme schedule created for NBC a task unprecedented in the history of theatre, film or radio – immediate volume production of live audio-visual entertainment (see Process innovation, this volume, p. 88). NBC built studio production facilities and, reversing the process of early radio, recruited staff from the advertising agencies to its new TV Program and Public Affairs departments. However, in-house production staff balked at the volume of output required:

> NBC executives argued strongly that it was manifestly impossible for the
> network to hire enough people to support an operation providing live pro-gramming from 6:00 pm to 11:00 pm seven days a week . . . it took months
> to produce motion pictures and Broadway plays, yet television's insatiable
> appetite for programming demanded fresh material every day.
>
> *Mashon, 2007:142*

Chapter 1 showed how researchers have used the "flexible specialisation" approach to argue that outsourcing decisions were driven by failure of the standard-ised, mass production of the networks and the need to access the greater flexibility and innovative potential of the independent producers (see Barnatt and Starkey, 1997). By contrast, this chapter follows the argument presented in Chapters 1 and 2 which emphasised a focus on talent "brands" (often originally developed by the studios and the networks) as a strategy to try to reduce audience uncertainty over individually differentiated media products and thus to try to increase the predict-ability of content in attracting audiences.

Chapter 2 explained how Hollywood stars, often encouraged by their talent agents (especially Lew Wasserman, at the largest agency MCA), had begun to transition from being employees, paying a potential 88% tax, to forming independent companies paying only 25% tax on their income from the studios. Anderson (1994:65) confirms that "talent agencies played a crucial role in this stage of the [television] industry's development". Although Screen Actors Guild (SAG) regulations forbade talent agents from becoming TV producers, a grey area allowed them to act as "packagers". By bringing a client and a production together, the agents were able to waive their right to a commission from the talent and instead earn a percentage of the TV product budget and of any profit made (Wilson, 2000). In 1952, Wasserman used his political connections (especially one of his clients, SAG president Ronald Reagan) to persuade the SAG to make an exception and allow MCA's Revue Productions to supply TV programmes for the networks.

Because the power of these independents was based on the brand recognition of their talent, in reducing the risks of production, outsourcing did not reward small, innovative independent producers. Instead it gave talent agencies, and some talent-based independent production companies, advantages in raising the significant levels of risk investment needed to finance early TV production;

> because of their reputations in radio or movies and the backing of established talent agencies, they often were able to get series commitments from sponsors and networks based on a single pilot episode. And as a result of these commitments, they found it much easier to arrange bank financing to cover production deficits and company expenses.
>
> *Anderson, 1994:65*

This financial power gave talent agencies and talent-based independents a competitive advantage over small independents, but also over the networks' own in-house production, since they could exploit the high-risk "deficit financing" model, where a producer sold a series to the network at lower than the cost of production but retained the rights to the profits from "off network" distribution (syndication) as "repeats". If the series was a hit, the producer could continue to make profits almost indefinitely.

Rather than providing innovation, as FS would suggest, Wasserman's initial successes involved moving two of NBC's successful flagship shows, *The Jack Benny Show* and *Amos 'n' Andy*, to CBS. However, this is not to say that quality or innovation were irrelevant in the outsourcing of production. NBC's in-house, live, variety shows were hugely expensive and yet the process of recording these New York productions, on film, for broadcast in other time zones, produced a much lower resolution image than a programme originally shot on film (Copeland, 2007). The huge success of the innovative sitcom *ILL* in building large, loyal audiences and habitual viewing established the dominance of this new model of TV production: outsourced, recorded, deficit financed, syndication-oriented and Hollywood-based. Again, the intervention of a talent agent, Don Sharpe, was influential in helping Lucille Ball and Desi Arnaz to start Desilu Productions. The increase in quality, compared with live studio shows, was made possible by the deficit financing model. Recording *ILL* on film cost $24,500, roughly five times the cost of live production. Since the network and sponsor would not meet all these costs, Desilu financed the rest of the cost, in return for retaining syndication rights (op. cit.). By 1957 Desilu was able to buy its own Hollywood studio.

Without the access to the deficit financing made possible by access to talent, most independents could not compete for network commissions or afford the potential losses of a failed series. Although there was some specialisation in particular text types (e.g. quiz shows), as Wilson (2000:406) noted: "only the major agencies are able to package". Anderson (1994) suggests the number of independents declined from 75 in 1951 to less than 30 a year later. By the end of the decade MCA was the dominant producer and "packager" of TV shows, owning 1,650 shows outright and 525 more as co-producer. At the same time, it was earning around $9.5 million more than its nearest competitor, the other large talent agency William Morris (Wilson, 2000).

By 1957 NBC's vertical integration strategy had failed; the network had out-sourced 14 series (8 and a half hours a week) to MCA alone, and *Variety* had declared "the end of the 'Milton Berle Era' of TV leadership" (Schatz, 1990:124). Rather than a pure demonstration of the superiority of outsourcing, this also reflected the extent of the networks' oligopolistic control over the advertising market. Public service regulations limiting prime time advertising minutes had pushed up the "cost per thousand" viewers and TV advertising spend had increased from $454 million to $1.6 billion between 1952 and 1960 (Meyers, 2011a). With this level of control, the threat that the independents might establish a competitor network had disappeared. Rather than trying to prevent independent production and the emergence of a programme syndication market, the networks used their oligopsony power (as buyers of programming) to gain control of it, negotiating "profit participation" contracts to gain a share of syndication income. By 1957 three quarters of prime time programming was outsourced to the large talent-based independents and (increasingly) the Hollywood studios.

As Chapter 4 shows, rather than flexible specialisation, other forms of vertical integration strategy influenced the coevolution of the film and TV industries. MCA took control of Universal Studios in 1962 and Desilu was acquired by Paramount. It should be noted that while outsourcing replaced in-house and advertiser produc-tion in prime time, outside of these hours advertiser-produced "soap operas" like *As the World Turns* (CBS, 1956–2008) and *Another World* (NBC, 1964–99) contin-ued for decades (Allen, 1985). Similarly, network in-house live studio production still dominated for prime time news, talks and variety text types.

The BBC faced few alternatives to the development of in-house production. Much of the live entertainment industry banned its performers from broadcast-ing and would not permit live broadcasts from its venues. The BBC was forced to try to develop its own talent. After a series of agreements with live entertain-ment businesses, in 1930 the BBC's new Revue and Vaudeville section produced the BBC's first "series" programmes directly drawn from live entertainment text types – *Songs from the Shows, Music Hall,* and *The Kentucky Minstrels* (Crisell, 2002:40). Outsourcing was not unknown however, and some of the BBC's biggest variety shows like *Monday Night at Seven* and the pioneering "sitcom" *Band Waggon* were produced by the independent theatre impresario Jack Hilton who bought the UK rights to the US show.

However, the live entertainment industries were central to establishing the legitimacy of commercial TV (ITV): two talent agents, Prince Littler and Lew Grade, establishing the ATV company. As with radio, the continuing critique of the commercialism of the US model was central to regulations preferring the "magazine" model of spot advertising (over sponsorship) and editorial control by the networks. Oligopolistic control of the advertising market brought ITV revenues of £50 million by 1957, enabling it easily to exceed the BBC's spending of only £14 million on TV (Potschka, 2012) The larger ITV companies were able to secure their in-house production via, "must carry" affiliation agreements requiring smaller companies to take their programmes (op. cit.).

Process innovation

As noted above, and in the terms used in Chapter 1, the immediacy of broadcasting and the extension of the programme schedule, created a requirement to maintain a continuous flow of programming which presented the networks with the challenge of achieving an output of live production unprecedented in the history of entertainment. The BBC increased its annual hours of programmes broadcast from 65,800 in 1927 to 79,525 hours in 1938 (Briggs, 1965). The average hours of TV per week increased from the BBC's 30 in 1950 to 50 each from both ITV and BBC in 1955 (Turnock, 2007:14). BBC TV staff numbers increased from 880 in 1956 to 9,640 by 1963 (op. cit.). However, the development of studio production techniques cannot be explained as an extension of mass production principles to broadcasting, to create "programme factories" (see Bakewell and Garnham, 1970). Instead, studio production reflects a range of technical and creative influences on studio design, in addition to the requirements of achieving the output necessary to sustain the programme schedule.

The first radio studios, developed to enable production of radio's initial dominant design – the "talks" programmes offered as part of the telephone "toll booth" model of selling airtime – contained the transmitter with the microphone and audio equipment. The demand for radio stations to increase programme hours, to have a full schedule, increased the volume and quality of programming required. To improve sound quality, studio designers sought to separate desired sound (performers on microphones) from unwanted sound (engineers and other non-performers working in the studio) through the development of studio control rooms, separating the two groups by a soundproof glass – communication achieved via radio, intercom and/or headphones (Eddy, 1945). Studios were able to achieve a continuous programme output through the introduction of the audio mixer, enabling transitions between performers and continuity announcers on different microphones in separate studios linked to the control room. These fundamentals of the radio studio design remain in contemporary radio studios and were adopted when networks transferred radio shows to TV studio production. In 1933 NBC developed studios at "30 Rock" aiming to achieve "forty-nine audience telecasts per week of thirty to ninety minutes in length" (Gleich, 2012:4). Even more than for radio, for TV production the control room needed to be constructed with a good view of the studio floor. The control room housed the vision mixer (or "switcher") used to select, balance and grade, and make transitions between audio and video inputs including microphones and cameras. In the 1940s, the networks converted theatres and other live entertainment venues into TV studios (op. cit.), however, proscenium theatres imposed severe space limits on movement of cameras and performers. In the 1950s the networks developed purpose-built TV studios eliminating the obstruction of the proscenium, to enable greater variety of movement and placement of multiple cameras (ibid.).

Studio productions in the UK, like the long running soap *Coronation Street* (ITV, 1960–date), were initially broadcast live. Even after the introduction of video recording in 1958, the difficulty of cutting the two-inch tape meant the BBC's purpose-built Television Centre (opened in 1960) was "designed around the principle of live transmission: '[t]he central concept was the necessity to train directors for live [studio] television'" (director Don Taylor, cited in McNaughton, 2014:391). Even pre-recorded shows were produced "as live" in narrative order "in a single run-through" (Briggs, 1965:832–9). These decisions largely involved adapting the existing system of studios producing the dominant text types of broadcast series.

However, by combining centralised production facilities with the volume of output required for a broadcast schedule, studio production enabled fundamental economies of scale. A contemporary BBC engineer explained:

> Just one day in the studio and all the scenery is whipped out overnight, all the lights are re-set overnight and the next day a whole new production goes into the studio . . . this is where the economy is – not in the use of the apparatus, not in the number of technical staff that you use, but in the amount of production that you get out of a given set of facilities.
>
> *Cited in Bakewell and Garnham, 1970:21–2*

As noted above, the series form had advantages over "one-off" "project" productions in encouraging repeat viewing/listening. Further, economies alone cannot explain for example the limited variety of locations in series production, or a radio soap opera, like the BBC's *The Archers*, would not confine itself to the familiar locations of Ambridge. Instead this must (as e.g. Hobson, 1982, suggests) reflect narrative techniques designed to achieve rapid familiarity for audiences. But the creation of the series form as the dominant design did also achieve economies of scale in production. Particularly in the soap opera and sitcom, the series enabled some of the economics of repetition of the long theatrical run. As Chapter 2 showed for

B-features, compared to project production, series production reduces "first copy" costs by reducing the search costs involved in each stage (writing, casting, set design etc.). Combining the series form with studio production enabled reuse of intellectual (characters, settings, stories), physical (sets, costumes, equipment) and even technical (camera and lighting set-ups) assets, across episodes and even seasons of a successful series. The series also enabled producers to balance the (sometimes unexpectedly) high costs of one episode with cheaper ("bottle show") episodes, with action limited to a small number of actors and sets. The studio series form was so dominant even single plays were adapted too, organised into anthology series like NBC's *Philco Television Playhouse* and ITV's *Armchair Theatre*, with a single production team (Baughman, 1997).

Similar economies of repetition were achieved with the discovery that audiences would accept repeat programming. This first occurred in the live era when, for example, the BBC produced repeats of live dramas "using the same cast, principal crew, scripts and technical specifications" (Turnock, 2007:89). The gradual lowering of the cost of recording on film and then on video opened up the possibility of retransmitting the original recording.

Unlike feature films, radio and TV studio productions were unable to use recording to decouple and achieve a detailed decomposition of the tasks of live entertainment. The difficulty of recording or editing video and the immediacy of the demand for hours of programming each day meant that live or "as live" TV production in studios (on the radio model), continued to be the dominant means of programme production well into the video era. Thus, TV studio production continued to follow the sequential, linear dependencies of the order of the narrative or performance seen by the audience. As shown below, radio and TV production have tended to preserve even the pre-production dependencies of live entertainment – writing, casting, staging, rehearsal, blocking and lighting. Furthermore, the nature of the series form meant that all these production tasks had to be performed to a weekly or even daily cycle time.

Only writing could really be decoupled from the "as live" production process. Broadcasting created a demand for a volume of original ("first copy") scripts unknown in live entertainment. And without the ability to record programmes, each production had only one opportunity to attract an audience or a sponsor. Thus, studio production was unable to follow live entertainment production in spreading first copy costs by extending the life cycle of a production for long runs of weeks or even years. Briggs (1965:80) noted that comedians unfavourably compared the economics of touring a live act with payment for a single broadcast, quoting the duo Clapham and Dwyer: "we had only one act at that time and we really didn't want to give it away to thousands listening".

Scriptwriting productivity was increased by vertical integration (recruiting in-house writers) and decomposing the writing task. In soap opera production, Irma Phillips closely supervised scripts – which "kept her from producing more than a few serials at one time" – while the Hummerts built up an inventory of completed scripts at least three weeks in advance of live broadcast (Meyers, 1997).

The Hummerts developed a process to supervise, simultaneously, the plot lines of the 125 series they produced over 30 years and achieve an output of 100 15-minute scripts a week. They exercised control over their series by originating something similar to the "scenario" used in features, an overall story outline (four-five pages) which they called a "theme". The next step was similar to the in-house screenwriting of Hollywood. They employed around 15 writers (many from newspapers serials) to develop this into a "storyline", detailing the key events over five or six episodes of a soap. To meet the output requirements, these "story writers" worked across several series simultaneously, producing storylines for 15–25 episodes a week. However, the crucial innovation was in decoupling this task of writing storylines from the task of writing dialogue, to achieve the large volume of dialogue required by a daily series. Once plot events and characterisations had been decided, the storyline could be handed over to a relatively new type of worker, the dialogue writers (some recruited from advertising copywriting), specifically tasked to generate the dialogue lines to deliver plot information (op. cit.). While relying on around 12 in-house dialogue writers, the volume of output meant they also used freelancers. This move to in-house, volume production was accompanied by a reduction in "piece-rates" (dialogue writers were paid $25 a script, half the freelance rate) but actors like Julie Stevens affirmed that by working across all the Hummert serials, this did add up to a "banner income" (Cox, 1999:19). Levine's (2001) study of *GH* confirms Meyers (1997:114) argument that these methods "provided the basis for nearly all subsequent soap opera script production". To generate sufficient script pages (roughly 30) for *GH*'s daily hour's output: "Head writers plan stories that outline writers break down into daily segments and scriptwriters translate into dialogue and action" (Levine, 2001:74).

It is instructive to compare the writing processes of these daily soaps with weekly sitcoms. Where the *GH* soap writers work in isolation, sitcom writing still tends to follow a more collective process often modelled on the famous writers' room. While many date this method back to the work of Mel Brooks and Carl Reiner on *YSS*, Isaacs (2017) notes its presence in earlier radio shows. US sitcoms may have "upwards of a dozen people turning out episodes that generate from a simple story idea to an outline to several drafts of a script" (Isaacs, 2017). But rather than purely productivity, this process seems to be required, like the studio audience, to continually control quality, testing out material on others to reject it or make it funny. Camporesi (1989:151) notes that the BBC initially attempted to develop sitcoms by appointing "a good American gag-writer", but the predominant approach in the UK has been to change the sitcom design, aiming to ensure quality by reducing the number of episodes and employing individual authors or two-writer teams. The BBC's Huw Wheldon contrasted this approach, more similar to writing for the stage, with the advertising influenced "copy writing" approach of the writers' room, "exact, sophisticated and brilliant work which – makes an immediate impact for a precise purpose" (cited in Phillips, 2005:21).

While these differences may reflect practices developed in different genres, they may also relate to the production cycle. In the UK soap *Brookside*, produced at the (relative to *GH*) leisurely pace of three episodes a week, the writers "developed and coordinated the 'storylines' (character, story and plot developments through a sequence of scripts) in *collaboration* with the executive and supervising producers" (Saferstein, 1992:64, my emphasis).

Without the potential for editing, TV production mirrored the conditions of live entertainment requiring performers and production teams to deliver a perfect performance. However, the weekly cycle of live and "as live" studio series production required a huge increase in volume of original performances without the time to rehearse these in advance or to build up an inventory in the way developed for script production. Thus, White (2015:235) notes "a standard six weeks' rehearsal" in 1936 for the three act farce *Stork Mad*. US Radio studios operated on the basis of providing "anywhere from five to fifteen hours of rehearsal for one hour of program on the air " (Hanson and Morris, 1931:17) and Kogan describes the one-day production cycle for the half-hour radio anthology drama series *The Mysterious Traveller* (1940):

> on the day of broadcast the cast and I would . . . read through the script . . . (then) we would have a first time read through on the microphone with myself and the engineer in the control booth . . . (then) a second run through with sound and music, with numerous pauses for level settings and directorial notes on interpretation . . . (then) a complete dress rehearsal.
>
> *Cited in Hand, 2015:63*

BBC radio drama productions followed a similar pattern (op. cit.). Thus, the Hummerts' restriction of rehearsals to one hour for a 15-minute programme represented a significant trade-off of quality for productivity.

The conversion of radio series to TV increased the range and complexity of tasks, both physical (acting, movement about the studio) and technical (makeup and costumes, scenery/sets, lighting and cameras). Unlike radio, actors and performers were not able to perform while reading their lines from a script. Unlike features, performances could not be perfected through recording and editing. Donald O'Connor, presenter of NBC's *Comedy Hour* compared its live production unfavourably with recording: "In films, a dance sequence can be shot over and over again until it is perfect. This doesn't hold up in television because it boils down to a one-take affair" (cited in Baughman, 2007:155).

We can now address the argument that scripts for soaps and sitcoms, and the TV studio (the "programme factory"), facilitated "the mass production of programmes which can be explicitly associated with the rise of serialisation" (Turnock, 2007: 42). The time devoted to rehearsals in studio production suggests, as Chapter 1 argued, that even after the most detailed scripting and planning, the inherent uncertainties of producing media products requires a process of discourse to decompose the overall task into specific steps. The cost of rehearsal time is justified by the economies gained by resolving uncertainties about the timing of the actions and interactions (dialogue and movements) of production inputs before more, expensive inputs (cast, crew, sets, props, studios) are deployed. Unlike in a real factory, where the positions of equipment and the flow of materials between them are planned and fixed, in studio production positions and movements are unique to each production and are developed collectively in rehearsal, through specialists applying their knowledge routines to the specifics of the script, rather than being written into it in advance. The camera rehearsal, for example, produces a cue sheet, which each cameraman amends and then translates into a series of marks on the floor to indicate the specific moves for a particular production (Mayerle, 1989).

The contingent nature of production also means, unlike in an assembly line, the dependencies between activities cannot be fixed in advance. Thus, the work of lighting engineers in planning the changes of lighting (the lighting "plot") cannot be completed until the actor and camera movements have been finalised. Similar dependencies affect the ability to pre-plan movements and placings of microphones, special effects and graphics.

The anthology drama formats, like NBC's *Philco Playhouse*, with a single production team but a changing cast, enabled a degree of "parallel working" creating a two-week production cycle; one day assigning the script, two days casting and planning, a day for the first reading, a day for dry run rehearsal and blocking, a further day's run through and then a day for blocking with heads of technical teams before the full, dress rehearsal, supposedly without stopping, and for rehearsing commercials (Hawes, 2001:63). The weekly live variety shows like *YSS* set the precedent for the weekly production cycle. Writing and set design (Monday), dances and musical rehearsal (Tuesday), main sketch rehearsal (Wednesday), further rehearsals (Thursday) and on the Friday "a run through without costumes, cameras or sets". Camera blocking and a full dress rehearsal both happened on the Saturday with transmission live that evening (Hyatt, 2010:75).

Comparing these shows to the inheritor of NBC's live variety tradition, *Saturday Night Live* (*SNL*), reveals the further limits imposed on rehearsal time by the process of writing topical comedy (Perkuny, 1980). Two and a half days are devoted to writing (in collective and individual modes) before the first read through decides which items are in the show. The contingent nature of the script affects key dependencies. Until the script is finalised, the final script is not available for decomposition in the form of script breakdown for the construction of sets, props and costumes. The time required for this work, in turn, determines whether the team can move into the studio for one or two days of blocking and camera rehearsal. Because the script is completed so close to broadcast, insufficient time is left for actors to learn lines and so they use prompt cards. If two days are available, the aim is to block the sketches on the first and musical numbers and remaining elements on the second day. As with *YSS*, the first run through happens on the Saturday (13:00) with the first dress rehearsal again at 20:00. Unlike *YSS*, there are then editorial (21:00) and technical (22:30) meetings before live transmission at 23:30 (op. cit.).

The real innovation in studio TV production involved the introduction of the potential of recording (first on film and then on video) to the multi-camera studio technique developed for live shows. Multi-camera production was not unknown in features. In the 1920s Cecil B. DeMille had:

> one camera at a long shot, a second one right next to it with a longer focal length lens for a close-up, and several other cameras at angles for more close-ups and two-shots. Thus, the scene could be played through, the various shots could be edited together to provide the classical establishing shots and cut-ins, and the action would match.
>
> *Bordwell et al., 1985:229*

This was not a method of reducing production costs, however, and the costs of cameras and operators largely prevented its widespread adoption. Instead DeMille believed filming in narrative story sequence enabled actors to improve the quality of their performances by developing "characterization and psychological intensity" (ibid.).

A crucial step in the evolution of multicamera filming was the phenomenal audience success, in 1951, of *ILL* which established a dominant sitcom design with a studio process which was adopted across the world. Much has been written about the efficiency of the *ILL* production system, with the inevitable "mass production" comparison (see, for example, Schatz, 1990). However, it should be recognised that much of the reasoning behind the speed of production of *ILL* (and contemporary studio sitcoms) concerned the need to record the show with a studio audience. At that stage, compared with radio, TV presented huge problems in gaining the attention of the domestic audience without losing the attention of studio audience. Bel Geddes wrote of Milton Berle's (NBC) show,

> No laughs due to lower floor audience being unable to see anything except the center set, because of cameras and mike crews . . . The crowd left the theatre in a disgruntled mood of having been cheated, openly talking to each other about it.
>
> *Gleich, 2012:8*

As an *American Cinematographer* article observed, in *ILL*:

> there are none of the interminable delays which mark the production of films in the major studios. Delays could not be tolerated because the show must proceed much the same as an actual live show telecast, inasmuch as there is an audience also present on the stage. This audience is an important adjunct to the show and its audible reaction as the show unfolds is recorded simultaneously with the dialogue and becomes an integral part of the production.
>
> *Allen, 1952:23*

Adapting the Hollywood "sound stage" for an audience of 300 entailed removing a wall and installing seating and fire exits and cost $50,000. The space required to give the audience a good view of the action had to be lost from the design of the three main sets (living room, kitchen and nightclub) preventing staging in depth and contributing to the "flatness" of sitcom style (Schatz, 1990:123). This is not to suggest that the Desilu production team did not see the potential to use the live multi-camera studio technique to eliminate delays in production (compared to single camera) and achieve an important cost advantage over others producing on film for TV. *ILL* produced 22–26 minutes of TV programme in an hour of shooting. Although it was developed to enable shot transitions for live video cameras, and involved an increase in the cost of inputs (three cameras and operators rather than one), the multi-camera process should logically reduce set-up times by at least a third compared to single camera production. In features, covering an action in wide, medium and close-up requires three 'set-ups' – arrangements of camera, lights, microphones, scenery, costumes etc. Multi-camera production enables these three processes (three shot sizes) to happen in parallel. While one camera (e.g. the equivalent of the live "on air" camera) takes the wide shot, the others can be setting up the next shots by moving or changing focus.

ILL's cinematographer Karl Freund was clear that the show's "almost continuous camera-on-dolly technique" was "adapted from standard TV camera operations for live shows" (cited in McNaughton, 2014:393). Each take, each piece of recording was achieved on average in between 7 to 8 minutes. Further efficiencies were achieved because most takes were filmed "right first time" and retakes were rare. And crucially, compared to feature production, "the elapsed time between camera set-ups averaged a minute and a half" (Allen, 1952:34). A number of elements of studio design were required to facilitate such rapid production. As in live TV, all lighting equipment was fixed at ceiling level so as not to slow the movement of actors, cameras and crew (as well as not obscuring the studio audience's view), with a uniform lighting plan, yet with lights mounted so changes (e.g. adding highlights) could be made quickly. Equipping cameras with zoom lenses and quick-change turrets enabled quicker changes in focus and thus increased the speed with which shots could be set up. The sets had to be designed to adjoin so that, as actors moved between sets, cameras could quickly move and rapidly set up and continue filming. Finally, the show also had to be edited and dubbed in a week. There is some ambiguity about whether all three cameras filmed continuously (op. cit.) or whether (as Anderson says) the cost of film stock and processing was such that "much of the editing was completed 'in-camera,' with only one designated camera running at any given moment" (Anderson, 1994:54–5). Most support Allen's account, in that the editing required three interlocking Moviola machines, matching the vision mixing process of live TV, with the editor having shots from all three cameras available and cutting from one to another.

Anderson (1994) suggests that it was the "rigorous pre-production planning" which enabled *ILL* to achieve such speed of shooting and such a low level of retakes. The movements of the whole production team had to be precisely choreographed in advance so they "tried to hit their marks on the first take" (Anderson, 1994:55). And *ILL* did spend significantly more time than *YSS* (two and a half days against half a day) on blocking and rehearsing the movement of actors, equipment and crew (although still much less than features or live entertainment) and also introduced the role of a script clerk with two-way communication, to cue sound and lighting crews from a control room above the stage.

The success of *ILL* brought a process of isomorphism which saw similar processes adopted across the US. The BBC's Aubrey Singer noted that DuMont produced two episodes of *The Honeymooners* sitcom each week. This was achieved by following a radio model where the cast only saw the scripts the day before shooting and then they would rehearse once, and then film before the studio audience that evening. Singer noted how this method created a preliminary edit (what would now be called a "line cut"):

> when the director switched from one camera to the next, the film was marked as a guide for the editor . . . providing a record of the shots selected for broadcast and used as a template for the editing of the filmed output of individual cameras.
>
> *Cited in McNaughton, 2014:393*

Butler (2012) identifies the continuation of this *ILL* weekly process in the production of NBC's *Friends*, and production journals show the same process for *Big Bang Theory* (*BBT*) with a day for the script reading, a day for rehearsal, a day for blocking on set, a day for camera rehearsal and pre-shooting/non-live taping of sequences which may be needed for the "as live" shooting on the final day. The key innovation with contemporary sitcoms like *Friends* is that they are "shot twice (in sequence) in front of two different audiences – the first called the dress show, and the second the air show" (Honthaner, 2013:403). To help the audience in following the live performance, the line cut is shown on screens in the studio.

For a daily soap, like *GH*, the production cycle is also daily; two separate production teams and studios working 12-hour shifts to produce "an entire episode each day of the week . . . shooting 25–30 'items' or scene segments, per day" (Levine, 2001:71). The difficulties of achieving this led to the necessity of developing a "buffer" inventory with episodes filmed "2 to 3 weeks in advance of airing" (ibid.). If *GH* relied on the limited number of sets used in *Friends*, audience figures would be affected by the lack of variety. Achieving this variety means *GH* works with a larger number of sets and this in turn precludes using the sitcom method of shooting episodes in narrative sequence. Instead the episodes must be decomposed and production scheduled out-of-sequence in a method more similar to feature production:

> Because only a limited number and configuration of sets can fit on the stage on any given day, and because the cast of approximately 35 contract players has a myriad of personal and professional scheduling conflicts, each day's production schedule is organized by grouping together related scenes, not by proceeding in a linear fashion through an episode.
>
> *Levine, 2001:75*

This means that soaps achieve vastly higher output and "productivity" than features. *GH*, for example, has increased its productivity since Levine's (2001) study: "we shoot 110 to 140 pages per day instead of 80 pages. We're in production roughly 35 weeks a year as opposed to 50. Our budget is down 30% of what it was back in 2009" (Dominick Nuzzi of ABC Daytime cited in Maloney, 2018).

As with feature film, early studio production involved an attempt to integrate the different production knowledge of specialists "the working methods and approaches drew explicitly on established practices in radio, theatre and cinema production" (Wyver, 2012:30). Managing these different production cultures required the creation of a new division of labour, a structure of authority, roles and responsibilities. Radio stations initially adopted the producer role from live entertainment and, at the BBC, this role initially carried over into TV: "key creative individuals in . . . television were producers, just as . . . in radio . . . being a producer also involved all the tasks later associated with a director, including refining the performances of the actors and planning and executing the camera script" (Wyver, 2012:28). In both radio and TV, the emergent dominant design of the series brought a distinction between producer and director which differed from that in features. The producer role, responsible for the series, developed into a more creative role, responsible for the series style and narrative. In the US, the producer role often became the powerful "showrunner" of US TV series, while the director remained, as in features, responsible for creative control of individual shows. Turnock (2007:37), notes that the BBC initially followed theatrical practice but the development of serialisation "meant that the producer had overall responsibility for the long run of script and budget but individual directors would be responsible for particular editions or episodes". Each writer, then, wrote the scripts for particular episodes within a storyline. The directors individually directed a number of episodes. This also represented a process innovation to achieve the required output levels. In soap opera or sitcom production each shooting day must complete a much larger number of script pages than a filmed series and this in turn must achieve a higher output ratio than a feature film.

Within this broad distinction, authority relations between senior managers and producers could vary considerably. Radio producers like the Hummerts kept a tight control over creative decisions and "did not permit directors to interpret [depart from] a script or use non-essential sound effects or background music" (Cox, 1999). Meyers (2011a) argues this related to cost control, but Allen (1985:55) noting a similar system in TV soaps – where directors are allowed "an extremely limited repertoire of visual flourishes" – also shows that this pressure for standardisation is largely one of quality, trying to achieve consistency across a huge number of episodes, rather than maximising output of a standardised product: "quality control cannot be assured if product design is altered on the shop floor" (op. cit.: 57). However, as Allen and Levine then show, it is also manifestly true that the "soap opera" design in the script must necessarily be altered on the studio floor. Thus, Allen confirms that the role of soap writers is similar to that of screenwriters (see Chapter 2) once the script is complete they are "powerless to influence its actualisation on the set" (Allen, 1985:54). As an alternative approach, NBC's Weaver saw the producer role as enabling innovation. He created "something like the unit producer system whereby the producer of any NBC property would enjoy considerable creative and administrative autonomy . . . [controlling] hiring, firing and salaries" (Kepley 1990:49).

The level of output required of a soap, for example, prohibits in studio production the degree of rewriting or reshooting of scripts common in features. However, rather than scripts guaranteeing standardisation, studio production of soaps presents real problems in achieving any consistency across the series. Instead "the continuity practices running throughout this daily work are the main method employed to stabilize . . . meaning" (Levine, 2001:73). Production meetings, a week in advance of shooting, are a "combination of practical or technical details and creative speculation" where the discussion ranges "from the kind of undergarments needed for a scene where a character disrobes to the maneuverability of the cameras in a new set" (op. cit.:71). Far from a mechanistic logic, "questions about character motivation and plot convolutions . . . are asked and answered throughout each production day" (op. cit.:74).

Thus, even in the most supposedly "mass produced" area of TV, production happens through the same process of negotiating meaning between individual interpretations of all the aspects of production – narrative, genre, visual sequences, setting, music etc. Levine quotes a *GH* staffer:

> certain writers . . . love characters so much that they would trade scenes . . . Writer A will say, "Oh, I'd kill for the Jason/Robin stuff in your day." And writer B will go "Well. If you do those scenes for my script, can I pick up your Kevin/Lucy scenes."
>
> *Ibid.*

We can trace this collaborative process of production in sitcoms from *ILL* – where open discussions of the production team would make "major changes" in action, dialogue or camera movements (Allen, 1952). We find this again in Mayerle's (1989:104) detailed description of a revision process, "key to the success" of *Newhart* which

> continues during production not only in script revision but in camera blocking where the type and composition of shots selectively capture the actors' performance. The process continues in postproduction through the selection of footage, editing decisions, and the blending of sound elements in the prelay session.

In his study of the UK soap *Brookside* Saferstein (1992:65) traces how these stages of production enable "management by discourse", exercise of authority, application of knowledge routines, collaboration and consideration of efficiency: "through the work of such script meetings, participants collectively developed mental and tangible models of scenes to be used in subsequent phases of production". Thus, when a writer, script assistant and director are discussing a scene the writer is struggling with a classic dilemma of series production, the need to inform new audiences about the relations between characters and the desire to dramatise the action of the episode:

WRITER: it's just — it's a big slab of information, after they arrested the lad [reads lines from script] "Get on the blower. Find out what happened Saturday three weeks ago. You've dropped yourself right in it, haven't you lad? We only wanted you for mugging that girl." It's information for the audience rather than what a copper would say, anyway. That's all.

SCRIPT ASSISTANT: I think you need . . . that . . . for the audience to get it . . .

DIRECTOR: [laughs]. I can . . . possibly, break that speech in two . . .

Cited in Saferstein, 1992:66

The director attempts to resolve the dilemma by drawing on his/her knowledge (and control) of the visual staging of the speech, looking forward to the filming stage of the production process.

Although the design of studio TV is not fixed until the final processes of post-production, and so the idea of the "programme factory" is clearly misleading, this is not to say that TV series studio production did not achieve efficiencies by imposing limits on design choices, compared with features. In particular, studio design achieved efficiencies through limits on the search process by transforming the general-purpose equipment of feature production for the specific purposes of TV series. Thus, lights were fixed overhead, rather than allowing lighting from the floor. The limited size of studio sets constrained the movement of actors and cameras and so reduced the range of potential camera set-ups, reducing the potential complexity of interdependencies between people and machines, and thus reducing "search costs" in blocking and for camera rehearsals. The "as live" studio process and the daily or weekly production cycle further limit the control a director or producer have over each shot. The lower search costs of these reduced shooting options were matched by reduced search in editing, via a form of "just-in-time" editing enabled by live and "as live" shooting and vision mixing. While this increases output, it reduces the ability to construct sequences using the techniques of continuity editing (such as matching shots on action). As discussed above, these limits on the "grammar" of TV studio production, compared to features, were not, initially, developed for reasons of efficiency, but the demands of volume production have reinforced these limits.

4

PRODUCING FILMED TV SERIES

Technological discontinuity

The Hollywood studios were interested in TV from the start. Some of the studios originally bought broadcast TV stations and Wasko (1994) describes two technologies they used to try to establish pay TV services, either by broadcasting films into cinemas or by installing pay TV in people's homes (Paramount's Telemeter). Instead, it was the development of the VHS system (and later DVD) which created the first alternative distribution mechanism for audiences to watch films at home. The DVD box set began the process of audiences binge-watching TV series which became a key part of the service offer of Subscription Video on Demand Services (SVOD) services like Netflix.

However, it was not until the emergence of cable and satellite systems, that the studios began to develop services capable of competing with the networks, such as the 1983 merger of Warner's The Movie Channel with Viacom's Showtime. Ironically, however, the technologies the studios developed to differentiate features from TV – digital graphics, Steadicams, special effects generators – would eventually enable filmed TV series (from *Star Trek*, to *Game of Thrones* (*GoT*)) to provide audiences with an experience which could compete with feature films (Caldwell, 1995).

Dominant design

This section analyses an episode, "The Old Gods and The New", from season two of the HBO series *GoT*, to describe the development of the dominant design of the filmed series. *GoT* is typical of this form of continuing drama, particularly in its attention to the "back stories" and complex narrative arcs of major characters. However, as this episode shows, these series have retained the convention, traditional in episodic TV, of resolving at least one plot within the individual programme. The design of the filmed TV series, in the experimental period of the 1950s, involved a range of alternative coherence structures for linking individual episodes into a series. Chapter 3 showed that initially the networks focused on live "anthology" drama series; stand-alone narratives, whose only series coherence structure was a common cast or theme (e.g. murder). Anthology series like *The Wednesday Play* continued longer in the UK than in the US.

The first step in the transition from anthologies to the filmed TV series came when the networks began to commission Hollywood studios to produce series for TV. The studios had experience of producing B-movie series, with continuing stories and characters and "cliffhanger" endings, such as MGM's *Andy Hardy* series (Henderson, 2017). However, for many years, Hollywood produced filmed series that followed the prime time TV convention that series would feature recurring characters, locations and plot devices but would ensure each plot was fully resolved within the episode. More complex serial narrative, with stories carrying across several episodes, had, been a part of the networks' daytime studio soap operas since the early days of radio. The first experiment in bringing serial storytelling to filmed prime time series came in 1964 when ABC broadcast *Peyton Place* (20th Century Fox Television, 1964–69). However, it was the success of *Dallas* (CBS, 1978–91) which began to establish serial narrative as a key element of the dominant design of filmed series (Sewell, 2010). Another important filmed series in this period, *Hill Street Blues* (*HSB*), developed "story arcs" for characters, sometimes lasting several seasons. Each episode usually contained an A-plot which was resolved within the time frame of that episode. After *Dallas*, in the 1980s, "it became increasingly common for prime-time fiction television to combine the single setting and episodic storylines which are components of the series form with the serial form's ongoing development of characters and storylines across episodes" (Bignell, 2009:11–12). Again, the US provided the template and, by the 1990s, UK filmed series had "become flexible in their employment of single or multi-episode plot strands and following American precedents they have developed complex, multi-strand narratives" (Corner, 1999:58).

The characteristic which most distinguishes filmed series from other designs is the relationship between the serial narrative of the plots and the development of regular characters across the series and different seasons. In US series especially, these character "arcs" are much longer and often more complex than would be possible in a feature film (Nelson, 1997). Unlike in the design of a soap opera, producers expect audiences to follow these arcs, which are often similar to a Hollywood "education plot" where the character learns to overcome a flaw in their make-up, enabling them to restore some balance to their lives.

Figure 4.1 is taken from an interior studio scene, set in the bedroom of Bran Stark (Isaac Hempstead-Wright). It is part of a shot-reverse-shot sequence similar to the example from *Pirates* described in Chapter 2. Its camera movement, editing and lighting are all much closer to pirates than the similar over-the-shoulder shot of Rachel and Monica in Chapter 3. Unlike *Pirates*, however, this scene is picking

FIGURE 4.1 Over-the-shoulder shot: Bran Stark, *Game of Thrones*

Credit: "The Old Gods and the New", *Game of Thrones* (HBO, 2012).

up the story from the previous episode. To help audiences understand the plot, the producers include a brief action scene, which is narratively "redundant", because it repeats the information that Theon (Alfie Allen) and his soldiers have taken the castle, Winterfell.

This scene is then able to progress the story with the episode's first dialogue where Theon attempts to persuade Bran to yield the castle. Theon's threat is that if Bran will not yield, he will have to take the castle by violence. This sets up the A-plot of the episode which is the threat to Bran Stark. As we will discover, this A-plot is one of three in the episode which involves a threat to the life of a member of the Stark family. This similarity in the three different plots gives the episode a thematic unity, above and beyond the thematic coherence of the series.

The next shot is taken from a small crowd scene, an exterior, filmed inside the walls of the castle. The location is a castle in Northern Ireland in the UK. Although *GoT* is, overall, an example of the modern fantasy genre, this location, and the large number of British actors in the series, draws on a long tradition of costume, period drama produced in Britain. Where the US networks commissioned Westerns and police series, both UK networks were producing multi-camera studio series like the BBC's *The Forsyte Saga* (1967) and *Poldark* (1977–9) and ITV's *Upstairs, Downstairs* (1971–5) (Jacobs, 2000). Initially UK drama production consisted of a mix of multi-camera studio shooting of interior scenes (on video) and single camera shooting of location exteriors (on film). As Alvarado and Buscombe (1982) describe in their study of ITV's *Hazell*, this created significant problems

FIGURE 4.2   Theon Greyjoy tries to lead the crowd

Credit: "The Old Gods and the New", *Game of Thrones* (HBO, 2012).

making transitions between interiors and exteriors. The equivalent would be a transition from one of the scenes shown in *Friends* (in Chapter 3), with its overhead lighting, shallow depth of field and minimal camera movement to the shot above, using natural light and 360° of movement.

The UK's move to filmed series production began when ITV began to copy the US network model of commissioning feature production companies. Again, they began with a costume drama, the swashbuckler, *The Adventures of Robin Hood* (1955–60). However, in seeking out the US audience, ITV moved onto a run of *James Bond*-based filmed series including *The Avengers* (1961–9) and *The Saint* (1962–9) (Sexton, 2013). However, the emergence of first PBS, in the 1960s, and then cable channels in the 1980s, along with cheaper, smaller film cameras, brought the first UK filmed period drama series including *Downton Abbey* (ITV, 2010–15) and *The Crown* (Netflix 2016–date).

This shot (Figure 4.3) is taken from a scene which is introduced to complicate the episode's A-plot; the threat to Bran Stark. The plot device used is similar to the complication used in the example from *Pirates* – the false double-cross. In this over-the-shoulder shot, Osha (Natalia Tena) offers to have sex with Theon in exchange for her freedom. This piece of misdirection leads the audience to suspect she will betray Bran and sets up a "plot twist", for the A-plot, in the last act. Serial narrative has to use many such devices in order to maintain interest in plots across hours of TV.

Another aspect of the shot concerns its use of sex and nudity. As a cable channel, HBO has been subject to less regulation of its content than the broadcast networks. It is very unlikely either a UK or US terrestrial broadcaster would have

FIGURE 4.3 Osha's offer sets up a plot twist

Credit: "The Old Gods and the New", *Game of Thrones* (HBO, 2012).

produced a series with *GoT*'s use of graphic violence and nudity or its moral balancing of events. However, this series reflects a process of change in the approach to these issues which began in network TV. In the US, in the 1980s, NBC's *HSB* broke the, then common, network convention that stories should communicate clearly whether characters are good or bad and that moral questions should resolve with good triumphing over evil. But it was cable TV, and in particular another HBO series *The Sopranos*, in the early twenty-first century, which established the

FIGURE 4.4 "Cinematic" shot: Ygritte in dramatic landscape

Credit: "The Old Gods and the New", *Game of Thrones* (HBO, 2012).

roles of graphic sex and violence and morally ambiguous heroes in the contemporary filmed series (O'Sullivan, 2017a).

The episode's second plot sets up another threat, to one of the extended Stark family, Jon Snow (Kit Harington), from Ygritte (Rose Leslie), a wildling captured on a raid. The first complication is quickly introduced to this plot. As the conflict between the two transforms into a relationship, a further plot is begun; a "romantic comedy". The scene is shot from Jon's point of view to maintain the suspense created by Ygritte's unclear motivations. The central romantic question of this plot is not resolved in the episode and so can be revisited in subsequent episodes. This plot also draws on a continuing theme of the series, as the families fight over the Iron Throne, they are ignoring the threat that "winter is coming". This theme adds a further complication to the relationship – will they be loyal to their warring peoples or follow their feelings? Figure 4.4 shows Ygritte escaping from Jon. Her figure is small in the frame of a wide shot, filmed on location in Iceland, to convey the harshness of the ungovernable world on the other side of the Wall, and thus the backdrop of the threat to them both.

This sequence, almost as cinematic as the sea sequences in *Pirates*, demonstrates the ambition of filmed series to compete with features. And, like *Pirates*, *GoT* makes extensive use of CGI to deliver on its overall fantasy genre promise. As noted, the potential for TV to develop a cinematic style emerged in the 1980 to 1990s when technologies originally developed to differentiate features from TV (like Steadicam) became inexpensive enough to use on a TV budget. Caldwell (1995) describes this aspect of the filmed series design as "televisuality" and argues that a key influence on its development, also from the cable TV industry, was MTV. In the terms of Chapter 1, Caldwell's argument is that filmed series gained an additional coherence structure, derived from the music video. In series like *Miami Vice* (NBC) the director Michael Mann began to use the music soundtrack to motivate shot changes, transitions and whole sequences. Like MTV videos, and also like older Hollywood musicals, the narrative coherence of the sequence was subordinate to the "performance" of the track: "the music is unrelated to the narrative and used for its discrete appeal, typically in *Miami Vice* dubbed over a car chase and used as a regular insert whatever the context of any particular storyline" (Nelson, 1997:184). Later filmed series successes on cable networks, like *Breaking Bad*, have continued to use this "maximum degree style" for filmed series (Mittell, 2015).

The episode's second act begins by introducing a third plot, again around a threat to a Stark (Sansa, Sophie Turner). This plot again references a continuing theme of the series, the legitimacy of competing claims to the Iron Throne of Westeros, and the danger to usurpers. The shot is taken from a riot whose inciting incident is an insult to Joffrey's (Jack Gleeson) legitimacy. When one of the crowd calls him a bastard, Joffrey's response confirms his unfitness to rule – calling for his soldiers to "kill them all". As Joffrey is saved, a group of rioters prepare to rape Sansa.

Figure 4.5 illustrates a third coherence technique used to structure the sequence; realism or actuality. The shot looks like it is taken with a held camera and the combination of camera and actor movement leaves Joffrey in focus in the foreground,

FIGURE 4.5 Hand-held shot: Joffrey's rescue from the rioters

Credit: "The Old Gods and the New", *Game of Thrones* (HBO, 2012).

with the Hound (Rory McCann) out of focus. The camera movements, the framing and the editing are motivated, as if the scene was being filmed by a news or documentary crew in the observational style (see Chapters 5 and 6). The audience accepts the camera whip-pan, the imperfect framing and the loss of focus as the consequences of the film-maker's attempt to cover an unpredictable event (a riot) which involves the greatest degree of task variability. In this case, the camera is filming as if in a point of view shot – attempting to locate the important characters as the chaos engulfs them, to establish who has survived and who is slain. However, the fact that this is a stylistic device, rather than actuality, is revealed as the shot develops and the camera pulls the Hound into focus for him to deliver his dialogue response to Joffrey; "They want the same for you!"

This style is used here to contrast the mood of this sequence with the more cinematic style used throughout the series. In other genres, particularly crime and police series like *The Wire* (HBO), this style may be used extensively. The origins of this style in news and documentary, following the availability of 16mm film cameras and later hand-held video cameras, are described in Chapter 6. In the UK, drama producers began experimenting with this technique in the 1970s; the police series *The Sweeney* (ITV) was shot by current affairs and documentary directors (Alvarado and Stewart, 1985).

An early pioneer of this style in filmed series, the US series *HSB* (NBC, 1981–7), adopted not just the visual coherence structure of observational documentary, but also its narrative coherence structure. As Chapter 6 notes, the series was inspired by a documentary, *The Police Tapes* (PBS, 1977). Watching this, *HSB*'s creators realised that audiences had accepted and could understand the events portrayed despite the discontinuities of space and time created by the filming technique (Bignell, 2009). However, they also realised audiences accepted and understood the narrative discontinuities, the breaks and gaps in the cause and effect chain, resulting from documentary filming. Bignell (2009) describes how *HSB* included these techniques by leaving out important story information, making other information ambiguous or even deliberately incomprehensible. As in the *GoT* sequence, *HSB* sequences tended not to be structured using the feature film method of progressively closer shots and clear shot-reverse-shot grammar, but instead, sequences appeared to try to "follow" characters, as if trying to cover an unpredictable news event. Again, the aim was to try to attract audience attention, by presenting the sequence as "actuality", where the meaning of events was unclear, and anything might happen. However, like *GoT*, this "hand-held" technique was used as a coherence technique, rather than as a method of filming. Although the series appeared to be filmed on hand-held video cameras, it was largely shot on 35mm cameras (op. cit.). In location sequences, the continuity conventions promoting audience comprehension (establishing shots of a new location followed by closer shots of the action) were replaced by the typical sequence created when a "ride on" documentary crew follows a police unit arriving at a scene. Three-point lighting was replaced by the use of "practical" and natural light typical of documentary (Corner, 1996). Rather than enabling comprehension by covering sound and dialogue clearly with directional microphones and multiple tracks, the soundtrack attempted to replicate documentary sound by the creation of a specially recorded wild track of background sound and conversation and by written dialogue which mirrored the sound created (several people speaking at once, failing to finish sentences, speakers interrupting each other etc.) by recording real conversation; "more radically than

FIGURE 4.6   Osha and Bran escape Theon

Credit: "The Old Gods and the New", *Game of Thrones* (HBO, 2012).

television had ever seen before, they ushered in overlapping dialogue" (Gitlin, 1983:256). Similarly, rather than cueing audience understanding or emotion with a music soundtrack, *HSB* used music only in its title sequence.

Figure 4.6, from the end of the episode, reveals the plot twist that Osha's relationship with Theon was actually a double-cross. It has allowed her to gain the trust of one Theon's soldiers, on watch that night, who she is then able to kill. The final reveal is that she has led Bran to the gate so she can spirit him away. Because it resolves the episode A-plot, and so is effectively the "end" of the episode, this wide exterior shot is held for slightly longer than other shots in the episode, covering Osha's escape with Bran past the corpse of the soldier.

This average length of the shots (ASL) in this episode is 3.28 seconds and the median shot length (MSL) is 2 seconds (shotlogger.com V2.0, accessed 2018). This makes *GoT* relatively fast-paced in its editing style, compared with *Friends* where an episode from season seven had an ASL of 3.7 seconds but an MSL of 3 seconds, a second longer than *GoT* (www.cinemetrics.lv/movie.php?movie_ID=7472, accessed 2018).

The pace of TV drama has increased significantly since its early years. Horwitz (2013) demonstrates that the ASLs used on TV fell "precipitously" from around 1960. A live drama like *Marty* had an ASL of 28 seconds while the ASLs of filmed TV series at that time were under 14 seconds (ibid.). These figures point to some of the differences in style, reflecting the different methods of multi-camera "as live" and single camera recorded production. Particularly in its early years, "a great deal of the drama (was) captured with an immobile camera" (Horwitz, 2013:43).

Although the main plot has ended, the serial narrative design is intended to hold audience attention for the next episode. Figure 4.7 shows one of three plots left

FIGURE 4.7 Tracking shot: theft of dragons sets up cliffhanger

Credit: "The Old Gods and the New", *Game of Thrones* (HBO, 2012).

as "cliffhangers", so audiences will be sure to watch the next episode to see how/ if they resolve. In one of them, Daenerys Targaryen (Emilia Clarke) is attempting to find ships so she can sail to Westeros to pursue her claim to the throne. She discovers she has been betrayed and many of her attendants murdered. The episode's final sequence builds to this the tracking shot (Figure 4.7) revealing the tower and a hooded figure carrying what looks like a cage. Under this shot we hear the audio of Daenerys (in a different location) delivering the episode's last line of dialogue, setting up the cliffhanger question – "Where are my dragons?"

The serial narrative design attempts to combine this need to leave plot questions unresolved, to retain audience attention for future episodes, with techniques to provide a coherent structure for the individual episode so it retains attention (especially for new viewers) and provides a satisfactorily dramatic experience as a stand-alone narrative. One coherence mechanism is the three (or sometimes four) act structure, which allows sub-plots to be integrated around the overall narrative arc of the A-plot, which resolves within the episode. Another method is the use of an identifiable theme for the episode. The events of the episode – Theon's incompetent killing of an elderly man, Jon's inability to kill Ygritte, Joffrey's tyrannical order to execute the protesters, contrasted with Arya Stark (Maisie Williams) and Osha's use of violence, to save their own lives or the lives of others – suggest that the people of the old faith will overturn the current, "illegitimate", rulers of Westeros.

Regulation and legitimacy

As noted above, the Hollywood studios were originally keenly interested in taking advantage of TV technology. However, as Hilmes (1999:133) notes, these visions of film industry involvement failed largely because of a "slow strangulation by federal regulation", the FCC and the courts deciding to protect the TV industry against potential market control by the studios. This was effective in enabling the networks to develop their control, both of the advertising market and, later, the syndication market.

This regulatory division between the studios and the networks was reinforced, initially, by the assumption among many in TV that filmed series were of lower quality than live TV drama. Similarly, US series imported to the UK "were disparaged by many British critics at the time, failing to meet the standards of 'quality' and 'value' that, they argued, could be found in the live or videotaped studio drama" (Sexton, 2013). It was the weakest network which, perforce, made a deal with the studios which, at the time, brought criticism; "for many contemporary lamenters of the demise of live drama ABC played the villain of the piece – a role reinforced by the protestations of the other networks of their commitment to live drama" (Boddy, 1985:32). But the success of Warner's filmed series for ABC began to transform opinions in Hollywood, where production of filmed series began to be seen as a natural replacement of the studios' B-movie production.

However, by 1970, the networks had reached a situation of dominance in the syndication market, owning the rights to syndicate 98% of their programmes

(Perren, 2004). The regulator, the FCC, decided that this market control had disadvantaged programme suppliers causing the "shake-out" of independent producers or their acquisition by the studios. A series of regulations, usually referred to as Financial Interest and Syndication Rules – or "Fin-Syn" – was introduced to limit the amount of prime time programming the networks could either produce themselves or own or have syndication rights in (op. cit.).

Regulation also weakened the networks' control over the advertising market. The 1984 Cable Act, and subsequent legislation, encouraged the growth of networks like HBO. Regulators allowed cable channels much more freedom from the content regulations governing the networks' ability to show sex, violence or morally questionable behaviour. This posed a fundamental challenge at the networks. As a producer of the UK series *The Avengers*, noted; in the 1960s the networks insisted

> each episode had to conform to the formula – right had to be opposed by wrong; the hero had to be menaced; violence had to be involved (usually with a murder); this was followed by a chase, a battle to create tension and an eventual climax.
>
> *John Bryce, cited in Sexton, 2013:75*

Caldwell (2006) shows that by the early 1980s, both trade press and TV critics had begun to celebrate "quality" TV filmed drama as a "critical industrial practice". At the same time, following Gitlin's (1983) study of *HSB*, scholars began to accord filmed series design greater legitimacy than other forms of TV programming, differentiating these series on the basis of their "quality" (McCabe and Akass, 2007), "televisuality" (Caldwell, 1995), "flexi-narrative" (Nelson, 1997:24), "cumulative narrative" (Newcomb, 2004:422), and "complexity" (Mittell, 2015). Finally, the success of HBO's *The Sopranos* (1999–2007) has been seen as indicating a turning point, a more general shift in public opinion about the legitimacy of dramas including sex and violence and anti-hero characters;

> a shift away from a Judeo-Christian governance of American television serials . . . more or less stable notions of judgment and justice . . . to a Greco-Roman governance – where humans behave in ways that are more capricious and less reconcilable with modern codes
>
> *O'Sullivan, 2017a:62*

Market control

Chapter 1 explained the way many media organisations operate in more than one market. Media producers create content designed to attract audience attention and "attention markets" then allocate that scarce resource, primarily through prices (measured as "cost per mille" (CPM) or "cost per thousand" (CPT) viewers)) and sales to advertisers. Media organisations also sell the products they produce directly to audiences. Chapter 1 noted that this kind of media product market functions more efficiently when the intangible content of the media product (the story, the news report etc.) can be stored in a tangible form (newspapers, cinema tickets, DVDs, etc.) or when technologies enable audiences to pay for the content "on demand" (cable and satellite channels, internet, mobile etc.). Chapter 1 also noted that media organisations may operate in "secondary" product markets, selling to other media organisations which in turn use those products either to attract audience attention to sell to advertisers, or to sell directly to audiences or to resell to other media organisations.

Chapter 3 described the broadcast networks' strategies for controlling the TV attention/advertising market. This section describes the networks' strategies for selling filmed series and also the emerging role of cable channels, like HBO, in selling filmed series directly to audiences as pay TV. An important feature of the US secondary markets in TV programmes (known as the "syndication" market) is the existence of local stations, and later cable stations, buying recordings of network studio shows and filmed series which can continue to attract audience attention when shown as "re-runs" or "repeats". Like the studios' "windowing" strategies for feature films, series could carry on earning profits for years, if not decades, starting off selling at higher prices to large urban stations before moving on to progressively smaller stations (Caves, 2005).

Chapter 3 noted that initially the networks had attempted to limit the growth of this syndication market to prevent the emergence of networks of local stations using "syndicated" programmes to compete for audience attention and advertising. The chapter noted that this created a bias towards live programming, to ensure that affiliated local stations would carry the networks' live feed and so allow the networks to sell national audience attention to advertisers. The chapter showed that, once they had established control of this market, the US networks were, primarily for financial reasons, keen to outsource production, and this gradually resulted in live studio shows being replaced in network schedules with filmed series. Secure in their control of the advertising market, the networks were now free to sell the filmed series they had acquired in US syndication markets and global TV distribution markets. This chapter explains the networks' strategies for controlling these markets.

In the mid-1950s, as explained above, the Hollywood majors saw TV as a competitor and so were opposed to "free" access to their products. In outsourcing production, the networks initially turned to independents like Ziv (*The Cisco Kid*, 1950–6) (Kompare, 2006). At this stage, the studios participated only by renting out their sound stages (underused since the disintegration of the studios and the reduction in B-movie production, see Chapter 2). During this period the US independent TV production sector grew rapidly, and by 1952 the networks were commissioning filmed series from 75 independent companies (op. cit.). The real attraction of series production for the independent producer was that if the series was a success, they would earn share of the revenue from selling the series on the syndication market. As Chapter 1 showed, the failure rate for filmed series, like that of features and studio series, remained irreducibly high. But, for those producers who could create a hit series, the potential rewards were great, as local stations, cable channels and overseas broadcasters would continue paying to show the series for years, or even decades (Lotz, 2007).

However, the networks' control of the TV market for audience attention placed them in a strong position to control this syndication market. Effectively, the networks were the only organisations capable of creating a demonstrable hit series. Only after a series had been a returning success over several years of prime time scheduling would local channels pay to show it as a re-run or repeat. As oligopsonistic buyers of programming, the networks were able to demand that producers both deficit finance filmed series, and allow the networks a share of the syndication revenues. The networks thus created long-term contracts with producers, typically for seven years, which included the network retaining a share in syndication revenues and an annual option to decide whether to continue the series, without giving the supplier the right to take the series to another network (Caves, 2005). The final element of the deal was that the networks expected them to "deficit finance" production of the series (see Chapter 3).

A typical budget for filmed TV in the 1950s was $20,000 an episode ($184,662.17 today) (Moore, 1980). Furthermore, the pattern of demand in the advertising market created pressures for producers to deficit finance a large volume of production. From the late 1940s, "sponsors began to demand thirteen to twenty-six episodes already filmed before they would consider buying a series" (Moore, 1980:29). Furthermore, the sponsors wanted to see up to 20 completed episodes before deciding if they would invest. Thus, an independent might be required to find up to $400,000 ($3.6 million today) in "deficit finance" without knowing whether they would find a sponsor to recover those costs (ibid.). Furthermore, the pattern of demand in the syndication market rewarded only proven hits which could be shown almost indefinitely. Most local channels were looking for series which had proven their success in prime time, over at least five seasons, which they could then "strip" – show on their own channel five days a week for around 20 weeks. This meant that the real demand in the syndication market was for prime time series which had continued to be successful and reached a substantial volume – around 100 episodes. Most independents faced difficulties raising this amount of money to finance production, especially since this was such a high-risk business, given the very substantial chances that the series might fail and the network's control over the process – the series could easily be cancelled by the network before it reached the number of episodes required to succeed in the syndication market (op. cit.).

The one source of filmed series production capable of supporting this level of deficit financing was the Hollywood studios. After regulation had effectively prevented studio ownership of TV stations, until the mid-1950s Hollywood had seen "free" TV purely as a competitor to paid movies. To protect their market, they had attempted to deny the networks access to Hollywood's content and talent. The change to their strategy of non-involvement in TV came, ironically, as a result of the very *Paramount* judgement which had helped to end their production of

B-movie series (Boddy, 1985). The ruling had required Paramount to disintegrate its cinema chain from production. The buyer was the ABC network and, as a result, the head of United Paramount Theaters, Leonard Goldenson, became ABC's president. ABC had been placed at a competitive disadvantage by the networks' focus on controlling the advertising market through live programming to their affiliates. Half of ABC's affiliates could not carry live programming, instead providing low quality tele-recordings. Goldenson saw that TV viewing had replaced audiences' habitual attendance at cinemas and, finally, how TV could be used to distribute filmed series; "we would put programs on film and show them on the network the same way we showed feature films in theaters" (Perebinossoff et al., 2012:5).

ABC commissioned a number of Hollywood majors to produce a filmed anthology series. The success of one element, Warner's *Cheyenne* (1955–63), encouraged Goldenson in 1955 to replace all of ABC's live dramas with filmed series principally from Warner, who revived its B-movie series division to form Warner Brothers Television (WBTV). *Cheyenne* paved the way for a run of TV Westerns (*Gunsmoke* (1955–75), *Maverick*, *Bonanza*, *High Chapperal* and *The Virginian*) lasting until the mid-1970s (Anderson, 1994). The experiment in filmed series production transformed ABC's ratings and by 1959 WBTV was producing a third of ABC's schedule, earning almost half Warner's total revenue, partly through its growing international syndication of these successful series. Warner became the model for other studios and "by 1957 the big Hollywood motion picture corporations were the largest suppliers of television programming in the United States" (Butler, 2012:223). After a period of conflict the two industries began a process of coevolution, such that by the 1970s the studios were earning more from TV than from cinemas (Anderson, 1994).

The studios' growing control of the market for filmed series production brought consolidation in the sector "as independent producers either went out of business or merged with larger firms" (Balio, 1990:35). Some, like Desilu, were able to use the continuing syndication revenues of a hit series (see Chapter 3) to deficit finance series production (although Desilu was eventually acquired by Paramount). Others, like Revue and Screen Gems, relied on the finances of parent companies MCA/Universal and Columbia Pictures respectively.

As other countries developed TV services in the late 1950s, the US networks supported the establishment of commercial broadcasters, like ITV, which would become major markets for the networks' international programme distribution arms (Hilmes, 2012). By 1964 the networks were selling filmed series in 80 countries, returning $70 million. International syndication was 60% of all US filmed series syndication revenues "and represented the difference between profit and loss for the entire US industry" (Sexton, 2013:101). The networks' control of these two secondary markets enabled the filmed series quickly to replace live studio shows as the dominant design in prime time. In 1957, the networks ran 100 filmed series (mainly Westerns). By 1960, film accounted for more than 80% of network programmes and no network was running live drama in prime time (Kompare, 2006). Chapter 3 explained how UK broadcasters had relied on studio shows to generate the volume of production required to fill the increasing transmission hours which regulators allowed. The alternative was to import US filmed series which, particularly for ITV, represented a good return, in terms of audiences, on investment. In the mid-1950s, the US networks sold filmed series for around £2,000 an hour, compared to at least twice that amount for a UK broadcaster to produce its own studio drama or five times as much to commission an hour of filmed drama from a UK film producer (Sexton, 2013). ITV immediately began to import the emerging US filmed series, especially the Westerns – *Cheyenne*, *Maverick*, *Rawhide* and *Bonanza*. US series have continued to be important for Channels 4 and 5 and for Sky.

However, regulation had restricted the amount of imported programming on UK networks (initially to around 15% of the schedule) creating a demand for home produced content (Chapman, 2002). Lew Grade's ITC saw the potential to use ITV commission income to cover production costs, and then make sales in the US to move into profitability. Working with some of the UK's surviving film companies (e.g. Sapphire Films) before acquiring Elstree Studios, ITC began by selling *The Adventures of Robin Hood* to CBS, following this with a range of series financed by US distribution; *The Prisoner* (CBS, 1968), *The Saint* (NBC, 1967–9), *Secret Agent* (CBS, 1964–6), *The Avengers* (ABC, 1966–9) and *The Persuaders* (ABC, 1971) (Chapman, 2002). The BBC has returned to this type of series in the co-production era with series like *The Night Manager* (BBC/AMC, 2016).

ITC's series were unusual in their success in the US, and in conforming to the requirements of the US market (e.g. for 20 to 25 episodes per season). Part of the reason for limited sales to the US networks has been because UK series have generally been closer to the US idea of a "miniseries" (4–13 episodes). However, an alternative source of US finance, prepared to consider this format, arrived in the 1970s with the creation of the Public Broadcasting Service (PBS). With much smaller budgets than the major networks, PBS strands like *Masterpiece Theatre* and later *Masterpiece Mystery* acquired or co-produced many BBC, and later ITV, costume drama serials. Beginning with studio-based serials like *The Six Wives of Henry VIII* (1970) they later transitioned to filmed series like *Brideshead Revisited* (1981) and *Pride and Prejudice* (BBC 1995). The cost of filmed series production means US co-production continues to be essential. Mediatique (2017:17) estimated that "in 2016, around 65% of all BBC drama titles were co-produced with an external party; for Channel 4, the figure was 90%. Partners included AMC, Amazon, Netflix and Sony".

The challenge to the legitimacy of network control over the US syndication market led to the fin-syn regulations, which gave greater ownership in syndication rights to the studios and independent producers, and created a secured market in prime time, requiring the networks to outsource production for this section of the schedule. This has been credited with changing this situation and leading to a period (a "golden age") of innovation in TV production by independents (Lotz, 2007), an argument which might appear to support FS theory.

However, despite the fin-syn rules, the networks' continuing oligopolistic control of the advertising market gave them effective control over the commissioning of filmed series. The continuing high failure rates of series and, in particular, of serial narratives during the '70s (despite the limited success of *Peyton Place*) "estab-lished a conventional wisdom that prime time audiences would not return to 'unfinished' stories" (Newcomb, 2004:421). Instead, both advertisers and network executives tended to prefer episodic series, requiring no prior knowledge, at prime time. Gitlin (1983: ix) described this "gatekeeping" process as resulting in the industry commissioning the "least objectionable programming".

The impetus to change this seems to have come from competition between the networks. First, ABC which, again from a position of weakness, engaged in experi-mentation which would ultimately establish the filmed series as a dominant design. Its audience research suggested its programming attracted younger viewers than its rivals, and that this demographic was more likely to purchase newly launched prod-ucts. ABC was able, despite its lower overall ratings, to get advertisers to pay higher costs per thousand (CPMs) than they paid the other networks (Cantor, 1982). CBS responded by commissioning series, particularly MTM's *The Mary Tyler Moore Show*, designed to attract younger, more female audiences, considered to be the target market for consumer goods. The network also had the sustained ratings achieved by Lorimar's *Dallas* (CBS 1978–91) to begin to alter the perceived risks of prime time filmed serials. When NBC recruited MTM's Grant Tinker as chairman, the net-work introduced the key innovation, MTM's *HSB*, which established the dominant design of the filmed series; serial dramas which could attract niche, but highly profit-able, audiences. And the MTM "alumni" have been credited with continuing this development across the networks through series like *Moonlighting*, *Northern Exposure*, *Twin Peaks*, *LA Law* and *Thirtysomething* (Feuer et al., 1984).

Apart from encouraging the networks to outsource more of prime time to the studios and some independents, the other beneficiaries of the fin-syn rules were the new entrants into the TV markets, cable/satellite channels like HBO and AMC. The business model of the cable channels enabled them to develop filmed series in ways which were not open to the networks. Rather than always requiring produc-ers to deficit finance production they could raise production finance, including for in-house productions like *GoT*, by "pre-selling" new filmed series to cable operators (Holt, 2011). This enabled them to establish the potential of channels using filmed series to attract niche audiences of subscribers, and by the late 1980s cable channels were attracting significant pay TV subscription revenue (30% of TV viewers were also cable subscribers) (Sewell, 2010). This, in turn, enabled them to sell this audience attention to advertisers looking to reach particular demographics, undermining network control of the advertising market. Finally, these channels were able to differentiate their product, offering audiences something the net-works could not. Their greater freedom (from regulations and advertisers) enabled HBO to commission *The Sopranos* (1999–2007), after it had been rejected by three networks because of its graphic violence, sex and anti-hero lead character. The subsequent success of the series established some of the final elements of the filmed series design, which has been adopted by more recent new entrants like Netflix and Amazon. The budget for the series ($2–3 million per episode) had an effect on budgets for filmed series which has continued – *GoT* was estimated in 2016 to cost $10 million per episode (Mediatique, 2017). Second, it freed producers from the volume constraints imposed by the advertising and syndication markets. *The Sopranos* introduced the 13-episode series to US TV and the absence of commercial breaks has enabled a wider variety of episode lengths.

Chapter 1 noted that a flexible specialisation (FS) theory would suggest that the networks would seek to innovate (functional flexibility) by choosing the best ideas from the widest range of independent producers. Initially, this was the pattern. Independents had been selling recorded series to local stations since the early days of radio. However, the "deficit finance" model and the demands of the syndication market quickly led to a shake-out of independents and the Hollywood studios' takeover of filmed series production. Lotz (2007) and others have argued that the fin-syn rules produced an increase in innovation and quality in US TV by requiring outsourcing. The classic example for this argument is the success of MTM with *The Mary Tyler Moore Show* and *HSB*. However, other frequently cited examples of innovation from this era, such as CBS's *M*A*S*H*, were produced by the studios (20th Century Fox). Rather than producing a diversified, competitive market of independent producers, the fin-syn regulations largely benefited the Hollywood studios (who could now add domestic syndication revenues to their international programme sales). And, of course, much of the innovation came from the new cable channels, like HBO, the majority of whose productions continue to be "in-house" (Küng, 2008).

A transaction cost (TCE) explanation would suggest TV networks vertically integrate production when the level of the uncertainty is so great that it becomes difficult to specify contracts with independent production companies. However, outsourcing by the networks was, in practice, the same as integration by the studios. The success of their work for ABC enabled Warner to restart the in-house production they had lost when the demand for B-movies had declined. By 1960, Warner's TV division, WBTV, had 300 permanent employees (producers, actors, editors, costumiers etc.) Rather than problems with contracting out to independents, Warner wanted to ensure it could meet the volume targets set by the networks for filmed series production. WBTV "wanted to guarantee that no single actor could throw a wrench into the machinery of production" (Anderson, 1994). Rather than uncertainty, it would appear to be the urgency of demand for volume production which brought integration at WBTV.

Process innovation

Chapter 1 suggested that after the emergence of a dominant design, we should expect an industry to develop a range of process innovations to achieve efficiencies in production. Chapter 3 showed how studio shows reduced the "cycle time", compared to feature production, because shooting took place live, or "as live" in a few hours, and therefore required minimal editing. The emergence of the filmed series, as the dominant design of prime time TV, replacing studio-based anthologies, generated more limited requirements for process innovation.

Process innovation in filmed series production developed through the coevolution of the TV and film industries described above. This has led many authors to draw on Bordwell et al. (1985) to describe TV production in the 1960s to 1970s as "mass production". Hilmes (2012:226) calls this era the "classic network system" because of its "highly systematic and rule-bound mode of production". However, other authors reject this idea that filmed series were "essentially a continuation of the Hollywood factory studio system" (Brook, 1998:27). Anderson (1994:269), for example, suggests an analysis of "mass production" which begins to undermine the theory of mass production of feature films; "the major studios often had been described as assembly lines, but the analogy was never more appropriate than during the late 1950s at Warner Bros. Television, where the series truly seemed to consist of interchangeable parts". Caldwell (1995:58) takes a similar view of Universal's production of series like *Columbo* in the 1970s which he argues was "systematized" with "uniform settings, lighting, looks and cutting . . . the only things that changed from week to week were stories, plots and guest stars". Gitlin (1983:240) describes Universal as "television's major factory".

These accounts of the mass produced filmed series have often been contrasted with the production of "quality TV" and the studies which highlight the complexity, televisuality and quality of some contemporary filmed serials, particularly *The Sopranos*, *The Wire* and *Breaking Bad* (McCabe and Akass, 2007; Mittell, 2015). Cardwell (2007:26), notes that such serials are distinguished by; "high production values . . . (and) a sense of visual style created through careful, even innovative, camerawork and editing, and a sense of aural style created through the judicious use of appropriate, even original music". By contrast Caves (2005:23) argues that mass production has continued into the twenty-first century:

> While cinema films ceased a half-century ago to be produced in assembly-line fashion on studio lots, that mode of organization remains congenial to the production of TV programs. It fits with their serial structure and their usual reliance on simple studio sets.

The next section compares a number of accounts (Anderson, 1994, Ravage, 1977, Griffin, 2007, Chase, 2009, Casau and Garin, 2015) to try to chart the extent of process innovation and production efficiencies across three eras of filmed series production (WBTV in the 1960s, Universal in the 1970s and HBO in the 1990s/2000s).

The "production function" approach allows comparison of the inputs and outputs of processes. In 1955 WBTV produced 40 hours of filmed drama at a cost of $75,000 ($700,000 in 2018 money) an hour (Roman, 2005:13) increasing to 260 hours in 1960. This represented a significant increase in efficiency compared to even low budget B-movies which cost around $250,000 ($4.4 million in 2018). In the mid-1970s the Universal "factory" produced *Ellery Queen* (45 minutes) at $400,000 ($1.8 million in 2018), almost the same as HBO's *The Wire* (55 minutes) ($1.5 million, $1.9m in 2018) but an order of magnitude less than *The Sopranos* (50 minutes) (reportedly $10m, $12.5 million in 2018) (see Ravage, 1977, Biskind, 2007).

We can compare the efficiency of the three eras of filmed series production using their "cycle times" – production schedules. At WBTV "production on an episode had to begin at least eight weeks before the broadcast date" (Anderson, 1994:251). HBO's *Sopranos* was 50% longer; "approximately 3 months from initial writing to the first episode" (Chase, 2009:ix). However, Universal was 50% more efficient even than WBTV with "three to five weeks" between production beginning and transmission (Ravage, 1977:59). The first core production element of the schedule is pre-production. It's not clear how WBTV divided up this stage, but we can see that Universal's six days, is not significantly lower than HBO's seven days for *The Wire* or eight days for *The Sopranos*.

Given that "quality TV" is often distinguished by its "cinematic" elements, we would expect the filming period to evidence the greatest difference between "mass" and "quality" production. Both WBTV and Universal gave directors six days to shoot an episode, with a shooting ratio of between nine and 12 script pages per day. Orr declared "a seventh day suggests that somebody does not know what they are doing" (cited in Anderson, 1994:250). At HBO shooting took between eight (*The Wire*) and nine days (*The Sopranos*) with a ratio of five to seven script pages filmed each day. While this represents a significant (30–50%) increase in expensive inputs, it is hardly evidence of a radical break between mass and quality production systems. Despite these shows being described as "cinematic", they more closely resemble series production of the "factory" era than the average one-two script pages a day typical of feature production.

Editing episodes at WBTV was limited to "no more than four cuts" (Anderson, 1994:251), which included director's and producer's cuts and two cuts seen by the production chief. Ravage does not fully describe the editing process at Universal, but makes clear directors were responsible for the "first cut". At HBO, editing *The Wire* followed the four cuts pattern of WBTV, but for *The Sopranos* the writer-producer noted; "I generate many cuts, all the way to the final . . . This process can take months and I always, selfishly, use as much time as the schedule allows" (Chase, 2009:x). The role of the director changed significantly for filmed series production at WBTV and has remained constant through the three eras of production. Rather than being the creative leader, directors are hired on "a one-time basis and a freelance artist" (Casau and Garin, 2015). At WBTV, creative control was exercised by production chief William Orr who managed a layer of supervising producers who then managed individual series producers. At Universal the roles were similar although the supervising producers were now called executive producers.

The key change in the "quality" era has been the merging of the role of writer and producer. At WBTV writers were often freelancers who "had only a marginal involvement with a series" (Anderson, 1994:269). The studio created the role of story editor to try to ensure consistency across the series, which Anderson describes as "taking out each writer's distinctive voice" (ibid.). Universal continued this approach to writing with the story editor responsible for rewriting to accommodate changes in budgets or locations while the writer, after selling the script, "is virtually never seen . . . or heard from again" (Ravage, 1977:58).

During the "quality" era, the development of the role of writer-producer (showrunners) has allowed greater creative control for the likes of David Chase and Shonda Rhimes. A related improvement in managing the volume of production has been the introduction of a practice from sitcoms. Writer-producers manage a writers' room – a team responsible for plotting episodes and writing scripts. As well as helping meet deadlines, writers emphasise the creative benefits of "breaking a story with six minds than with one" and the potential to improve continuity across the series "you have to be in the room with all the writers so that everyone knows what is going on" (writers cited in Phalen and Ossellame, 2012:9). In the UK, where the volume of episodes is much lower, series are still written by an individual or pair of writers. We should distinguish this from the idea that, even in the quality era, writer-producers have creative "freedom". In general, HBO requires approval of the writers' initial story outlines and final scripts. And once a writer has been assigned an episode, "no matter who writes [it] they are all based strictly on the outline that's been given to them" (Chase, 2009:ix). Nor should we assume that this contrasts with an era of close supervision and intervention by network management. Even at Universal's "factory" there was never "a hint of force or pressure from the network or advertisers to (radically) change the content of the program or the characterizations" (Ravage, 1977:57).

Chapter 1 outlined a number of concepts (including the variability and analysability of the overall task, and the interdependencies between production tasks) useful in explaining how media organisations achieve process innovations and efficiencies, following the establishment of a dominant design. For filmed series, Anderson (1994:267) shows how WBTV attempted to increase output by reducing variability; "production at Warner Bros. Television . . . sometimes seemed, to see how far the studio could go in standardizing its products before it alienated viewers". The writers Richard Levinson and William Link said that at WBTV:

> writers were tailors, cutting bolts of cloth to a rigid set of specifications. They would be provided with an existing group of characters and a format, and any flexibility within these parameters was severely limited. The key words were "jeopardy" and "conflict," and the emphasis was almost totally on plot.
>
> *Cited in Anderson, 1994:269*

The same pressures were applied to the decomposition of the script into scene shots. Most scenes were filmed on WBTV's backlot, with "locations" provided by stock footage or very occasional location shoots. Producers controlled costs by minimising the number of characters and the number of scenes which required crews to move from one set to another. Directors were limited to three takes of each shot and to standard sequence construction to try to ensure all scenes could be edited without the need for reshoots.

However, WBTV's experience seems to demonstrate the limits to the control of task variability in filmed series production. Each script scene is different and thus requires a different decomposition into shots and a different "set-up" of equipment and blocking (layout) of actors for each shot. Unlike studio shows, the variation of interiors and exteriors limits the degree to which these tasks are analysable through the process of rehearsal. In many cases, each shot must be rehearsed individually.

Much of Anderson's account actually demonstrates that WBTV was unable to operate like a factory, "balancing" interdependencies between tasks so work flows smoothly along the assembly line. The attempt to film multiple series on the same backlot, while saving in travel costs, created bottlenecks in shooting, with several crews waiting to use the same soundstage. Similarly, editing such a volume of episodes with a small in-house staff created bottlenecks in post-production. WBTV also encountered limits to the analysability of filmed series production. Frequently, episodes came in either too long or too short for the network slot. Orr scolded his staff; "establishing lengths of shows is such a basic element of producing that I hope it will never be necessary to mention it again" (cited in Anderson, 1994:251). The resulting delays and consequent overruns in production brought overtime charges from film developing labs and penalties from the networks.

Rather than the formulaic and systematised assembly line process suggested by Gitlin (1983) and Caldwell (1995), Ravage found production at Universal to be stalled at the earliest stage of task analysability. With four days to go before filming was due to start, the script was still being rewritten. The four major parts had not been cast. Rather than conforming to Anderson's description of actors as "interchangeable parts", Ravage's (1977) account illustrates how limited is the knowledge producers can apply in solving the problem of which actor will best fit a particular part. Universal producers spent many hours considering a large number of new and established actors, discounting some as "difficult" or "inappropriate", without solving the problem of who to cast.

Other decisions raised complex trade-offs which were specific to the individual episode and for which there was no "formulaic" solution. The producers attempted to schedule all the scenes involving extras on one filming day, to save the cost of paying them for an additional day. But the director calculated that this would require filming 28 script pages in a single day. The difficulty of finding adequate solutions to these problems cost the producers time and money. Four days before the shoot they were $12,000 ($56,000, 2018) over budget and still without a final script (op. cit.). The nature of interdependencies in filmed series production meant this reduced the time available to analyse subsequent tasks. Without a script it was not possible to construct a set, this, in turn, prevented creation of a continuity script (ordering the scenes into filming as opposed to story sequence). This further prevented specification and booking of filming equipment and creation of call sheets to reserve actors and crews and for days needed on set. With all of this still uncertain, the director was in no position to think about the details of blocking actor and camera movement, lighting and sound etc.

David Chappelle describes an almost exactly similar process as typical in the production of *The Wire* for HBO:

> What I do when it [the script] comes in late is work nights and do what it takes to get through the first five days [of shooting] and then I'll take the

weekend to prep for the next week. [Without a script] I have to work from a "beat sheet" that at least tells us our locations, so we can at least do location scouting . . . when the script comes in, hopefully nothing will change.

Cited in Griffin, 2007

Ravage (1977) attributes these problems to the limited preparation time allowed in filmed series budgets. But the need for this preparation time is generated by the uncertainty of analysing film production tasks, and this in turn relates to the different types of knowledge employed in different production tasks. *Homeland* director Lodge Kerrigan gives an idea of the relational interdependencies between writing and directing;

> Usually . . . scripts are too ambitious, they're too large to the amount of shooting time you have, and you have to ask the writers to make certain changes . . . one of the most important skills is to be able to analyze and determine how long a scene will take to shoot, with a crew and a cast that you've never worked with before, in fifteen minutes.
>
> *Cited in Casau and Garin, 2015:29*

A key means of managing this interdependency is for a writer to attend the shoot, so that problems translating script into shots can be resolved jointly;

> the director will have to say to the writers, "OK I know that the beat is this, you want to get this guy to escape out of this space, but there is no door that leads out." So, we show the writers what we have to work with and nine out of ten times they'll say "that works"
>
> *Chapelle, cited in Griffin, 2007:28–9*

Chapter 1 highlighted the importance of such "mutual adjustment" in managing reciprocally interdependent production processes. As the chapter also noted, such management operationalises the tacit knowledge – of text types and discourse strategies– relevant to media production: "What might appear to be an unstructured 'free-for-all' conversation is really highly structured by professional norms and expectations" (Phalen and Osellame, 2012:12). The difficulty of managing such interdependencies was apparent even in WBTV's "mass production" process; "most directors don't even take the trouble to understand the script . . . If a director plays the characterization wrong . . . the total effect of the teleplay is destroyed" (Jules Schermer cited in Anderson, 1994:251).

Attempts to achieve efficiencies by standardising production come up against the problem that, unlike tangible products, the dominant design of a media product, like "the filmed series", offers only the most general guide to the production of each individually differentiated episode. "Formulas" constitute series-specific solutions to some of these problems, but they are not unique to the kind of programming produced by WBTV or Universal; "Negotiation with formula operates at all ends of the televisual spectrum . . . Indeed, the greater the rebellion against formula – as in, say, the FX series *Fargo* – the more apparent does formula become" (O'Sullivan, 2017a:55). Specifically commenting on the work of celebrated HBO showrunners, O'Sullivan notes that whatever "the master plans that the likes of Chase and Milch may cook up . . . by the end of the season, the scramble to turn scripts into shots into episodes typically accelerates as the gap between process and airtime shrinks" (O'Sullivan, 2017b:46).

5

PRODUCING NEWS REPORTS

Technological discontinuity

Beginning in the 1830s, technical changes created the potential for mass news-paper markets. Printing costs were reduced by the development of first rotary and then steam presses. The speed of text editing increased with the intro-duction of linotype machines and then word processors. Newspaper design innovations were enabled by photocomposition, lithographic printing and finally digital desk-top publishing and pagination systems. Telegraph networks gradually increased the speed and reduced the cost of global newsgathering and distribution (Winston, 2002).

The emergence of film and broadcasting enabled new organisations to enter news production (and the news advertising market) with newsreels appearing in cinemas and bulletins on radio and TV. Because of the difficulties of recording and editing video, most location news reports were produced on film, imposing delays (because of the processing time needed) and high costs. The development of videotape reduced the cost of recording and pre-recording news (op. cit.). The combination of satellite distribution and solid-state lightweight video cameras – electronic news-gathering (ENG) – reduced the time taken in transporting, processing and editing film and audiotape, enabling broadcasters to compete with the immediacy of teleg-raphy and news print.

Satellite transmission to printing plants facilitated rapid national and interna-tional distribution of newspapers but also enabled further new entrants as cable and satellite broadcasters established dedicated 24-hour news channels. The combina-tion of internet and mobile platforms enabled a large number of digital-only new entrants to news production, without the costs of printing or distribution borne by "legacy" news organisations (op. cit.).

Dominant design

News organisations produce factual content in a range of designs or text structures (editorials, opinion columns, investigative reports, features, listicles, live blogs etc.). This chapter identifies news reports as the form which distinguishes news from other forms of media production, and so focuses on this dominant text type.

Like the designs in other chapters, the news report evolved in competition with alternatives, each attempting to attract audiences in markets where attention is scarce. Chapter 1 explained how different text types use alternative structures to try to achieve coherence for readers. Thus, Jucker (2005) describes sixteenth-century newsbooks comprising sequences of letters – dispatches from foreign "correspondents" whose sole "organizing principle" was chronology. The disadvantages of the chronological structure have been classically illustrated by reference to news reports which began with Archduke Franz Ferdinand's carriage ride and only in the last sentence revealed the information (his assassination) which started the First World War (Pöttker, 2003). In the eighteenth century "partisan" newspapers used a rhetorical model of coherence, structuring news to develop an (ideological) argument. The legitimacy problems of the press in the nineteenth century, and the developing libel laws (see Legitimacy and regulation, this volume, p. 130), encouraged publishers and reporters to seek an alternative to the rhetorical structure. This alternative, which became the dominant design – the inverted pyramid – aimed to achieve coherence by metonymy (relating elements of a report to one another) rather than chronology or rhetoric (Ytreberg, 2001). It offered a solution to the coherence problems of chronological structures by ordering elements of news in a hierarchy of importance, relevance or "newsworthiness" (Pöttker, 2005). Its solution to the legitimacy problems of rhetorical structures was to adopt techniques designed to ensure the "objectivity" and "impartiality" of these news values. The inverted pyramid is, thus, fundamentally different from the narrative designs discussed in this book, because by revealing the most important information at the start, it precludes use of narrative techniques of withholding information to create suspense.

The following section illustrates the use of the inverted pyramid in reporting the allegations against the British film producer, Harvey Weinstein, which first appeared in an investigative report in *The New York Times* (NYT). The next section shows how *USA Today* used the pyramid structure to report these allegations. The subsequent section shows how the ITV evening news bulletin used the TV version of the inverted pyramid structure to report the spread of allegations which grew into the #MeToo movement.

"NYT"; Producer Harvey Weinstein has a 30-year history of sexual harassment

Andrea Mandell and Jayme Deerwester *USA Today* Published 11:08 PM EDT Oct 6, 2017

In a blistering report published Thursday, *The New York Times* detailed nearly 30 years of reports by women accusing Oscar-winning movie producer Harvey Weinsten of sexual harassment.

FIGURE 5.1   Shot of Harvey Weinstein: report of #MeToo allegations

Credit: *News at Ten*, ITN, 2018.

The headline and first sentence (or "lead") give a basic outline of the most important facts (who, what, where, when) needed to understand the event and its importance. This creates an invisibility of technique similar to both scientific articles and the continuity system (Chapters 2 and 3). The ideal is for the reporter to remove his or her role in the production and narration of the report; "he will make literally no reference, however modest or oblique, to his own person" (Weaver, 1975:88). This is achieved through the use of descriptive language, writing in the third person, with limited use of adjectives and adverbs. An exception occurs when reporters witness events first hand, and so write in the first person ("reportage"). Because *USA Today* closely followed practices in US TV news, it adapted its descriptive language from past to present tense (as shown in the excerpt below, "The *Times* reporters . . . write") (Logan, 1986).

The *Times* reporters, Jodi Kantor and Megan Twohey, write that they learned of legal supplements with at least eight women.

Many of his accusers have been young female employees of his production companies, the Weinsten Company and Miramax, the *Times* reports. However, they also include actress Ashley Judd who says Weinsten, 65, invited her to his Beverly Hills hotel room for a breakfast meeting some 20 years ago and then suggested he gave her a massage or she watch him shower.

The next section of the *USA Today* report uses bullet points, rather than full paragraphs, to summarise "other allegations" in a list. Descriptive language is used to convey the verifiable facts, and follows the principle of objectivity, attempting to verify this information, by attributing it to authoritative sources – in this case the *NYT* investigation which itself cites documentary evidence relating to legal settlements. Although the internet has enabled greater access to documentary sources, much newsworthy documentation is either private or its publication is prohibited. An alternative means of sourcing information became the interview – ideally with "eyewitnesses" or at least two independent witnesses, "in a position to know". One of the problems faced by the *NYT* investigation was that the legal settlements prevented the actresses from making attributable allegations in news reports. Instead actresses and former employees were quoted anonymously.

The inverted pyramid design has enabled newspapers to achieve spatial, as well as textual, coherence. By the eighteenth century, as the news publishers identified a habitual demand for the consumption of news, the quantity of news published became determined, not by the supply of newsworthy events, but by the specific number of pages which could be sold (to advertisers and readers). As demand for advertising space developed, newspapers began trying to achieve coherence across this space – the "news hole" – through the layout of reports and the use of visual aids, typography, illustration, photography, layout and design. Unlike cinema or broadcasting, newspapers are non-linear and the reader is free to navigate *between* stories. This means most people read a fraction of the newspaper's total content and read few reports to the end. To try to capture audience attention, newspapers prioritise spatial over textual coherence. Whereas features and TV series prioritise narrative continuity, newspapers habitually allow discontinuities in news reports. To try to maximise papers' attractiveness to audiences, newspapers start a number of stories on the front page and then continue them on other pages. For the same reason, newspapers may, at the last minute, put the most recent ("breaking") story on the front page (Weaver, 1975).

The inverted pyramid helps overcome these spatial discontinuities because it links a series of more or less self-contained sections in order of importance ("newsworthiness"). Rather than a linear (narrative) structure, the news report has an almost cyclical structure, telling the story more than once, with increasing elaboration. This allows journalists to edit reports to the available length (much more rapidly than would be possible in a feature or TV series), without losing coherence, by removing paragraphs starting with the last one. It allows readers to follow stories across (multiple) pages, or depart before the "end" while still retaining a basic comprehension of the event.

Because they were consumed in linear time, the cinema newsreel and later the radio and TV news bulletins did not have the newspapers' ability to retain audience attention by allowing them to switch between stories. Instead, they severely limited the time demanded of audiences (both of the bulletin and of each report, producing a much smaller number of reports than newspapers). This imposed much greater constraints on selection. Rather than following journalistic news values (such as immediacy), cinema newsreel "gatekeeping" focused on entertainment and dramatic visual action (sports, disasters, celebrities, crimes and punishments etc.) which would still be relevant when shown at second and third run cinemas; "newsreels were not in the business of being first with the news, or of breaking stories – they were supplementary and dependent on their audience already being aware of the story" (Taylor, 2002:68). More than radio, TV news retained these news values. The linear nature of TV news also encouraged differences from the pyramid form. Rather than structuring reports to create departure points for the audience, TV reports attempt to hold audience attention, building up to the "end" of a story.

However, the immediacy of TV broadcasting, with live newsreading, enabled news bulletins to include breaking news reports, using headlines, wire service copy, photographs and caption cards. The potential for "editing from the bottom" was to combine elements of the pyramid – especially "objective", descriptive writing – with those of the feature and the studio show. Broadcasters replaced the anonymous newsreel voice with a named anchor, increasingly the "star" of the bulletin (Sendall, 1983). Both anchors and reporters are faced with a dilemma, compared to the newspaper reporter, in the extent to which their performance is "invisible" and objective, is "authoritative" and uses personal reputation to establish trust and legitimacy, or is "dramatic" and intended to attract and retain audience attention.

Most bulletins have an opening sequence (Figure 5.2) similar to the newsreels' titles, logo and "musical score of earnest strings and fulsome horns" (Althaus, 2010:202). This provides the main opportunity for news producers to use "non-diegetic" music to help communicate the genre of the programme.

This is followed by an establishing shot of the news "anchor/s" (Rageh Omaar, Figure 5.3) showing the studio setting and the location of key props; the newsdesk, a screen for graphics and live interviews, and often the newsroom in the background.

FIGURE 5.2 *ITV News at Ten* opening credit

Credit: News at Ten, ITN, 2018.

FIGURE 5.3 Establisher studio layout and newscaster

Credit: News at Ten, ITN, 2018.

The next sequence covers the headlines starting with a close-up of the anchor reading from a teleprompter in a direct address (breaking the fourth wall), cutting away to very short recorded sequences from the featured stories.

The first story adds new information to the *USA Today* report, by reporting the increasing number of actresses prepared to make "on the record" allegations against Weinstein. It begins in close-up, with the anchor reading the equivalent of the first paragraph of the pyramid. The transition (a vision mix) to a live video shot of a reporter on location is motivated by the newsreader, with a "look" away from

FIGURE 5.4 Medium close-up: Rageh Omaar reads #MeToo headline

Credit: News at Ten, ITN, 2018.

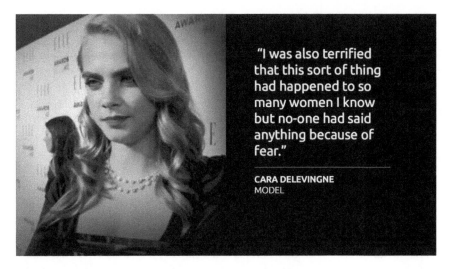

FIGURE 5.5   Close-up: Cara Delevingne reporting allegations

Credit: News at Ten, ITN, 2018.

the camera, similar to the "looks" used by film or TV actors to enable a match on action. This is followed by a transition to a graphic (Figure 5.5) with an image of the model Cara Delevingne, who is one of those who has spoken "on the record", and a quote from her statement.

In a typical news bulletin, a second story might consist entirely of a recorded sequence of either actuality (shot documentary style, see Chapter 6) or planned action (often generic establishers of buildings, transition shots of people walking or writing at desks, nodding shots of reporters etc.).

Compared to many studio shows, news bulletins involve very limited movement either by the presenters or the camera (see Redfern, 2014). TV news interviews (between the anchor/reporter and an interviewee or the anchor and a reporter on-screen – a "two way") are a presentational (delivering information as dialogue) as much as a newsgathering technique. Movement and dialogue are covered in the multi-camera "proscenium" style (Chapter 3), observing the 180 and 30° rules.

TV news magazines like *Panorama* (1953–) and especially *60 Minutes* (1968–) also moved from the inverted pyramid structure to a narrative structure of more or less dramatic scenes (such as the "stake out" or "door-step") filmed and narrated from the point-of-view of the star presenter (Ytreberg, 2001).

The emergence of 24-hour news services first on radio and then on cable and satellite channels, from new entrants (CNN) and existing broadcasters (BBC News 24) increased the proportion of "live" to recorded news reports and of (low cost) news "analysis" to reporting. This accentuated a trend towards reliance on "experts" as opposed to "eyewitnesses". "A century ago, outside experts almost never appeared in the news . . . Today . . . almost every story includes an official source, and outside experts appear in one fifth of the stories" (Barnhurst, 2005:249). In the US, this has brought the re-emergence of partisan news reporting with cable channels (e.g. Fox and MSNBC) dedicated to the political inclinations of a niche audience.

Online journalism has enabled further structural innovations, including the use of categorical (listicles) or chronological (live blogs) reports. It has also enabled changes to the established reporting conventions of newsworthiness and the provision objective or verifiable facts. Websites like the *Drudge Report* and *Breitbart* have returned to the ideological selection and rhetorical structuring practices of partisan political reporting. Others have abandoned the convention of objective facts ("fake news") or adopted purely commercial conventions ("clickbait") (Parks, 2017).

Legitimacy and regulation

Many authors identify US Defence Secretary Edwin Stanton as the inventor of the pyramid form (see Mindich, 1993). As Mindich's account makes clear, however, Stanton's use of the form was not intended to replace partisan bias with objectivity but to create a more legitimate form of promoting the government's agenda. By structuring facts into a hierarchy, apparently based on "objective" criteria of newsworthiness, he was able to set the news agenda. Mindich (1993) shows how Stanton was successful in persuading newspapers both to reprint his reports with minimal changes and to imitate his terse, compact pyramid form. A similar explanation ties journalists' adoption of the pyramid to their experience of court reporting which "included retrospective accounts of the crime or the criminal's life" (Jucker, 2005:13).

Whatever the origin of the pyramid design, its widespread adoption appears to have occurred in response to the legitimation crises of the alternative model, sensationalist reporting (or "yellow journalism") which had enthusiastically been adopted in the 1890s by Pulitzer's *New York World* and Hearst's *New York Examiner*. While commercially successful, this approach generated numerous controversies, particularly when one of their "serious" journalism competitors, the *New York Sun*, accused Hearst's papers of inciting the assassin who shot dead US President William McKinley in 1901 (Sachsman and Bulla, 2017:11).

The periodic "moral panics" following such excesses threatened to undermine the legitimacy of the industry. As Nerone (2017:99) argues, the professionalisation of journalism represented a solution accepted as legitimate by the key participants in the industry:

> the publishers wanted to remain free from . . . industrial regulation . . . the outraged public wanted the news system, which they considered vital to democratic governance, to be insulated from the self-interest of the moneyed class who owned the media; the newsroom workforce wanted prestige, income, and creative autonomy. A professionalization project for news was the result. That professionalization project took the work of making the news and turned it into journalism.

Although less immediately commercially successful than sensationalist approaches, the pyramid was a more successful commercial product than other "legitimate" forms which had been practiced by the "prestige" press. Pöttker's (2005:63) historical analysis of *The New York Times* and *New York Herald* suggests that the pyramid succeeded in gaining audience attention because it improved the "communicative quality of the journalistic product". He found that between 1875 and 1895 inverted pyramid reports increased 300%, bringing an increase in the use of headlines and a reduction in the average length of both reports and sentences. Stensaas (1986) shows an increase in "objective news reports" from around 50% (1884–95) to around 66% (1905–14) to around 80% (1945–54).

Schudson (2001) shows how newspaper organisations and journalists supported the development of a profession whose core methods and values were promoted in trade publications, codes of ethics and in practitioner guides. Shuman (1894, cited in Mindich, 2000:65) explained that "a well-constructed story begins with its most important fact and ends with the least important". The (1926) Code of Ethics of the Society of Professional Journalists stated that "news reports should be free of opinion or bias and represent all sides of an issue" (cited in Shoemaker and Reese, 1996:93).

US and UK regulators have traditionally accepted the argument that professional news reporting should be a mandatory part of any broadcast schedule. Vianello (1985:35) argues that the broadcast news bulletin itself is a result of FCC regulation. "The Supreme Court interpreted the Communications Act of 1934's famous dictum – 'in the public interest' – as requiring news within the day's programming". Although resisted by the newspaper publishers, the emergency of the Second World War made the legitimacy of the case for broadcast news seem unquestionable. For commercial broadcasters, regulatory requirements were more important than market concerns in supporting news services; one NBC executive noted: "without the FCC, we couldn't line-up enough affiliates to make a news program . . . worthwhile" (cited in Vianello, 1985:35).

In the 1950s, academic studies began to question the legitimacy of the journalistic profession's claims to independence and objectivity. The journalist's power to select or reject stories created the potential for individual bias (White, 1950). Later studies noted the constraints on professional autonomy. The original relationship between the inverted pyramid and bureaucratic sources of information acted as a strong external influence on news reporting (Shoemaker and Reese, 1996). Institutional studies detailed the influence of the news organisation hierarchy on the decisions of journalists (Schlesinger, 1978). Finally, the shared professional culture and working practices of journalists were observed to "construct" news in particular ways, categorising some events as "hard" and others as "soft" news (Tuchman, 1973). This idea of genres of news drew attention to the influence of narrative structures on the framing and construction of events to tell a particular type of story (Jacobs, 1996).

These critiques of the independence and diversity of news reporting have led US and UK regulators, at times, to attempt to limit news organisations' ability to control news markets. Even during periods of extensive deregulation and marketisation of broadcasting, regulators have often included measures attempting to protect the continued production of news reports from the potentially damaging effects of competition (DNH, 1995). To some extent, therefore, the regulation and protection of news reporting has reinforced the legitimacy of the pyramid design and encouraged standardisation of reporting practices across news organisations. Compared to genres such as documentary, for example (see Chapter 6), the news genre has experienced very little innovation and change.

Beginning in 1982 *USA Today* introduced a range of innovations in news reporting, quickly adopted by many other US newspapers (McNichol and Carlson, 1985b:48). However, for some, this widely adopted approach exemplified the limitations of "objective" reporting; "*USA Today* excludes all commentary, personal columns, interpretive writing and investigative reporting. Not a single story, column or paragraph on the other pages takes a critical perspective toward anything" (Ludlow, cited in Berry, 1993:25). From this perspective, professional journalism based on the pyramid, lacked legitimacy because it "refused to examine the basic structures of power and privilege" (Schudson, 1978:160). This critique led to an argument that "alternative media" (Couldry and Curran, 2003), and particularly the internet, "would democratize news production and reinvigorate democracy" (Redden and Witschge, 2010:184), creating a new, more legitimate "public sphere". However, recent studies have suggested that the internet has brought an increase in unverifiable or even intentionally "fake" news, while professional journalists have less time for face-to-face meetings to hold politicians to account (Fenton, 2010).

Market control

Chapter 1 explained how the low marginal costs of media distribution work to create spectacular hits, which compensate for the many misses associated with experience goods. The demand for news has required extreme "individual differentiation" of products, in the sense that there has never been a demand for a daily news product the day after its release, and so news has faced the most limited "window" to achieve mass consumption of its "first copy". This has imposed a very limited cycle time (the "daily news cycle") on production, which has in turn led to the heavy emphasis on deadlines in the development of journalism production routines.

However, demand for news has retained its habitual character longer than most other media products. Thus, many US and UK newspaper brands have survived for two centuries or more; *Observer* (1791), *The Times* (1785), *The Daily Telegraph* (1855) and *The Guardian* (1821). This habitual demand has enabled the newspaper industry, at times, to achieve reliable profits, particularly where competition can be reduced or eliminated.

The initial development of mass markets for newspapers brought significant competition. By 1850 the US had 200 daily newspapers, more than the rest of the world combined. Both US and UK markets saw a period, roughly between 1880 and 1920, when increasing sales encouraged new entrants. US daily readership grew tenfold, from 3.5 million to 33 million (Schudson, 2001). UK annual sales increased from 85 million to 5.6 billion (Curran and Seaton, 2009). New entrants expanded the number of newspapers published in the US, from 850 to a peak of 2,200 (Hannan and Carroll, 1992). In the UK, local dailies increased from two to 169, local weeklies from 400 to 1,700, with a "substantial" increase in national papers (Curran and Seaton, 2009). This period saw the foundation of the *Daily Mail* (1896), *Daily Express* (1900) and *Daily Mirror* (1903).

As radio stations entered the news market, both the US and the UK newspaper industries acted to protect themselves against competition from broadcasters. The American Newspaper Publishers Association (ANPA) limited broadcaster access to wire services, while in the UK the Newspaper Proprietors Association, the Newspaper Society and the UK news agencies (Reuters and PA) "successfully lobbied the government to restrict BBC Radio's hours of and sources of live news" (Crisell, 2012:13).

The outbreak of war undermined the legitimacy of the newspaper industry strategy; public service arguments (the importance of informing the public in wartime) prevailed in establishing radio news bulletins. However, despite this competition US daily newspaper sales continued to grow, from 41 million to 63 million between 1940 and 1974. UK national daily sales increased from 5.4 million to 10.6 million from 1920 to 1939 and from 1938 to 1947 total circulation (including local dailies) increased from 17.8 million to 28.6 million (Ellis, 2011). This convinced the industry that radio news bulletins were not a "free" economic substitute for paid newspapers (op. cit.). Instead, as the broadcast networks created national markets in advertising (see Chapter 3) the newspapers began to horizontally integrate, acquiring other newspapers to create newspaper "chains" (as opposed to networks) with individual titles exercising monopoly control of local advertising (Camporesi, 1990). As advertising markets became more sophisticated, self-styled "quality newspapers" like *The New York Times*, *The Washington Post* and *The Wall Street Journal* (*WSJ*) could become target affluent demographics. "By the mid-1930s, over two-thirds of quality newspaper income came from advertising generated by charging high rates to reach small, but affluent audiences" (Curran and Seaton, 2009:44).

Chains were not a new phenomenon. In the UK, in 1884, the Carnegie syndicate controlled eight dailies and ten weeklies (op. cit.). UK newspaper chains began to acquire national and regional titles. The creation of five major regional newspaper chains increased their market share from 12% to 44% of local morning papers and 8% to 40% of evening papers between 1921 and 1939 (ibid.). By 1937 three publishers controlled 50% of national daily circulation and 59% of national Sunday newspaper circulation This market structure, with three or four newspaper groups controlling between 60% and 80% of national daily and Sunday sales, has continued to the present day (Ellis, 2011, Schlosberg, 2013). In the US, after 1930, chains increased their control of newspaper titles from 16% to 32% between 1930 and 1960. Chain ownership of US newspapers continued to increase to 77%

(1990s) and over 90% (2000) (Rhomberg, 2012). The eventual outcome of this consolidation was the creation of monopoly control of local newspaper markets across the US and UK; "a steady downward trend toward a single daily" (Hannan and Carroll, 1992:217). The number of US cities with competition in daily newspapers declined from 61% (1880) to 20% (1930) to 1.9% (1981). By the 1960s, 90% of firms operated monopolies (Rhomberg, 2012). The chains competed to acquire papers which, as "the only viable advertising option for local businesses", achieved profit margins of 20–40% (Abernathy, 2016). "Gannett was one of the first to embrace this business model and it would come to define the paradigm of the publicly traded newspaper chain" (Rhomberg, 2012:30).

Audio-visual news initially posed a less direct competitive threat than radio. The newspapers responded by horizontally integrating into film (e.g. Hearst Metrotone). The first "television newsreels" continued this coevolution, using film supplied by the global newsreel companies (Althaus, 2010). Their decline left the TV networks to establish their newsgathering systems for international reporting. The high cost of this, until the emergence of ENG in the 1970s, meant the US networks lost money on TV news reporting, but maintained the bulletins to meet public service regulations (Vianello, 1985).

Thus, in both the UK and the US, TV news did not significantly substitute for newspaper purchasing, and national newspaper circulation stabilised at around 60 million (US) and 20 million (UK) until the mid-1990s (Ellis, 2011). However, TV advertising seems to have substituted for newspaper display advertising. As display advertising revenue fell, the proportion of US newspaper income from classified advertising increased from 18% to 40% between 1950 and 2000 (Picard, 2002).

The strategy of developing oligopolistic control of newspaper markets had built on the industry's inherent barriers to entry. The vertical integration of reporting and printing enabled newspapers to achieve economies of scale, creating a "virtuous cycle" of lower cover prices and increased sales. This combination of high start-up costs and low margins deterred new entries to the industry. However, in the 1980s, digital technology lowered start-up printing costs and satellites reduced distribution costs (Winston, 2002).

These lower costs and the succesful model of *USA Today*, encouraged the speculative entry of a raft of new national daily and Sunday papers in the UK including *Today* and *Sunday Today*, *The Independent* and *The Independent on Sunday*, *News on Sunday* and *The Sunday Correspondent*, and a London paper the *London Daily News*. As Curran and Seaton (2009) show, many of the new entrants failed to appreciate that the low margins available meant, even with reduced costs, newspapers needed to quickly achieve significant sales to break even. The incumbents were able to tip the scales further, by making dramatic reductions in cover prices, preventing their new rivals from building an audience of habitual consumers. The pioneer, *Today*, was sold to a multinational within weeks of launch and eventually the new entrants all ceased publication, except for *The Independent* (albeit in multinational ownership) largely because it succeeded in attracting an affluent demographic, generating sufficient advertising revenue to compensate for low sales.

As noted, these new entrants had been attracted a model established in US markets and typified by Gannet's successful use of digital and satellite technology to launch a new national paper – *USA Today*. Prior to the launch, Gannett had recorded growth in quarterly earnings for 15 consecutive years (Rhomberg, 2012). Each new addition to the chain received the same management approach "raising prices and advertising rates and cutting costs including staff" (Rhomberg, 2012:31). Unlike the UK's new entrants, however, Gannett possessed the financial resources to deal with price competition and to incur significant losses, until its TV-influenced redesign of the newspaper format succeeded in attracting a new newspaper audience additional to that of the other nationally distributed US papers. Launched in 1982, by 1986 its daily circulation was second to the *WSJ* (1.4 million) and by 1992 it was the market leader (6.6 million). It became the highest selling English language daily newspaper in the world (WAN-IFRA, 2016).

Gannett's success with *USA Today*, "became the model to be followed by many titles in the USA and Europe" (Saltzis, 2006:34). However, rather than enabling new entrants, this model revitalised the incumbents. In the US, the model involved adopting *USA Today*'s news format innovations (colour, graphics, "factoids" etc.). A survey of 230 large US dailies found that a broad range of chain-owned papers had done this (Berry, 1993). The second step was financing the investment, through a transition from family ownership to becoming publicly traded corporations. The capital raised enabled extensive acquisitions, greater market control and rapid profit growth. Between 1970 and 1989, Gannett acquired 69 daily newspapers (as well as horizontally integrating into other media markets), and increased annual revenues and from $186 million to $319 million (Ellis, 2011).

The Gannett model attracted publishers around the world. In the UK, established publishers, like News International (*News of the World*, *The Times* and *The Sunday Times*), financed the initial investment by selling their premises in central London and building new printing plants on the outskirts of the city. However, the potential of satellite technology created a new competitor. In the 1980s, new entrants like CNN and Sky, and the established UK and US broadcast networks, began to launch 24-hour national and international news channels reaching global audiences via satellite and cable networks. Digitisation and the emergence of online news affected the "private good" nature of the print newspaper, giving it more of the characteristics of a "public good" and thus increasing the difficulty of monetisation. The immediacy of 24-hour cable, satellite and online news enabled it to act as a cheap or free substitute for newspaper purchase. The internet also provided a cheap, effective substitute for the newspapers' monopoly of classified advertising.

Between 1995 and 2005, US newspaper circulation fell 11%. By 2005, UK national newspaper sales had fallen 30% against their 1965 figure (Picard, 2008). The web's massive expansion of advertising space, hugely increased supply and competition, driving down prices of classified advertising. In the same period, the newspapers' share of overall advertising spend fell from 36.9% to 28.9% in the US and from 40.4% to 35.5% in the UK. Iosifides (2016:429) notes: "the cumulative loss of circulation of popular and quality dailies was 29% and 31%, respectively, owing among other factors to the rise of television and the Internet". The US chains responded to falling sales with more acquisitions, including their online competitors, to try to achieve further market control. They were joined in the twenty-first century by private equity firms like Digital First and New Media. By 2016, along with Gannett, these companies owned almost twice as many newspapers (898) as the three largest chains in 2004 (Abernathy, 2016). As Chapter 6 shows, increasingly newspapers became part of the horizontal integration strategies of global media conglomerates, as established operators "converged" production and distribution across multiple (print, TV, online and mobile) platforms.

Process innovation

Chapter 1 illustrated the relationships between the volume of output required and the degree of specialisation and division of labour in production. Until the late nineteenth century, apart from "prestige" papers like *The London Times* and *The New York Times*, most papers limited their size to four pages (Nerone and Barnhurst, 2003). The task of filling this "news hole" was to squeeze in as many stories as possible. The growth of the advertising market, lower paper costs and the success of yellow press encouraged newspapers to increase the number of pages, and managing this greater volume of output encouraged process innovations including greater specialisation of labour and greater mechanisation of production.

Chapter 1 differentiated media products from other information goods (such as a software system), describing them as "communication" goods, because media consumers want new information each time they consume. The demand for first daily, then hourly, and now "minute-by-minute" news, has imposed on news production the most rapid cycle times (and thus production schedules and deadlines) of all the media industries. Since the beginnings of daily newspapers, the "news cycle" has required, as a minimal definition of news, an event which has occurred since the previous deadline and before the next deadline (Shoemaker and Reese, 1996).

Örnebring's (2013) study of news production at *The Times* in 1860 gives an idea of the early organisation of production (by a flexible workforce of between 150 and 200 writers) required to fill the news hole in a prestige newspaper in the UK. Some of the specialisms continued practices from the earliest days of newspapers, such as the 10–12 senior writers working at *The Times*. The role of editor, whose name appeared on the newspaper, followed the logic of the early one-person operation partisan papers but developed to take on the functions of the editorial page editor (Nerone and Barnhurst, 2003). The leader-writer's role also continued the traditions of the partisan press, bringing in the opinions of politically active professionals (politicians, lawyers etc.). Similarly, the pseudonymous correspondent (22 foreign and 21 provincial), with a separate full time job, originated in the seventeenth century (Örnebring, 2013).

However, producing the volume and range of news types needed to fill the news hole called for a a significant quantity of original reporting and this in turn required a large and separate reporting staff, at lower levels in the legitimacy/status and pay hierarchy than the senior writers. To reduce the variability of the task of finding and producing news, reporters were usually based at an institution (parliament, court, police station, stock exchange etc.) considered a dependable source of news events. This in turn led to specialisation of reporters in covering these institutions/subjects and to the establishment of different reporting "beats". Thus, *The Times* employed reporters at court (28), parliament (16), with police (14), business (11) and arts and literature (10–15). However, a large amount of the content was produced by generalist newsgathering reporters ("penny-a-liners").

This legitimacy and status hierarchy was reflected in the way copy was edited for the paper. The work of editors and correspondents held a prominent position across the middle pages. Reporters competed for space within the remaining pages. The link between writing and technical staff came through the foreman of the composing room, who was the ultimate arbiter of which reports would fit into the available space.

The professionalisation of journalism was encouraged by a number of trends, particularly challenges to the legitimacy of yellow journalism, broader social trends in white collar work (Schudson, 1978) and the desire of newspaper managers both for quality (to attract audiences) and for a quiescent workforce (Kaul, 1986). This coincided with a reduction in the volume of output required from journalists. Barnhurst's (2005:245) study of three typical newspapers showed a reduction in the output of reports required to fill the news hole, noting "a dramatic decline in the number of stories that newspapers publish on their front pages". He dates this change, in particular, from the 1930s and notes that "journalists wrote longer stories, and editors . . . allowed stories to expand in length" (ibid.).

Until this point there had been, "no clear lines of separation between news and criticism . . . so many journalists are . . . both reporters and commentators, and frequently are both at the same time . . ." (Fox Bourne, cited in Örnebring, 2013:401). But during this period, two types of writers used by *The Times* converged to form the modern professional journalist, whose work was clearly defined as "reporting". "What we call journalism came from the merging of the roles of correspondent and reporter . . . beginning I think in the mid-1890s, but . . . consummated suddenly in the second decade of the twentieth century" (Nerone, 2008:142).

As the reporting practices which would become the basis of the inverted pyramid (such as interviewing and quoting sources) became generally accepted, a second key motivation for the establishment of a journalistic profession came from the desire to control the labour market and gain some form of "occupational closure" (Örnebring, 2018). No formal training was required to work as a journalist, although experience in local newspapers had become an established "training ground" before reporters came to work for *The Times*. Örnebring's account also makes clear that, in the 1860s, newspapers practised "numerical flexibility". While the editors and publishers were employed on a permanent salary basis, most other writers worked as freelancers. Leader-writers were usually paid a weekly salary, but might work for several different newspapers. Most reporters (so-called "penny-a-liners"), either wrote copy to order or sold their reports "ad hoc", and were paid by the line.

As the writers with the highest legitimacy, in terms of content, some parliamentary reporters were employed on temporary contracts with *The Times*, which excluded parliamentary recess. This need for supplementary income became part of the campaigns (of organisations like the Newspaper Guild) for permanent employment for professional journalists. "Washington correspondents routinely supplemented their newspaper income by clerking for the very Congressional committees they wrote about" (Schudson, 2001). The call for editorial independence thus supported arguments for financial independence.

Many studies of journalism have noted that the similarities in the way different organisations report news demonstrate that news reports cannot be an objective recording of aspects of reality, but must reflect similarities in their production process. Some argue that these are ideological similarities – whether conscious partisan bias or the unconscious influence of the profession's ideology of objectivity (Hall, 1982). Many newsroom studies, however, have noted how similarities in reporting processes enable efficiencies in production. Journalists reduce "task variability" by locating close to "institutions which generate a useful volume of reportable activity" (Rock, 1981:64). Rather than autonomy, journalism is characterised by following rules and is specialised into news beats and "routinized" work processes (Tuchman, 1973). This has been interpreted as evidence of a Taylorist rationalisation of reporting into a mass production process. Bantz et al. (1980:59) describe "the development of a factory news model, with its assembly line approach, in conjunction with the trends toward routinization". Golding and Elliott (1979:119) described news production as "a highly regulated and routine process of manufacturing a cultural product on an electronic production line".

Since Gutenberg, the task of print production had been divided into two subtasks – arranging movable type blocks into lines of text (composing) and then applying ink to their surface to press paper against them (the press). These tasks required experience and skill, gained through apprenticeships with existing workers, which limited the substitutability of such labour. In the context of the limited cycle time of news, and the very limited window for distributing newspaper content, this gave print unions the power (as with TV) to use a strike to prevent publication and thus inflict heavy financial penalties on publishers. For many decades, newspaper owners ceded control of recruitment, training, pay scales and many aspects of the production process to print unions (Mendel, 1991)

The late nineteenth-century boom in newspaper sales encouraged owners to introduce a range of typewriter-based, process innovations, especially the linotype machine. This further divided the work of the compositors into two subtasks – arranging the type into words (typesetting) and composing the page. This mechanisation increased the throughput of typesetting by between 300 and 1,000% (Jaske, 1981). This weakened the position of print workers since newspapers could now more easily substitute cheaper, untrained, inexperienced labour for these skilled workers. Thus, the unions did not oppose the new technology, instead they sought to maintain their key terms and conditions through its introduction. The unions largely succeeded in retaining their control over both the labour market and the production process, by securing agreement that the typesetting jobs would still be reserved for union members who had completed the full (4–6 year) apprenticeship (even though this was not strictly necessary to to the job) and by restricting the number of apprenticeships available (Kalleberg et al., 1987).

Increasing use of the telegraph enabled newspapers to increase the volume of news output by outsourcing newsgathering (and a certain amount of report writing) to the news agency oligopoly. But agency fees and costs of telegraphy encouraged newspapers to restrict the length of agency reports (Schudson, 1978). US newspapers employed copy editors ("sub-editors" in the UK) to manage the volume of incoming "wire stories" by editing them ("from the bottom") – reinforcing the use of the pyramid structure (Nerone and Barnhurst, 2003).

Studies suggest telegraph usage, between 1856 and 1906, also reduced the "cycle time" of news production. Wilke (1998) found that newspaper reporting of events, within 24 hours of their occurrence, increased, from 11% to 95% in Germany. This competitive, 24-hour, news cycle, increased the requirement for last minute changes in text, layout and photography (especially front pages), and copy editors increasingly replaced printers in performing this quality assurance (proofreading) and design role. By the 1930s, copy editors were routinely laying out pages (showing location of text, photos and headlines). These "maps" were produced manually and were then used as guides by compositors and printers (Keith, 2015).

The extension of the chains' market control enabled them to develop process innovations to change this situation; "consolidation has provided the capital necessary for research to develop automated technologies . . . (and) the networking capacity provided by newspaper chains allows member firms to gain access to advanced technologies" (Kalleberg et al., 1987:53).

The gradual introduction of computers and satellite technology enabled the dis-integration of some elements of production process (uncoupling some key sequential interdependencies) and their reintegration in ways which achieved both process efficiencies and product improvements. Satellites enabled the separation of editorial and printing processes, reducing distribution costs, as papers could be printed at a number of local plants. Computers enabled automation of elements of the sequential tasks of reporting, editing, page make-up, typesetting and printing. But it also enabled a reintegration of these tasks to reduce duplication of effort. Systems were developed so that all the "pre-press" tasks – reporting, editing stories, proofreading and layout (columns, spacing, hyphenation etc.) and page make-up – could be done on computer or even automated (Holloway, 1987).

Unlike the linotype revolution, computerisation directly removed the typesetting work of compositors, removing duplication as journalists were able to input copy directly ("single keying") into a form suitable for layout, and page make-up was used to remove the jobs of compositors. This greatly diminished the training time required to set the type, thus obviating the need for long apprenticeships. This direct challenge led, in the early '60s, to a range of strikes at US newspapers. However, the balance of power had changed and, in Florida, the publishers were able to train non-union labour to print the paper using the new technology (McKercher, 2002). The professionalisation of journalistic work meant the culture and ideologies of the journalism union (the Newspaper Guild) was different from the printers and they were more likely to accept the new systems (ibid.).

This set a pattern of newspaper chains forcing their workers to accept "buy-out" agreements, often involving de-ecognition of the union and mass redundancies. Dertouzos and Quinn's (1985) study of a large sample of US newspapers found compositor employment fell 52% between 1970 and 1983. By replacing more expensive union workers with non-union workers, the industry reduced its pay-roll costs per employee between 1977 and 1992 (Benedict and Ogden, 2002). In the UK, Rupert Murdoch's News International implemented this model in 1986, using non-union labour and equipment long-established in the US. 5,500 workers were dismissed and a year-long strike ensued but eventually the model was adopted by the other major UK newspapers (Marjoribanks, 2000).

But satellite technology also enabled a major competitor and revealed a huge demand for 24-hour news, vastly increasing the output required to fill this 24-hour news hole and hugely reducing the cycle time by enabling constant live news. The production processes of audio-visual news began with the newsreels. This film process was both slow and expensive until the combination of video cameras and editing and satellite transmission created the potential for ENG. This automated some of the elements of camera work (focus, white balance etc.), lowered the costs of film-ing stock and enabled news crews to be much more mobile. The shorter cycle times and unpredictability of news events reduced the extent to which news crews could follow the standard conventions of features or TV series in performing central filmmaking tasks of lighting, mis-en-scène, blocking and dialogue. This created a restricted "grammar" for news footage which together with use of less skilled and experienced labour created an acceptance of poorer quality standards, particularly when filming "actuality". As Chapters 4 and 6 note, this "wobbly camera" aesthetic fed first into "fly on the wall" documentary and then back into filmed series.

The emergence of online media further shortened news cycle times, with a demand for minute-by-minute updates of continuing news stories, encouraging further process innovation in news production. While digitisation of newspaper production had enabled a reduction in printing work, it facilitated an increase in newspaper design work and online news has continued to explore the potential for graphical representation of news. To reduce costs and meet demand, many news organisations have abandoned copy-editing of online news stories and also pursued vertical disintegration and outsourcing of layout and design (Keith, 2015).

The impact of online content on newspaper sales and advertising brought an attempt to achieve process innovation in the "first copy" costs of news reporting. Traditional publishers like Gannet and Reuters have outsourced reporting to so-called "content farms" while digital entrants have operated with a similar model (such as the *Bleacher Report*) (McKinney, 2018). An alternative approach has been to attempt to "repurpose" the first copy of the report to try to engage audiences for it across multiple platforms. To this end, news organisations have introduced content management systems and low cost video equipment, and trained reporters to be "multi-skilled" – able to produce versions of their reports in TV/video, radio/audio and text/image formats.

The movement towards multi-skilled, multiplatform reporting has been inter-preted as evidence of a transformation – either from mass production or professional control – to flexible specialisation in news production; "flexible specialization of the labor process has resulted in the decline of the news media professional as crossmedia synergies, technological convergences, and corporate conglomerations have blurred the boundaries between information and entertainment" (Rose and Nesbitt-Larking, 2010:285).

This chapter has argued that the pyramid structure emerged because of its ability to gain audience attention, its role in the legitimacy of the press and its adoption by market leaders. It then enabled efficiencies principally by reducing task variability and increasing analysability. As noted in Chapter 3 for TV studio production, there is evidence that the combination of vertical integration of processes and the short cycle time for output created the potential for organised labour (particularly among printers) to limit the extent of process efficiencies (creating some "rigidities" in news production). Multinationals, like News International, saw the contrasts between the levels of productivity of their US and UK operations. Holloway (1987:136) notes of the three Royal Commissions on the Press since the end of the Second World War, "All three were highly critical of the national newspapers of Fleet Street; overmanning, restrictive practices and outdated equipment were singled out as the main causes of very low productivity".

Digital technology clearly increased the degree of "functional flexibility" in news production, with copy editors taking over many design and layout tasks from printers and, later, text-based journalists taking on production of video and audio content, and vice versa. But the account presented in this chapter suggests it would be a fundamental error to interpret the changes in journalism as a transformation from "mass production" to flexible specialisation. As Chapter 1 argued, the existence of standardisation in products or production "routines" is not necessarily evidence of the kind of routinisation of work proposed by Taylorism and Fordist mass production. While newsroom studies have stressed the degree to which planning and routines enable news organisations to reduce uncertainty, a comparison of news reporting with the scripted forms of drama and entertainment described in Chapters 2, 3 and 4, demonstrates that news production retains a high degree of uncertainty and variability, even by the standards of media production.

For this reason, the changes towards multiplatform production cannot represent a transition between mass production and flexible specialisation. Chapter 1 argued that, rather than a Taylorist imposition of management control, it is more helpful to understand the efficiency gains of routines and attempts to reduce task variability as part of the process of producers applying their knowledge of dominant designs, genre rules and professional ethics to the production of individually differentiated products designed to attract an audience. Rather than being standardised and routinised, this knowledge provides a more general guide whose exact application is usually resolved in a process of discourse and mutual adjustment with other workers.

6
PRODUCING TV FORMATS

Like media studies of newsrooms and news production, studies of factual media production have tended to focus on questions of legitimacy, particularly the way real events are represented in documentaries. This leads to understanding documentaries largely in terms of their different approaches to this ethical question (see Nichols, 1991). The emergence of factual formats and reality TV has brought further attention to these issues (Biressi and Nunn, 2005).

Factual TV is also an area where academic theories of flexible specialisation (FS) have moved from academic into policy and industry discourse. This is because factual genres were most affected by UK regulations which enforced vertical disintegration of production by broadcasters. Industry and policy advocates drew either explicitly on the theory (see Harvey, 1989) or implicitly on the language of flexibility to argue that this measure would increase innovation in TV production. The subsequent emergence of a new dominant design – the reality or entertainment format – was taken up by academics (see Barnatt and Starkey, 1997) and industry lobby groups (see Oliver and Ohlbaum, 2011) as evidence that deregulation had promoted flexibility which had unlocked the innovation of independent producers: "British creativity was widely believed to be central to the success of UK television exports" (TRP, 2014).

Using the theory outlined in Chapter 1, this chapter analyses a recent entertainment format success (*Love Island*, ITV) and explains the emergence of this newly dominant design. This begins with key technological changes, bringing new entrants to the market, then looks at the contrasting views of industry and policymakers in the UK and US about the legitimacy of vertical integration of TV production and distribution. The resulting regulations influenced the changing market control strategies of companies, with the US forming large, multinational media conglomerates while UK TV production saw the growth of a large number of independent producers. However, the emergence of the reality/entertainment format as a dominant design, capable of attracting audiences globally, and the UK's adoption of the US rights' regulations, saw consolidation of UK producers, and then the acquisition of most of these "superindies" by US or other foreign multimedia corporations. The chapter concludes by reviewing the impact of these changes on TV production.

Technological discontinuity

In the 1980s, the "mature" TV broadcasting industry, based around a small number of terrestrial analogue TV networks, was destabilised by technological changes, permitting a phase of new entrants to the TV market which continues to date. In the mid-1980s regulators permitted new analogue channels (C4 and C5) in the UK, and Fox in the US. The emergence of satellite TV distribution created the potential for both for new direct broadcast channels (like Direct TV in the US and Sky in the UK) and also for national distribution of US cable channels like HBO (see Chapter 4). The development of Digital Video Broadcasting (DVB) permitted the entry of new free-to-air terrestrial channels. Over the course of two decades, the TV market changed from one where most viewers could choose from a handful of free-to-air channels, to one where most viewers could access hundreds of free or pay channels (Holt, 2011).

The digitisation of TV transmission was accompanied by a parallel digitisation of production equipment. As noted in Chapter 5, the availability of lighter, more mobile cameras (whether 16mm film or ENG video cameras) in the 1970s began to reduce the level of technical skill required to perform basic camera operations. In the 1980s, Sony pioneered cheap, lightweight digital videotape cameras (camcorders), capable of broadcast quality, resolution and contrast. The mobility of TV production increased considerably with the development of radio microphones which could transmit sound to a remote recorder or mixer (Bignell, 2005).

The final step in the TV production process was video editing and postproduction. As Chapters 3 and 5 noted, the emphasis on live TV in the 1950s reflected the difficulties in editing videotape. Through the next three decades the analogue editing of tape consisted of a lengthy, linear process of copying clips back and forth between generations of videotape. In the 1990s the advent of digital, non-linear video editing software (like Avid and Final Cut Pro) enabled much greater flexibility in editing, with producers able to change edits almost as quickly and easily as with wordprocessing software (op. cit.). As this technology progressed, computers were able to store and access vast quantites of video. Separately, the development of multiplex systems (enabling a large number of cameras to be viewed or recorded simultaneously) and government crime reduction policies encouraged the spread of CCTV installation in the 1990s in the UK and US. The combination of this ability to record the output of many small cameras, and the capacity and flexibility to rapidly edit this footage facilitated the emergence of the "fixed rig" system of multi-camera filming reality shows.

Dominant design

In the mid-2000s, reality TV formats began to replace sitcoms and series as the means of achieving "hit" ratings on TV. In particular, *American Idol* enabled the Fox network to take over leadership of the Thursday night schedule which NBC had controlled through *Friends*. This section analyses the most recent reality hit, *Love Island*, which ITV developed for its digital network ITV2. The series enables the target youth audience to "binge-watch" a factual series, in the way they would a drama series, across their summer. ITV produced six hours of the main show every night for eight weeks, along with a range of digital content including an "aftershow" programme which encouraged viewers to discuss the talking points of the series on social media. The live final attracted ITV2's biggest audience ever and the series averaged 5 million viewers per episode, across all platforms. *Love Island* attracted the UK's largest ever audience, among 16–34 year olds, to a digital channel (ITV, 2019). The format has been exported to CBS in the US, and (so far) five other countries and Netflix have acquired previous series of the UK show.

This shot demonstrates the similarities between *Love Island* and the TV beauty pageants and competitions which originated in the nineteenth century (Riverol, 1992). The contestants are selected partly on the basis of their physical appearance and spend much of their time on screen in swimsuits and makeup. The programme sponsors also provide contestants with clothes and makeup as part of their product placement campaign. This shot (Figure 6.1), one of the scenes where the male and female contestants choose a partner, is similar to those used in the swimsuit sections of *Miss Universe* (Fox). The scene is covered using a multi-camera approach (see Chapter 3), but with

FIGURE 6.1   Crane shot: *Love Island* contestants in swimsuits

Credit: Love Island, ITV2, ITV Studios, 2018.

the addition of cameras on cranes and a temporary studio gallery (here housed in portakabins) which has been used in "outside broadcast" filming of sports and other live events since the early days of radio broadcasting. This exterior uses the natural lighting of the location (Spain) but most interior spaces are lit like a multi-camera TV studio for even coverage of a range of shots from different cameras.

The "reality" nature of the format is revealed by the visible presence of the radio microphones, around the contestants' necks, which are attached to transmitters on the belts around their waists. The convention of both multi-camera factual and feature production has been for "invisibility" of technique, to assist audiences in suspending disbelief, so sound is recorded either on microphones mounted on booms held out of shot or on radio microphones concealed under clothes. Reality shows often dispense with these conventions, partly for convenience of filming, but also because the visibility of techniques like microphones and CCTV cameras emphasises the sense that "reality" formats enable audiences to observe, "uncut", the private lives of the contestants.

The game show elements of the format go back to the earliest days of radio. As Figure 6.2 illustrates, *Love Island* partly follows the format of "stunt" shows (like NBC's *People Are Funny*, on radio from 1942 and TV from 1954 (Holmes, 2006)). The voice-over narration, in addition to performing usual documentary roles (such as recapping events after advertisement breaks) at this stage becomes a cross between the commentary developed for sports events and a comedic parody (see the discussion of "letsplay" videos, Chapter 7). In choosing narrators, reality shows often use comedians (where documentary films often use actors) to indicate the humorous intent of these challenges, a tradition of TV reflected in both game shows (like *It's a Knockout*, which began in 1966) and docusoaps.

FIGURE 6.2   Crane shot: contestants compete in game

Credit: Love Island, ITV2, ITV Studios, 2018.

The predominant game show influence, however, is the dating show; with contestants selecting partners, audience participation, prizes and moments of jeopardy. These core elements were established in formats like *G.I. Blind Date* (NBC) which began on radio in 1943 and transferred to TV as *Blind Date* (NBC, 1952 and ITV, 1985). Unlike beauty competitions, dating game shows centre on the contestants' romantic technique (Dubrofsky, 2014). As the title suggests, in *Blind Date* the contestants could not see each other and so the competition focused on their ability to flirt with and improvise "chat-up" or "pickup" lines. The second element is the more formal date, where more complex social skills are tested. The jeopardy of these formats is generated by the possibility of being rejected by a potential partner, left alone and facing elimination from the competition (op. cit.).

These format elements identify a key feature of reality TV; the way its unscripted and therefore unpredictable nature creates suspense and win-or-lose jeopardy. As a contemporary commentator noted, this draws on: "what quiz-industry tycoons call 'the unrehearsed, unwritten ending.' The biggest ratings in radio and TV, they point out, invariably go to special events whose outcomes are in doubt and whose scripts are unprepared" (Ira Peck, cited in Mittell, 2002:329). As Mittell points out, often this appearance of unpredictability (and thus task variability) conceals a degree of control enabled by the format: "tied to the convention of spontaneity, quiz shows presented situations that invited audiences to believe that anything could happen, even when audiences and producers both knew that the overall results were quite controlled to follow the patterns of previous programmes" (ibid.).

Figure 6.3 shows how, outside the villa, the *Love Island* couples are filmed using observational documentary techniques (see Chapter 2). Many early factual films

FIGURE 6.3 "Documentary" shot: contestants outside the villa

Credit: Love Island, ITV2, ITV Studios, 2018.

simply recorded an event ("actualité") and tended not to follow the conventional continuity structure of feature sequences. Instead they resembled live TV:

> single-shot street scenes, panoramic shots taken from the fronts of trains, and unbroken gazes at waves pounding rocks on the shore could easily have been read in their time as live; the films' arrangements of time and space . . . potentially simulated a televisual viewing experience.
>
> *Uricchio, 2008:296*

While documentary had been a significant genre in early network TV production in the UK and the US, by the mid-1960s, the US networks had largely abandoned the form as unprofitable. However, the availability of lighter cameras had enabled the development – in 1950s France – of an alternative design for the documentary; *cinéma-vérité*. The establishment of PBS in 1967 created a market for the US version of this form of film-making, "direct cinema", and one PBS series established this as the dominant design for documentaries in the 1970s. Alan and Susan Raymond, practitioners of direct cinema, were employed to film *An American Family* (PBS, 1973) a series which demonstrated that the drama of ordinary life – the breakdown of a marriage, divorce, a son's revelation of his homosexuality – could rival the drama of the networks' fictional soap operas (Bignell, 2005). By acting as a two-person crew the Raymonds dispensed with the attempt to match the lighting, sound and continuity of feature films or soaps. Instead, they used "fly on the wall" techniques, where the camera would "follow" characters – at work, at home or in other locations. The popularity of the series demonstrated that audiences would accept the shakiness of handheld cameras, occasional inaudibility of dialogue, and breaks in the continuity of action (through jump cuts, for example) or narrative (sometimes accommodated by voice-over) as the price of showing "real life" on TV. The BBC made its own series, *The Family*, the following year (op. cit.).

This focus on filming in the family home, to capture the drama of family life, evolved into the development of reality formats bringing together a "TV family", in a filming-friendly home, for the purpose of showing their daily lives. MTV's *The Real World* (1992) illustrated the minimal difference between the real, shared living experience of its young, target audience and shared lives of strangers brought to live together for a TV format (Dubrofsky, 2014). Again, the BBC produced a UK version (*The Living Soap*) the following year. In some respects, the popularity of the sitcom *Friends* (which began in 1994) may reflect the attention gained by these reality formats based on similar narrative subjects. The *Family* series also influenced a range of "social experiment" reality shows, in many ways similar to earlier "stunt" shows, where people were deliberately taken out of their usual context (to a house, an island, a prison) to understand how this would change behaviour. Often these series were historical experiments such as *Living in the Past* (BBC, 1978) and *1900 House* (C4, 2000), but others explored social class (*Wife Swap*, C4, 2003) and hierarchy (*Back to the Floor*, BBC, 1997) (Bignell, 2005).

In 1976, the Raymonds began "fly on the wall" filming with the New York Police Department for the PBS documentary *The Police Tapes*. As Chapter 4 notes, the drama they captured inspired the filming techniques used in *Hill Street Blues*. But these were later adopted in "docusoaps" and reality series where the crew would "ride along" with the emergency services (Fishman, 1998). The Fox network demonstrated the potential of these formats to attract regular audiences, with *Cops* (1989), followed in the UK by series like *Blues and Twos* (ITV, 1993).

The shot above (Figure 6.3) illustrates some of the compromises involved in "fly on the wall" filming. To help the audience understand the narrative and the movements of the characters (Dani Dyer and Jack Fincham), the sequence follows a structure similar to that of a feature. It begins and ends with exterior "establishing" shots of the high street and its buildings, followed by closer shots of the characters approaching the shop. Perhaps to emphasise that this trip is an escape from the competitive environment of the villa, the "invisibility of technique" convention of features is also followed in that the characters' radio mics are not in vision, and their sound is covered by a boom microphone held out of shot. The comedic purpose of the scene is underlined in the post-production soundtrack; with jokes in the narration and "comedy" music. However, this structure is combined with the compromises of the "fly on the wall" conventions. In a feature the action would be filmed out of sequence, from a range of angles, to create a continuous sequence. In a studio it would be filmed "as live" with three cameras at different angles to ensure all the action and dialogue is covered. But both cases would take the characters out of their own environment and require them to act. To try to capture the characters' authentic actions and words, the "fly on the wall" technique is used. The action inside the shop is filmed "as live", with one camera and a one or two person crew. This means only natural light is used (so the contrasts and some of the depth of field are reduced) and the action (the dialogue between Dani, Jack and the shopkeeper) is not stopped and started so that it can be covered by filming a shot-reverse-shot sequence. However, the shot is framed over-the-shoulder of the shopkeeper to help the audience understand the discontinuities of space, and filiming is stopped after the "as live" shooting of the action, so that cutaway shots (such as Jack's hands counting out money) can be filmed, Although the cutaways do not provide matches on action in the way a feature would, they do help conceal the discontinuities in time created by "as live" filming on a single camera.

The wide shot below (Figure 6.4) is taken from a high angle, with no directed lighting, and its composition is mostly constituted by the flooring. This means it does not provide the audience with a great deal of information about the characters' identity and emotions, their location or the setting of the series. However, audiences have become used to such shots indicating that we are watching people who may be unaware they are being filmed and/or their voices recorded. Again these conventions began on radio, with *Candid Microphone* (ABC), which became *Candid Camera* (CBS, ITV) (Andrejevic, 2014). While tabloid newspaper paparazzi provided audiences with voyeuristic shots of celebrities, investigative journalists used hidden

FIGURE 6.4 CCTV-style "hidden camera" shot

Credit: *Love Island*, ITV2, ITV Studios, 2018.

cameras and microphones to provide evidence of wrongdoing, sometimes involving elaborate "sting" operations in series like *Macintye Undercover* (BBC) and *Rogue Traders* (BBC). The use of CCTV footage in TV began with this evidential approach, in the mid-1980s, with crime appeal shows like *Crimewatch* (BBC, 1984), *Unsolved Mysteries* (NBC, 1987) and *America's Most Wanted* (Fox, 1989). CCTV footage of emergency services began to be used as actuality, to tell crime stories in docusoaps and shows like CBS's *Rescue 911* (1989) and the BBC's *999* (1992). This extended to footage of "antisocial" behaviour in series like *Stupid Behaviour Caught on Tape* (Fox).

This CCTV approach and the reality-house format were brought together most successfully in Endemol's *Big Brother* in Holland (1999) and the UK (2000). The cost of digital cameras and control systems had reduced to the point that it became possible to replace the "house" of the *Family* series with specially constructed locations which were part residence and part TV studio (Bignell, 2005). While the contestants are in this location, everything they do can be recorded by a system of cameras (a "fixed rig") controlled from a remote studio gallery. This approach has advantages over the observational documentary film crew, since although the contestants know they are being recorded, they are less immediately aware of this. The advantage over multi-camera studio production is that it is not necessary to block and predict action. The capacity of digital storage systems enables producers to record the outputs of many cameras simultaneously and select the footage required to tell the story. When *The Family* series returned in 2008 it used a fixed rig system.

To generate the volume of content required to enable the six-nights a week "binge" viewing experience, *Love Island* used around 70 cameras, a crew of around 200 and located post-production facilities in portakabins on site (Percival, 2018). Such an expensive operation, a world away from the small documentary film crew,

FIGURE 6.5 "Diary" shot: in the Beach Hut

Credit: Love Island, ITV2, ITV Studios, 2018.

is required to enable the multiplatform prescence of reality shows with live broadcasts to niche digital channels, online or to mobile devices. It is also required to enable hundreds of hours of video to be edited into a one-hour episode for broadcast on the main channel's prime time – either the same evening or with a delay.

Figure 6.5 shows an emotional interview with Dani in the Beach Hut. Documentaries often add interviews to actuality sequences to enable characters to articulate their thoughts and motivations and their immediate reactions to events. These would be recorded with an eyeline match to an unseen interviewer, preserving the fourth wall. The direct address technique shown here has a long history in theatre, where actors would deliver a monologue, directly to the audience, but the audience would understand the convention that this indicated the character was "thinking aloud" (Boltz and Clemen, 2013). In factual TV documentary, this technique appeared in *Video Diaries* (BBC, 1990), and became a space for private reflection on personal crises in reality shows through the creation of small studios – literally a confessional in the "confession booth" for *Real World* (CBS, 1992) but also the "diary room" for *Big Brother* (C4, 2000) (Bignell, 2005).

This kind of confessional or emotional interview is typical of "tabloid" talk shows which emerged in the 1980s with *The Oprah Winfrey Show* (ABC) and became more focused on creating conflict in *The Jerry Springer Show* (NBC) and UK equivalents like *The Jeremy Kyle Show* (ITV). As Grindstaff (2002) shows, creating this form of "unpredictable" conflict in a studio show requires considerable intervention and even manipulation by producers:

> producers who encourage guests to exaggerate their emotions or prioritize the more sensational aspects of their stories do so in the name not of

deception but of producing good television; this requires a certain amount of manipulation. For their part, some guests exaggerate or embellish their stories with little or no encouragement from producers, because they, too, know what constitutes good television within the parameters of the genre and are eager to provide their performative competence.

Grindstaff, 2002:248–9

In reality shows, like soap operas, these moments of conflict and emotional reaction drive an extended version of the traditional TV "watercooler" discussion and debate, first as other contestants are filmed reacting to events, and potentially intervening in a relationship, second, online, as audiences react to the events they watch, and then in "aftershow" studio programmes (like *Love Island: Aftersun*) where panellists give further comment and debate and audiences are again encouraged to contribute via social media.

As Grindstaff (2002) suggests, much of this "manipulation" of contestants in reality shows is explicitly agreed with contestants and again follows documentary traditions where characters would be filmed talking about an issue which could cause conflict. However, unlike documentary, the reality format allows producers to build conflict and jeopardy into the rules of the game – most notably by eliminating contestants. Equally, producers may create an unexpected "plot twist" by changing or adding rules. As a dating format, *Love Island* focuses on creating moments when contestants will be rejected (for example, by having an odd number of characters) or "betrayed" (when an existing partner abandons them for another). To isolate them from the online commentary the contestants are prevented from accessing social media or using a phone. The phones on *Love Island* only work to allow the characters to communicate with each other and to enable the producers to invisibly deliver a new instruction. In these moments, reality shows (like *Faking It* and *Wife Swap*, both C4) often claim to be "social experiments", where the question posed is whether a TV show can produce a positive change in the lives of the contestants. In the case of dating shows like *Love Island*, the experiment is to see whether a TV show can help one or more couples find a relationship which continues after the series. This motivates the changes in rules and creation of conflicts and potential betrayals as "tests" of the strength of the relationship. It also motivates the confessional monologue as evidence of the success of the experiement: "the monologue, as with reality programming in general, contains an ambiguous interplay of the pre-scripted and non-scripted, individual and collective, performed and non-performed and fake and real" (Aslama and Pantti, 2006:181). Bignell, (2005:13) traces this concept back through the history of documentary; "the notion of the makeover, and the ideology of self-improvement, are implicit in both American direct cinema and French cinema verité".

Figure 6.6 demonstrates a shift in the nature of the format as the live final episode brings the soap opera narratives to a conclusion by choosing the winning couple (Dani and Jack) from those who have survived elimination. The presenter,

FIGURE 6.6 "To camera" shot: presenter addresses audience for live final

Credit: *Love Island*, ITV2, ITV Studios, 2018.

Caroline Flack, performs to camera, and to the studio audience, where in previous episodes she has observed the documentary conventions of eyeline matches with contestants and the fourth wall. This live episode illustrates the extent to which the series is also a form of talent show. This again emerged as a media design in early US radio – with *Major Bowes and the Original Amateur Hour* (1934) inspiring the BBC's *Amateurs' Hour* (1936) (Holmes, 2014). The form combined the central elements of the quiz show – ordinary people in live competition for cash prizes, a studio audience, and audience voting (by phone or post) – with the studio variety show. Rather than performing, as in a conventional talent show, the contestants are performers in the traditions of docusoap stars who (usually briefly) became celebrities. Of the 150,000 people who applied to be on the show, several of those selected were models or performers and the eventual winner, Dani Dyer, is the daughter of a famous soap actor. If she or Jack do have celebrity careers, the series producer, ITV Studios, will be involved.

Regulation and legitimacy

The requirement to legislate for technological changes, principally the availability of first new analogue and then new digital channels, has provided policymakers and practitioners with opportunities to debate the legitimacy of different policies, in terms of their cost effectiveness, the degree of innovation they produce and the degree to which market competition supports diversity and audience choice. The 1981 Broadcasting Act, which established a fourth analogue network in the UK followed a long-standing approach (which had recently been confirmed in the reports of the Pilkington (1962) and Annan (1977) Committees), recognising the legitimacy of "public service" regulation as a defence against the homogenising effects, on programming, of (American) commercial broadcasting and advertising market forces. The Act therefore provided that Channel 4 (C4) would not sell its own advertising but be financed from a proportion of ITV advertising revenue. To counter potentially homogenising influences, C4 was specifically required to encourage innovation, educational programmes and programmes for minority interests (Potschka, 2012).

However, a new influence on policymakers came via a campaign by independent producers to preserve this section of the market for their own members (Darlow, 2004). The campaign was hugely successful. First, the 1981 Act required C4 to outsource all its non-news production. Second, the policymakers began to be persuaded that independent producers could be the solution to problems they might identify with the UK's other networks – ITV and BBC. The independents challenged the legitimacy of the BBC's and ITV's vertical integration of broadcasting and production and proposed that these networks be required to outsource 25% of production to themselves.

However, while the policymakers were convinced about the problem (integration) and the solution (outsourcing to independents) they were less clear about the underlying reasoning. The Peacock Committee's report critiqued vertical integration as a form of market control which undermined competition and consumer choice (Peacock, 1986). However, the subsequent White Paper (1988) argued that the problem with the "excessive degree of vertical integration" was that it resulted in high labour costs in production; "the inefficiencies of the established duopoly producers and restrictive labour practices operative in the industry" (HMSO, 1988:41). Whatever the reasoning, the 1990 Broadcasting Act implemented the solution, requiring the BBC and ITV to outsource 25% of their production. The policy critique of the perceived inefficiency of vertical integration continued with a Green Paper in 1992 which encouraged further outsourcing at the BBC. The broadcaster took up the proposal and created an "internal market" where in-house departments were placed in competition with external suppliers of technical resources, studios and other production inputs (Born, 2004).

After this point, the independent producers' campaign against vertical integration began to shift from its perceived high labour costs and inefficiencies to its alleged constraints on innovation in programme production. The broadcasters' commitment to factual programming, for example, which combined public service and the documentary tradition of focusing on social issues, could now be contrasted with C4's independent producers who had begun "reconstituting the documentary mode" in programmes like the Black Audio Film Collective's *Handsworth Songs* (Harvey, 1989:73). Set against the work of video activists commissioned by C4, the BBC's expository documentaries – from Kenneth Clark's *Civilisation* (BBC) to strands like *Whicker's World* (BBC) and *The Philpott File* (BBC) – appeared to confirm the image of the broadcasters as dominated by an Oxbridge and public school professional elite. There was "a widely held view" that the main broadcasters "had become boring, complacent, routinised and bland" (op. cit.:62).

The problem was still identified as the vertical integration of the BBC and ITV and the solution remained outsourcing to independent producers, but the reasoning had fully transformed to identify this agenda as a mechanism for innovation. As the discourse developed, commercial influences were now no longer seen to be homogenising. Instead, in 1993, C4 was required to compete with other networks for advertising revenue. Rather than homogenising programming, it was confidently asserted that "competition in the supply of programmes will tend to provide a better product for audiences" (DCMS, 2005:86). And competition meant requiring further outsourcing of BBC and ITV production to an independent sector now identified as the "marketplace of ideas". With independent producers as the "motor of creative change", outsourcing would increase innovation (House of Lords, 2005:paras 255, 259). Faced with this policy consensus, the BBC chose to impose its own vertical disintegration rather than waiting for it to be imposed, voluntarily increasing its potential outsourcing quota (via the Window of Creative Competition or "WOCC"). The broadcaster ceased attempting to defend the legitimacy of its in-house production and instead claimed outsourcing would "deliver range and diversity . . . across a wide range of output" (DCMS, 2006:41). This logic reached its apogee in July 2014 when the BBC announced the vertical disintegration of all of its in-house production into a commercial subsidiary, creating "one of the leanest, hungriest, most flexible organisations [. . .] a production powerhouse that is a beacon for creativity, risk-taking and quality" (Hall, 2014). The final step in the independents' campaign saw the abandonment of the main elements of the original critique. In this phase, the independents began to defend their own vertical integration strategies, dismissing criticisms of vertical integration as "myths" (Oliver and Ohlbaum, 2015). Furthermore, rather than promoting market competition in terms of its importance in delivering programme innovation and choice for UK audiences, commercialism was now advanced as an end in itself. The independents now championed their sector not as a solution to lack of innovation in UK broadcasters, but as a key contributor to the UK's creative industries, providing employment, earning export income and spreading the UK's "soft power" abroad. The key regulatory measure proposed to achieve these policy goals was a change in the "terms of trade" between broadcasters and independents. Essentially, the independents began to argue for a change to the US system (see Chapter 3) where producers, rather than broadcasters, benefit from the syndication market of "off network" sales (Faulkner et al., 2008).

This demand, however, concealed a significant difference between the situations of producers in the UK and US. As Chapter 3 noted, US programme production was outsourced, in the main, to large companies, especially the Hollywood studios. This was because programme production was based on a system of deficit financing, whereby the broadcaster paid less than the cost of production, and in return the producer retained syndication rights. The production company took a significant risk, however, because syndication rights would only yield a profit if the series passed the 100 episode threshold. Series which were cancelled before this point could leave the producer with a significant loss. The so-called "fin-syn" regulations prevented the broadcasters from acting as their own production companies (in prime time) to enable them to retain these rights (Lotz, 2007). It was this requirement for significant finance to invest in production which brought the shake-out of small and medium independents from US broadcasting.

By contrast, the UK followed a "cost plus" model; the broadcaster paid the independent the full cost of production plus an additional production fee of between 5% and 15%. In this instance, the broadcaster took on the risk of financing production, including the potential that the series might be cancelled having made a loss, but also retained the potential to earn from international syndication (Owen and Wildman, 1992). In the period when the UK broadcasters, and UK audiences, had been the main market for independent producers, their interest in the syndication market was limited. But the sudden international success of a number of UK factual formats had dramatically changed this situation. The first of these, *Who Wants to Be a Millionaire?* (Celador, ITV), had earned significant revenues for the UK broadcaster ITV when the format was sold to the US's ABC and many other countries. The production company Celador had also made a profit of £4.8 million, on a turnover of £22.7 million, between 1998 and 2001, from that format alone. Such potential profits led independent producers, through their association PACT, to campaign to retain all rights to international syndication (Faulkner et al., 2008). The policymakers implemented the PACT proposals in the 2003 Communications Act which established "a move away from 'full funding' contracts to a 'licensing' model whereby producers would meet the costs of production but retain ancillary rights to the future exploitation of licensed programmes" (Turner and Lourenço, 2010:9).

The crucial element of the UK model had been its ability to support the growth of small production companies (who had no ability to distribute programmes internationally), and ensure continued competition in the "marketplace of ideas". The new model threatened the existence of these smaller companies, encouraging a consolidation similar to the shake-out in the US. Nick Rosen, PACT's former vice-chair, claimed he was suspended for advocating the interests of small producers. In particular he criticised the way that in the new system:

> the most urgent problem is lack of finance for smaller and medium-sized indies – the big money is chasing only the biggest companies. It is best not to leave the seed funding to the largest indies, which are looking for ways to reduce competition.
>
> *Cited in The Guardian, 2007*

By contrast, in 2005, as PACT was involved in discussion of the "terms of trade" with broadcasters, its chair Eileen Gallagher floated Shed Media, her production company (Turner and Lourenço, 2010).

The government minister, Tessa Jowell, summarised the intended impact of the regulations in terms, not of a diversity of voices, but of public investment in the creative industries, making the UK:

one of the most attractive TV production markets in the world, with a high level of investment in original programming, a high level of renewal and innovation in on-screen IP and a rights framework that allows producers to own their works.

Oliver and Ohlbaum/PACT, 2015:5

Ironically, in the same year, 1990, as the UK regulators were imposing vertical disintegration on UK broadcasters, the US regulators were reversing their own approach and permitting the vertical (and horizontal) integration of TV production and distribution. This change, again, resulted from the sophisticated lobbying of a special interest – in this case Rupert Murdoch's News Corp – and again, the requirement to regulate for new technology provided the opportunity. The Cable Communications Act (1984) was a "tipping point", supported by further regulation, securing the cable operators' franchises, enabling them to compete with the broadcasters and encouraging vertical integration, as they began to replace network shows on their schedules with their own programming (Morris, 2007). At this point, "cable became the driving force for the media industries" (Holt, 2011:67).

As Chapter 3 outlined, US cross-ownership and fin-syn regulations had been introduced to prevent the three major networks from achieving market control through vertical integration. Murdoch established the Fox network in 1986 through his acquisition of 20th Century Fox and a group of TV stations in the major US markets. News Corp successfully persuaded the FCC to grant it a special waiver from the fin-syn rules, enabling it to act as a vertically integrated producer, combining a Hollywood studio and a broadcast network, able to syndicate its own shows to cable and terrestrial stations. Fox achieved particular success in syndicating its reality series *Cops* (Perren, 2004).

In response, the networks argued that Fox should not receive special treatment and that the prohibitions on vertical integration should be seen in terms of the national interest – the US networks' need to compete in international markets with emerging foreign-owned multinational entertainment conglomerates operating in the US market, such as Sony/Columbia, Matushita/MCA-Universal and News Corp/Fox. By 1995, the FCC accepted this argument, the fin-syn rules were removed and US networks were free to vertically integrate production, broadcasting and syndication. Immediately, the networks began producing more of their programming in-house and owning syndication rights in these programmes. That summer, the first of the original networks, ABC, was vertically integrated with a Hollywood studio when Disney acquired it for $18.5 billion. This process has continued with all the networks now part of vertically and horizontally integrated corporations like Comcast (NBC, Universal, Dreamworks) and 21st Century Fox (21st Century Fox, Fox Networks, Sky Channels) (Forbes, 2018). An unintended consequence of this deregulation in the US market (allowing competition from cable and then enabling vertical integration of broadcasting) was the creation of an international market for reality TV formats, which emerged in the 1990s (see Market control, this volume, p. 157). Deregulation in the UK market, disintegrating broadcasting and production, enabled UK independent producers to enter this market, and further deregulation, enabling independents to own syndication rights, brought the emergence of the format as a dominant design.

However, the legitimacy of factual entertainment formats has not been uncontested. The emergence of the format as a dominant design, between 1998 and 2003, coincided with a dramatic decline in the factual genres from which the hybrid had been constructed; education (−53%), arts (−23%), current affairs (−22%) and religion (−12%) (Ofcom, 2004: 35). Even within the constraints of the dominant design, regulators began to note that "new" formats were increasingly imitations of previous successes (*Popstars, Pop Idol, Fame Academy, X Factor, . . . Got Talent*). The UK regulator found that audiences had begun to "resent being repeatedly presented with similar versions of the same format" (op. cit.:59).

Moreover, formats opened up the ethical questions – the representation of "reality" and the manipulation of participants and viewers – referred to at the start of the chapter. *Love Island* itself illustrated this continuing debate as contestants revealed they were "given a nudge to talk in certain areas" or "asked to refilm scenes" that the crews had missed (Tyla Carr cited in Lindsay, 2018). More serious criticism followed allegations that the producers had edited footage to mislead contestants into believing that their partner had cheated on them with another contestant. Dani's emotional outburst in the Beach Hut (Figure 6.5), a result of her gaining just such an impression, brought more than 2,600 complaints to the regulator Ofcom (*The Guardian*, 2018). However, the regulator argued that the nature of reality formats legitimated just such manipulation; "viewers are likely to expect emotionally charged scenes that have been engineered to test contestants' relationships" (ibid.).

Market control

US cable pay TV networks grew from a few dozen in the 1980s to 531 in 2005. They quickly became popular, rising from a presence in 10% of households (1973) to 34% (1983) and 70% (2000) (TVB, 2008). Most of these households thus changed from three available channels to more than 30. The additional major new entrant in the US was Fox, in 1986, which immediately established itself as the fourth network, with only the big three networks having a larger number of stations. The impact on these established networks was dramatic; their combined market share fell from more than 90% of the audience (1977) to 69% (1985) and 29% (2002) (Morris, 2007). The pivotal moment occurred in 1990 when the cable channels' share overtook the networks'. This high level of new entrants had a rapid effect on the US networks' business; in 1986, only NBC reported a profit (Nielsen, 1989). Compared with years of 12% growth in advertising revenue, in 1984, the networks experienced 3–4% growth. The impact of satellite and then digital TV in the UK produced similar results: "audience share for the major terrestrial broadcasters has been steadily falling since the 1980s" (Lee, 2012).

Faced with this new competition for domestic audiences and advertising revenues the networks began to look to the international TV market as a source of growth and to consolidation of the sector as a way to limit competition in the domestic market. Within the cable sector the regulations had already allowed a number of major mergers but the changed regulations in the 1990s effectively gave the green light to the networks and studios to re-establish oligopolistic control, this time of an integrated feature film and TV market, which had been prevented by the Paramount verdict and the fin-syn regulations. As noted above, this was justified on the basis that the new multimedia conglomerates formed would be more effective in resisting competition from foreign-owned conglomerates (like Murdoch's News Corp and Sony/Columbia) and exploiting the international market (Perren, 2004).

The mid-1990s saw a period of major horizontal integration – of networks, studios, cable channels and related businesses – through mergers and acquisitions, to enter new markets. The most important of these was Disney's 1996 acquisition of the ABC network which not only horizontally integrated Disney's film and media businesses with a TV business, but also vertically integrated a TV broadcaster with a TV production powerhouse. In 1999, Viacom purchased CBS, horizontally integrating the broadcast channel with a range of cable channels like Showtime, MTV, Comedy Central and Nickelodeon, and vertically integrating with the production company Paramount Television (Holt, 2011).

The next step in the process of vertical integration was for these new network/studio/cable conglomerates to begin taking production in-house. The big three all established in-house production divisions and, by 1994, "had all become their own biggest suppliers" (Perren, 2004:315). By the 2000s, all ABC's soap operas were "network-owned" (Levine, 2001:60). In prime time, 30% of programming was produced in-house (the rest produced by the Hollywood studios) and the networks "owned or co-owned over three-quarters of the series scheduled to debut" (Bielby and Bielby, 2003:587). In 2004, the process of vertical integration of the networks was completed when NBC merged with Universal Studios; "by 2004, each of the established three networks had merged with a major film studio, and produced most of its programming in-house" (Lin, 2007:79).

This change effectively ended the idea of a "marketplace of ideas" in US production by closing out most of the remaining independent companies. As noted, the US system created a barrier to entry, restricting production to those companies which could afford to deficit finance production of their own series. The increase in in-house production created a further barrier, reducing the remaining independents' share of prime time by 30%, and leading to a further shake-out of independent companies (Perren, 2004). This also removed the independent sector as a source of competition in international markets. Unable to sell to the networks, the independents were thus unable to develop successful new shows which they could sell on the international programme market. US participation in this market was essentially limited to eight companies, mainly the Hollywood studios, which received 80% of the income from foreign syndication (ibid.). However, the networks did not predict the rise of the reality TV format as a new dominant design in the international TV market. Even today, as Chalaby (2015:465) notes, "the international trade in audiovisual products remains dominated by finished programming". Much of this consists of popular genres like drama and localisable genres like children's animation.

The experimentation with the reality format design in the US was led by one of the new entrants. Facing intense competition for TV advertising sales, the Fox network attempted to maintain profitability by keeping programme production costs low. As a result, the network created a number of, largely in-house produced, reality hits – with series like *Cops* and *America's Most Wanted*. Faced with similar pressures (from new terrestrial and satellite channels) in the late 1990s, UK broadcasters also began to develop low cost factual programmes, again largely in-house, which also proved to be prime time hits. Docusoaps like *The Cruise* (BBC) and *Driving School* (BBC) attracted audiences of 11 million and 12.5 million respectively. So important were these shows that by 1999 the BBC had 12 such series in production at the same time (Bignell, 2005).

The US networks saw the UK market as a source of revenue, from international syndication of their own programming, rather than as a place to buy content. And as Steemers (2004) shows, the vast majority of revenue still flows from the UK to the US. The entry of new channels, particularly Sky, to the UK market, had only exacerbated this, with Sky acting initially as a vertically integrated broadcaster bringing its Fox network content to the UK. As Chapter 4 noted, UK sales had traditionally been to the US public broadcaster PBS, and had especially focused on costume drama. Although there had been examples of UK entertainment sales (for example ITV's *Sunday Night at the London Palladium* was taped live in colour for a US audience), for the major networks the majority of such transfers had been in the other direction. Camporesi (1989) details a whole range of US game show formats which the BBC and ITV acquired from US networks in the 1940s to 1950s alone, including, *Amateur Hour*, *Spelling Bee*, *It Pays to Be Ignorant*, *Twenty Questions*, *What's My Line?*, *This Is Your Life* and *Opportunity Knocks*.

Again the experimentation was led by a new entrant – the cable network Discovery. For its first four years, Discovery's programming, like other cable channels, was entirely acquired from the libraries of other producers. However, as noted above, Discovery faced the problem that the US networks produced very limited factual programming, and so less than half its output could be acquired in the US. The BBC's huge catalogue of documentary (and particularly natural history) programming made it a natural partner. In the mid-1990s Discovery and the BBC signed a joint venture to launch digital channels in Europe and Latin America and to joint fund production (Chris, 2002). When Discovery relaunched The Learning Channel as TLC to try to attract broader audiences, its partnership with the BBC led it to commission US versions of the successful BBC makeover shows including *Changing Rooms* (Bazal/BBC) – which ran for eight years on TLC as *Trading Spaces* – and *What Not to Wear* (BBC).

Two UK formats demonstrated that this strategy could work for terrestrial networks, and so transformed the US market. The first was *Who Wants to Be a Millionaire?* (Celador/ITV), a game show which, in its first series in 1998, achieved a 44% audience share (Chalaby, 2011). ABC acquired the rights to produce the US version, which averaged 28.5 million viewers in its first year and in the 2001 season ran for four hours a week (Caves, 2005). The second was *Pop Idol* (19 Entertainment/ITV), which first broadcast in the UK in October 2001 and whose season finale gained 10 million viewers (Hill, 2014). Fox acquired the rights to make the US version and, in its first year, the format helped the network become the second most viewed in America, ahead of NBC and ABC. Its second season finale, in 2003, reached 38 million viewers, and the following year *Idol* became America's highest rating TV series (op. cit.).

The success of these formats, effectively created the international format sales market. First, they lowered the risks of media production. This was partly because they reduced the "first copy" costs of production. For producers, compared to a sitcom, soap or drama, these formats represented a very low-cost, low-risk form of development. In production, by using ordinary people instead of actors and writers, and "fly on the wall" shooting rather than studios or sets, a show like *America's Most Wanted* could cost around $300,000 an hour, in 1989, compared to $1.5 million an hour for *Star Trek: The Next Generation* (Beattie, 2004). For broadcasters, the combination of low production cost per episode and potentially high ratings made formats potentially hugely profitable. Although they did not quite earn the CPM advertising rates of top dramas or sitcoms, the sheer number of episodes and cumulative size of audience made them potentially more profitable overall. ABC earned around $556 million in the first year of *Millionaire*, and during 2001, reduced its annual programme development costs by half (Caves, 2005). Finally, a successful format was a more reliable guarantee of the volume of production needed (the 100 episodes, see Chapter 3) for international distribution than other genres,

More fundamentally, the format transformed this market by effectively turning programme production from a service into a product. Chapter 1 described the process of servitisation (Harjo et al., 2016) by which the characteristics of a production can be transformed from an intangible service into a tangible good – a "thing" – which is much more easy to trade and to which property rights can be attached. The creation of the dominant design of the TV format transformed the factual TV programme *concept* into a tangible product, whose value buyers and sellers can assess, and which is, therefore, easier to trade. The format transforms a service – the production of a "hit" factual entertainment series – into a product, the production bible, the marketing strategy, the scheduling and audience information etc. As Chalaby (2016a:21) notes: "the format trade has become a multi-billion dollar industry because broadcasters feel reassured by buying shows that come with a proof of concept and an established track record". In the terms of Chapter 1, formats constitute a new way to reduce the uncertainty, and therefore risk, for broadcasters, producers and audiences attached to buying individually differentiated media products;

> above all, TV formats enable broadcasters to manage risk, as they acquire them on the basis of their ratings . . . (and can) peruse ratings data that detail the show's performance in a large array of territories, scheduling scenarios, channels and audiences, before committing themselves.
>
> *Chalaby, 2016b:7*

A broadcaster can buy and produce a local version of a format without repeating information or reducing the degree of individual differentiation of the products. Audiences can simultaneously know more about what their experience will be than they would discover from knowing the genre of a drama, but also can expect to be surprised along the way. Finally, by creating a tradeable information product which does not reduce individual differentiation, the format also incurs less "cultural discount" than a finished programme or a script, making formats more capable of penetrating global markets than even the Hollywood blockbuster.

The number of formats traded reached 259 between 2002 and 2004 and 445 between 2006 and 2008 (Esser, 2010). In 2008, British companies sold 98 of the 295 formats traded (Chalaby, 2012). In 2013, UK companies' format sales increased 17% and the combined turnover of the top 150 companies reached £2.1 billion. With the change in the terms of trade, the rights to a format like *Millionaire* became a continuing income stream (around £25 million a year) for the rights owner (Faulkner et al. 2008). However, rather than achieving the growth of UK creative industries, the regulatory changes enabled the US media conglomerates to extend their reach into the UK market, and to extend their control over global media markets to include the trade in TV formats. As in the US, the deficit financing model created barriers to entry, leading to a shake-out of UK independents and consolidation of the sector into a number of "superindies". These companies then controlled much of the secured market for independent production which had been created by the vertical disintegration of the UK broadcasters. Many of these superindies, with libraries of successful formats, were then acquired by the US conglomerates – most notably Endemol and Shine (21st Century Fox), Carnival Films, Monkey Kingdom and others (NBC Universal), Shed (Time Warner) and All3Media (Discovery/Liberty). The result is that much of the UK public service broadcasters' spending on new UK production (35% of their TV revenues in 2016), including the public licence fee of the BBC, supposedly the "seed funding" for UK creativity, is actually the development funding for US-owned companies to develop entertainment formats which they can sell globally. It is not too much of an exaggeration to say that UK broadcasters and the UK licence fee payer are deficit financing US format production. These companies have become focused on finding such global "hit" formats, to the exclusion of other genres. The proportions of their business devoted to factual or factual entertainment production is; Endemol (64%), All3Media (64%), Zodiak (64%), Shine (90%) and Fremantle (100%) (Oliver and Ohlbaum, 2014:25).

Process innovation

Chapter 2 noted that early films were recordings of live events – often variety performances or short dramas – but also recorded the unscripted activities of "ordinary" people. Uricchio (2008:296) notes "the preponderance of nonfiction in early film production and exhibition". Nor did an extensive division of labour occur, and for some time, the cameraman system continued to operate, "a camera operator would journey to the subject, record the action, and then edit it together" (Gomery, 1997:46).

The advent of broadcasting brought documentary production from film first to radio and then TV. A key element in the organisation of production was the organisation of trade unions around the original process of studio production established in radio: "By the end of the 1930s, the division of tasks was clearly defined and labor groups secured respectable compensation" (Curtin and Sanson, 2014:137). This partly reflected the bargaining power of the unions, when a strike could shut down a network: "both network and station managers seemed well aware that labor unrest could be especially costly for an industry that faced insatiable production demands" (ibid.).

A second important influence on TV production, described in Chapter 3, concerned the technology of video compared with film or audiotape. First, the difficulties of recording and editing video meant that between the 1950s and 1970s most TV genres were produced live or "as live" in a multi-camera studio. This form of production established linear dependencies which were inherently less flexible to process innovation than (for example) recorded (film) production. But another factor concerned the state of development of the video camera. Quinn (2007:126) quotes a description of the complexity of basic camera operation in this era: "You had so many controls and perhaps fifty parameters to control to get pictures. The associated equipment required to light (high voltage bulbs) and carry (cables with 36 fine pins) and carry the video signal to the mixer was fragile, often temperamental and slow and expensive to replace". Even when video signals could be recorded, Quinn (2007) estimates that a third of production time was lost to some form of technical interruption or delay.

Production tasks were often strictly controlled by occupational groups; "An electrician would not touch a sound cable, a sound guy would not touch an electrician's cable or a camera cable, a cameraman would not touch a sound cable or an electrician's cable" (McKinlay and Quinn, 1999:5). Broadcast unions had significant ability to determine both the minimum number of production staff required on given genres of programming, and the specific tasks they could perform.

Faced with such an idiosyncratic and unpredictable production process, there were "compelling production imperatives to maintain full crews of skilled and experienced technicians" (Quinn, 2007:100). ITV thus accepted the practice of the "closed shop", requiring all workers to join the union, and occupational job demarcations, enshrined in national agreements which enabled production staff regularly to claim overtime payments or to stand idle ("downtime") during technical breaks in production (Campling, 1995). In the US, as Christopherson (2011:133) shows, "apart from the 'talent' portion of the workforce, the broadcast network workforce was employed in longterm jobs in large corporations (CBS, NBC, ABC) and highly unionized". As with the newspaper industry (see Chapter 5), broadcasting unions were largely able to absorb new production technologies within this existing organisation of production rather than technologies being used to achieve process efficiencies. This meant that crew sizes remained the same, even as new technologies allowed a single employee to perform tasks that had previously occupied one or more specialists.

Vertical disintegration, outsourcing of production to independents and out-sourcing studios and non-production activities (initiatives like the BBC's Producer Choice) dramatically changed TV production in the UK and had a huge impact on employment in the main broadcasters. BBC managers, rather than accepting union-determined crew sizes, made technical crews and facilities compete for work against freelance providers and commercial companies (Born, 2004). In ITV, between 1985 and 1995, "the broadcasting trade unions were decimated [. . .] the job controls established over almost three decades were obliterated" (McKinley and Quinn, 1999:13). Between 1980 and 2016 the BBC shed around 12,500 full time permanent jobs (NAO, 2017). ITV seems to have "hollowed out" at the same rate, shedding around 10,00 full time permanent jobs in the shorter period from 1987 to 2017 (Citywire, 2017).

However, we cannot simply conclude that vertical integration was the cause of production inefficiencies and disintegration produced process efficiencies. This is because the same process of shedding jobs occurred in the US broadcasters, where much production was already outsourced, and the general direction was towards greater integration. In 1986 alone, the networks cut jobs at their studios and news departments, again mainly technicians and engineers, shedding around 10% of the total workforce – or 2,500 jobs (1,000 at ABC, 700 at CBS) (Perren, 2004). By 1992, "NBC had eliminated 30% of its News Division" (Raphael, 1997:104). Nor were these simply removing jobs which had long enjoyed union protection, since the new network Fox reduced its studio workforce by 20% (ibid.).

There is evidence that some of these job reductions were achieved through process efficiencies made possible by newer video recording and editing technologies. Simpler, more reliable cameras and the ability to record and edit videotape created the potential for alternatives to multi-camera studio or single camera film production. From the 1980s onwards, factual TV production in particular was changed through the replacement of expensive live, studio-based programmes with low cost ones, recorded on video, on location. These changes particularly affected the jobs of technical staff. The new video technology enabled greater multitasking and multi-skilling of production staff. In particular, the division between creative/editorial and technical functions was eroded –with creative staff performing technical tasks (shooting and editing their own footage). The low cost of videotape reduced the requirement for skilled camera operation, since the cost of reshooting was so low. Digital non-linear editing software also enabled a single operator to take on a number of previously specialised skilled post-production tasks (editing, dubbing and sound mixing, graphics etc.). This new model of production was particularly suited to factual and documentary production. Essentially it allowed broadcasters to introduce the "fly on the wall" technique, developed on film, to the production of low cost, but high audience, docusoaps like *Cops* and *Driving School*. In many respects, this returned factual and documentary production to the "camera man" mode with which it began – a single "shooter director", possibly with a sound recordist "following" documentary characters. As Kerrigan and McIntyre (2010:118) recently noted, "the documentary filmmaker/practitioner constructs the documentary from its inception through to its completion".

The emergence of entertainment formats as the dominant design altered this trajectory. The volume of programming to be produced, and the range of skills required, has returned some forms of factual format production to something resembling the large labour force and complex division of labour seen in the first three decades of factual production. Some long-running formats – such as *Come Dine With Me* (C4)/*Dinner Takes All* (TLC), *Supernanny* (C4/ABC) and *Wife Swap* (C4/ABC) – are produced using the single camera, "fly on the wall" technique. However, many of the most successful entertainment formats have returned to the live or "as live" multi-camera studio mode, to provide either the element of variety shows like *Idols/X Factor* (ITV/Fox) and *Strictly Come Dancing/Dancing with the Stars* (BBC/ABC) or of game shows like *Masterchef* (BBC/Fox). Still others depend on specially constructed environments, like *Big Brother* and *Great British Bake Off/The American Baking Competition* (BBC/C4/CBS). As the analysis of *Love Island* demonstrated, many formats combine several of these production methods.

TV production on this scale, at this volume (for example *Love Island* transmitting six nights) and with such short cycle times (faster than soap opera or sitcom production) has resulted in a return to some of the specialisation and inflexibility of the earlier era of TV production, albeit now under managerial rather than union control;

> very frequently in an indie now the director is brought on after the pre-production work has been largely done, they're brought on just before the shoot. They do the shoot, they take the material into the edit where, because it's a highly-formatted piece, they stay for the first two thirds of the edit and then leave for it to be completed by the series producer and editor. You may only be on contract to that production for eight, ten weeks; you will never see your programme completed. You are absolutely a gun for hire to do a job and the job's not a very creative one.
>
> *Producer interview cited in Turner and Lourenço, 2010:18*

In the introduction to this chapter, it was noted that the FS theory had been adopted by academics, and at least implicitly by policymakers and industry lobby groups, to support the argument for vertical disintegration of the UK broadcasters and the adoption of the US deficit finance model in the UK. This final section considers whether the evidence suggests that these changes in regulations have produced greater flexibility and innovation in UK TV production.

The review of TV production in the vertically integrated UK broadcasters in the 1980s, did suggest production was unnecessarily inefficient. The original reasons for these inefficiencies were technical but, as in newspaper production, they became entrenched in trade union agreements and established working practices which made TV production inflexible to change. Producers had very limited flexibility to adapt production, or use workers with specialist skills, to innovate in programming. The unions were also able to limit management's ability to use new production technologies (first video recording and editing and then non-linear digital systems) to reduce labour costs or increase flexibility in production.

This evidence supports the view of the policymakers and the independent producers association, that UK broadcasters were unnecessarily inefficient and that costs could be reduced, particularly through the effective use of new technology. However, the chapter suggested that the policymakers and independent producers association were incorrect to argue that the cause of this inefficiency was the vertical integration of TV production and distribution. The comparison of the UK situation with US broadcasters, above, found broadly the same situation, despite the vertical disintegration of production and distribution in the US at that time.

Chapter 1 argued that it is "functional flexibility" in production which FS associates with innovation. This chapter also analysed production after the vertical disintegration of UK broadcasters to see if flexibility increased. Again the review supported the FS argument, suggesting that after vertical disintegration functional flexibility in TV production had increased, largely through the introduction of new technology, but also through the decline of union organisation within TV production, particularly in the independent sector. In particular, new technology allowed productions by very small crews based on multitasking. However, the emergence of the entertainment format as the dominant design was found to have brought a return to some of the specialisation and inflexibility of the earlier era

The proponents of FS also argued that vertical disintegration would increase innovation by enabling broadcasters to choose the best programme proposals from across the "marketplace of ideas" rather than being limited to those of their in-house production divisions.

There is some evidence that the vertically disintegrated model chosen for C4 did result in innovation through the broadcaster being able to choose ideas from the widest range of producers. In 1986, the channel outsourced production to more than 230 independent production companies and by 1990 the number had risen to more than 520 (Bennett et al., 2013). But the regulatory change in 1993, requiring C4 to compete for advertising sales, reintroduced the "homogenising" force of commercialism which the original structure had been designed to prevent. A new CEO focused on targeting affluent young audiences with programming acquired from US producers. By 2007 the channel was outsourcing to fewer independent producers (around 300) and by 2013 this had fallen to 230 (Mediatique, 2015). More significant than the absolute numbers of producers is the amount of production commissioned from these producers. Between 1998 and 2003 "by nearly every measure, Channel 4's dependence on large indies has increased" (Mediatique, 2008:18). The data about the BBC's outsourcing of 50% of its production shows that it also was not choosing the best ideas from across the marketplace. Although, in 2007, the BBC outsourced programming to 279 producers, it largely relied on the same section of the market as C4: "the BBC's apparent reliance on a limited range of suppliers to deliver the majority of independent programming does not necessarily accord with the plurality of provision desired" (Mediatique, 2015, Turner and Lourenço, 2010:19). ITV followed the same approach, working with

70–80 independents (Mediatique op. cit.). Altogether, from 2008 to 2013, half of all UK independent TV production was outsourced to large independent producers and another 30% to medium-sized producers (Oliver and Ohlbaum, 2014:6). On this basis, we should conclude that vertical disintegration did not lead to the flexibility and innovation which FS advocates had proposed.

One could argue that it was still the fault of the broadcasters. That the new structure did not produce the new flexibility because the broadcast management remained inflexible and uncreative. However, during this period, one of the most important constraints on the scope of the "marketplace of ideas" was the systematic process of larger independent companies acquiring smaller ones. Second, rather than flexibly innovating, the independent producers began to focus their development efforts on one or two channels and on a narrow product range: "by 1997, 84 per cent of UK IPCs [independent production companies] did not produce for more than two channels and many IPCs had moved into the field of genre production, i.e. production of only one type of programming" (Quinn, 2007:215).

Rather than innovation, the independent sector had become purely about commercialism. Quinn quotes two independent producers. The first noted: "I've long since stopped worrying about having my name attached to a great piece of investigative documentary, I simply don't care what I make as long as it makes money" (op. cit.:205). Another said:

> instead of pursuing an ambition to be a big director I decided to focus on building the company. We want to be able to develop our own content and own the rights. We want to go from supplying a service to owning a product.
>
> *Op. cit.:217*

Some independents have abandoned the creative process completely, to devote themselves to the world of format trading: "they find the (format) easier to sell than their own, new ideas. They have something to show to the broadcaster: a pilot or, even better, a finished program and audience ratings from another country" Esser (2010:288).

This change to commercialism rather than innovation was made irreversible by the adoption of the US model of deficit financing and the subsequent shake-out of smaller independent producers. Rosen argued: "the large number of small, powerless production companies have seen their access to broadcasters diminish and a handful of large, powerful companies have strengthened their relationships considerably" (*The Guardian*, 2007). Industry analyst Mediatique (cited in Turner and Lourenco, 2010:26) concluded that "the industry's overall capacity for innovation and creativity may actually have declined".

The evidence presented in this chapter suggests that the attempt to introduce a form of FS to UK TV production did not produce the flexibility required to liberate creativity and innovation. If the changes in UK TV production were not the result of an increase in functional flexibility and the operation of a "marketplace of ideas", it remains to explain what was driving these changes. Here, it is important to note that the large reductions in jobs in TV production were similar in both the vertically disintegrated US networks and the vertically integrated UK networks. The chapter noted that the new entrants to the TV market – particularly cable, satellite and digital channels – had dramatically reduced the established networks' share of the audience and severely impacted advertising revenue. In the US, the networks became the TV divisions of vertically and horizontally integrated, multimedia conglomerates, targeting global markets. One of their first strategies for coping with declining audience shares and revenue growth was to cut their fixed costs, particularly permanent staff. In the US this was achieved: "through union-busting (and) subcontracting to freelance employees" (Nielsen, 1989:26). Vertical disintegration of the UK broadcasters allowed them to reduce their dependence on permanent, unionised employees by outsourcing to independents employing non-union, freelance workers.

This, in turn, severely weakend the bargaining position of permanent employees and their trade unions within the broadcasters. This allowed the broadcasters' managements to introduce internal markets (like Producer Choice) requiring permanent employees to compete with freelance workers. The broadcasters began replacing permanent jobs with the use of freelancers. In 2016 the BBC used the full time equivalent of 2,500 freelance and agency workers (NAO, 2017). The growth of the independent sector has been built on freelance workers. UK independent producers now employ almost as many workers (around 27,000) as the rest of the industry (broadcasters, cable and satellite) combined. However, in the independent sector, 52% of workers are freelance compared to 36% across cable and satellite and 25% across the broadcasters (Skillset, 2016).

This adoption of numerical flexibility was successful in reducing costs, but it quickly began to undermine the perception of independents and flexibility as forces for innovation; "from being considered a progressive force in television [. . .] with the accent on 'new voices', independent producers have come to be seen by many within the television industry – including some producers themselves – as agents of rationalization" (Davis, 1991:17). The data from the UK independent TV sector show the transformation of the industry from predominantly secure employment to, in the independent sector at least, predominantly freelance work.

In the early 1980s, when C4 was outsourcing across the sector, independents faced great uncertainty about future revenue and were unable to employ production staff until they had a project commissioned. There was at this point a relationship between the attempt to use the "marketplace of ideas" as a source of innovation, and the need for numerical flexibility (and thus greater precarity) in employment of media workers. However, as this chapter has shown, this relationship quickly changed, and UK independent producers became divisions of (largely US-owned) multimedia conglomerates. Rather than achieving flexibility to generate innovation and creativity, the changes in UK TV production have produced "numerical flexibility" for both broadcasters and these UK arms of global media corporations. As the quote from the format producer, above, demonstrates, flexibility allows producers to pay production workers for the minimum number of days required. Such cost reduction measures may be supplemented by exploitative and even unsafe working conditions, as production teams are required to work long hours on the days they are paid, often being required to accept so-called "buyout" deals which prevent them claiming overtime payments (Evans and Green, 2017).

7

PRODUCING DIGITAL CONTENT

The digital media "industry" is not defined in the same way as the other industries we have discussed. Instead, there is a broad sector which may include (among other things); video games, video-on-demand services, social media, music streaming and e-publishing. As well as lacking a precise definition, this sector has not reached a state of maturity comparable to other media industries. Instead, it is experiencing "a state of what the software industry refers to as 'permanent beta' – a state of rapid prototyping, or 'fail fast, learn, pivot'" (Cunningham et al., 2016:379). Thus, the digital media sector remains at the stage of technological discontinuity and experimentation noted in the early development of other media industries. No dominant design has gained acceptance with producers and consumers, around which firms with significant market share could stabilise and exercise control. Instead, a range of designs have emerged – for internet search, social media communication and entertainment – whose legitimacy is increasingly contested. Dominant businesses have emerged, but because of "the fast pace of innovation cycles present in these markets", successful entry is still possible (Chirita, 2017:121). This opens up questions for the life cycle model which has been adopted in the previous chapters. It is possible that, in this sector, no dominant design will ever emerge which stabilises digital media production in a way comparable to features, TV shows and series or news reports.

This chapter, then, takes a slightly different approach, focusing not on a "dominant design", but on one of many emergent designs of digital media product which have achieved some success during this experimental phase. The example chosen, the letsplay video, is interesting because it is a design which shows the relationship between "user generated" video content and the professionally produced (video game) content which has been the subject of the previous chapters.

Technological discontinuity

The ability to record and store media content as digital files, which can be manipulated with computers, has transformed the fundamental technical process of *recording* text and live performances – which began with the printing press, film and video. Parallel technological changes involved the development of computer software for directly *producing* digital images (rather than making analogue or digital recordings of "real" images). This ability to use computers to *generate* images (CGI) transformed production of animated films and programmes (Brookey, 2010). Compared with creating images through recording multiple manual drawings or stop-motion images of models, CGI radically reduced the costs and increased the potential quality of animation. The development of digital software for manipulating digital audio and video files has also reduced the costs of *post-production*. In the mid 2000s, game capture cards and software became more easily available and video editing software like Adobe and Final Cut Pro became more affordable, enabling UGC production of videos using game footage (Christian, 2018b). Together these changes have enabled radical reduction in the cost of producing the "first copies" of media products, such that non-professionals can produce text, audio and video content.

The marginal cost of *reproducing* content – making additional copies from this first copy – was reduced from almost zero (with DVDs) to effectively zero (with digital files). The growth of the internet has transformed the process of *distributing* media products, reducing the (marginal) costs of distributing content to almost zero (the cost of servers for example). The spread of broadband internet in the early 2000s enabled people to download and stream video on a domestic internet service. The emergence of smartphones, with Apple's iPhone in 2007, and the connection of mobile phones to the internet via operating system like IOS, has enabled distribution of content to people wherever they are (Campbell-Kelly et al., 2015).

These technological changes have not, however, been straightforwardly beneficial to media companies since, as the previous chapters have noted, it was the existence of some of these costs, creating barriers to entry, which helped them to exercise some control over their markets and stabilise their market shares. The reduction of these costs, therefore, has enabled massive new entry to media industries. Many of these new businesses entered the already existing "informal economy" based on illegal reproduction and distribution of copyrighted media products. But there has also been huge entry into media production by non-professionals creating UGC.

A further impact of digitisation was in altering the relationship between producers, media products and audiences. Enabling audiences to interact with media content generates information about that content (metadata) and about how audiences are using it. This can reduce the uncertainty media producers face in determining which content to produce and how to promote it (or recommend it) to target audiences. Interactivity also enables audiences to search for and consume media products on demand, after (or even before) their linear distribution via news publication, cinema release or TV broadcast.

Finally, digitisation has enabled aggregation of content, the collection of huge quantities of text or video in a single database. YouTube was designed, in its earliest period of experimentation (in 2005), as a means of storing home videos originally describing itself as "Your Digital Video Repository". But the digital aggregation of content created the potential for on-demand access to a "long tail" of media products (including home videos) which in turn created a relationship between producers and audiences which was an alternative to the model of professional editorial selection, imposed by the limits of newspapers and linear cinema or TV distribution, described in the previous chapters. This potential emerged, after a period of experimentation, in 2007, when Google began to promote YouTube as an alternative to TV, now describing its offer as "Broadcast Yourself". The combination of aggregation and metadata enabled automation of advertising sales, creating economies of scale which, in turn, have created new barriers to entry to the digital advertising market.

Dominant design

Chapters 4 and 6 briefly discussed the role of filmed series and entertainment formats for online video platforms like Netflix and Amazon. These designs are not discussed here because they represent much less significant innovations (essentially adapting existing dominant designs to the new platforms) than does UGC. Chapter 5 briefly mentioned the rise of new designs (like the listicle and the live blog) for online news services. Analysis of the wide variety of new text-based social media designs (tweets, posts, comments etc.) is beyond the scope of this chapter.

Instead, this chapter focuses on user generated online video. Even here, distinctions are needed. An important user generated digital content design, capable of achieving large, "viral" audiences, is the short humorous video, often featuring animals. Social media platforms like Instagram and Snapchat, designed for use with mobile phone cameras, host large quantities of this UGC design. Burgess et al. (2013:4) go further and refer to "the paradigmatic amateur video genre – the cat video". However, there is a strong case that this design is not an innovation which is specific to digital media. Some of the earliest films ever made, at Edison's Black Maria studios in the 1890s, included not dissimilar designs, like *Professor Wilton's Boxing Cats* (Jacobson, 2011). In the early twentieth century, critics of film newsreels described them in terms similar to those used by contemporary critics of online videos;

> there is a tendency . . . to include, instead of news . . . views of a cat playing with a canary . . . of a sign-post with a word spelt wrongly . . . or an intensely uninteresting view of an exceptionally large egg laid seven years ago by a three-legged chicken.
>
> *Ruah 1914, cited in Althaus, 2010:198*

User generated videos of comic slapstick accidents at home, often featuring animals, have long been the key source for entertainment formats like *Funniest Home Videos* (ABC/US) and *You've Been Framed* (ITV/UK) (see Chapter 6).

Budzinski and Gaenssle's (2018) analysis of the output of 200 YouTube UGC producers (excluding people who were already successful in other media sectors, like the musician Taylor Swift) suggested four main genres of UGC video – comedy, gaming, how-to and style, and people and blogs (or "vlogs"). Analysing the audience attention gained by these genres showed that gamers averaged 7.9 million subscribers and 2.4 billion views, and comedy 5.7 million subscribers and 1 billion views. Both these genres came some way ahead of the other two categories. These findings confirm the view expressed by UGC pioneer Hank Green, who argued that in online video "narrative content has existed mostly as aspirational, money-losing, pre-pilot pilots for TV shows. Even content that TV people consider dirt cheap (like game shows, talk shows, and reality shows) is hard to produce with online video budgets" (cited in Poell et al., 2017:17). Green suggests that three emergent media product designs – vlogging, gameplay and style tutorials – are the "only . . . genuinely new cheap-to-produce, high-quality content that viewers really, really love" (ibid.). Part of the reason gameplay videos are able to achieve both high quality and low cost is because the gameplay video combines both professional content and UGC.

This chapter examines one of these designs, the gameplay video (and in particular the letsplay video), because this design appears to be more clearly differentiated from "reality" TV formats like the video diary and the makeover show (see Chapter 6). There is still a case that this form of UGC owes much to the pre-digital era. Jenkins (2006) describes UGC video parodies of Japanese anime TV series, distributed through VHS tape exchanges, which clearly influenced the machinima ("machine cinema") videos which prefigured the letsplay design. However, the combination of game footage, video and audio commentary and online distribution does make letsplay UGC videos a genuine innovation of the digital media era. The sequence

FIGURE 7.1 "Face-cam" shot of PewDiePie

Credit: UNBELIEVABLE GAMEPLAY!!! *Uncharted 4* FULL GAME Part 1/Walkthrough/Playthrough, YouTube, Felix Kjellberg/PewDiePie, 2018.

analysed below was produced by the world's most successful letsplay video producer, and probably the world's most successful individual producer of any form of UGC, Felix Kjellberg aka PewDiePie.

The first shot (Figure 7.1) illustrates the core element of the letsplay design which focuses on recording commentary rather than action. The shot mirrors the classic "sports commentator" presentation, directly addressing the camera with headphones and microphone in vision. In this respect, the letsplay design draws on the live commentaries on sports, games and events originated in the earliest days of radio. The purpose of the shot is not to cover PewDiePie's physical actions in playing the game – which would involve choices of shot and so require camera movements – but only his facial expressions, in commentating on and reacting to the game events. This design – with little or no camera movement – is similar to that of the single-shot movie of the silent era. However, rather than covering silent action within a proscenium shot, the design covers commentary in a static, close-up. Because the camera does not move and the shot size or angle does not change, there is no requirement to edit the recording (although PewDiePie clearly does) nor to observe the rules of continuity and film grammar characteristic of features and filmed series. The limited movement also reduces the requirement for lighting, while the loss of any form of stage or the studio set – just a curtain as background – removes the requirement to create 3D effects through lighting. The shot is lit with a fixed single-point light rather than the three-point principles discussed in other chapters. The only sound recorded is the commentary, reducing the complexity of recording audio, since a single, directional microphone can be fixed, close to PewDiePie's mouth, screening out the sounds of his manipulation of the game controller (although he also uses the camera mic as a back-up in case of problems with the main microphone). Headphones enable him to hear the game audio without this also being recorded by the microphone onto the commentary track.

The episode begins with the greeting; "Are you sitting comfortably? Good. 'cos it's about to begin!" – a parodic reference to a classic British children's show (the radio series *Listen with Mother*, BBC, 1950–82). He then introduces the game, describing how he's "just really excited for a new letsplay" of the game (mirroring his text comment next to the post; "So pumped to play *Uncharted 4*, this game looks incredible!"). This DJ-style language is routine and so acts as a kind of script, however, most of the commentary appears improvised, as live during the playing of the game, like a sports commentary. This ability to entertain simply through his improvised "live" commentary underlines PewDiePie's "authenticity" as a media personality. A key distinction between letsplay videos and the director commentaries recorded for DVDs and games magazines, is the extent to which the commentary and even the game footage serve as a vehicle for letsplayers to create an entertaining show (see Kerttula, 2016). The distinction between PewDiePie's success and many less successful letsplay channels, is that his personality, particularly his improvisational comedy, has placed him ahead of the likes of Justin Bieber and Taylor Swift in the audience he can attract to online videos.

The title also illustrates specific elements of the social media form of distribution of YouTube UGC videos. As with any media product, the aim of the title is to communicate information which can resolve some of the uncertainty all audiences have in deciding to consume an individually differentiated product. Using a superlative in the title – "unbelievable gameplay" – is similar language to that of tabloid newspaper headlines, which has carried over into the "clickbait" of social media news. The second element, the phrase "*Uncharted* FULL GAME . . ." may have more to do with the status of copyright content on YouTube. This phrase may attract viewers looking to illegally download the game. Finally, the "Part 1" in the title illustrates that letsplay videos tend to follow the dominant series design of TV, with letsplay "episodes" organised in playlists as a series (for the alternative role of music playlists see Dwyer, 2013).

In choosing *Uncharted 4: A Thief's End*, PewDiePie is selecting a popular title which conforms to the dominant design of the games industry – the so-called AAA game. *Uncharted* was one of the biggest selling action-adventure games of 2017 in the "serious" gaming section of the market (Batchelor, 2017). By showing the logos of the game title and the producer Naughty Dog this sequence provides "product placement" for the parent company, Sony. Although known for featuring games by small, independent companies, in this case PewDiePie was able to attract audiences to his channel by drawing on the power of a hit series or franchise (like other successful games that year – *Grand Theft Auto V*, *Halo 3*, and *Call of Duty Destiny*).

The next audience-building element of the letsplay sees PewDiePie use his "influencer" status to try to increase the audience for the video. The "as live" process of starting the game involves neither story action nor gameplay interaction, leaving little to comment on, so PewDiePie can ask "why don't we kick this off with a 'like', share this video with your friends and family?" Although recorded, and edited, PewDiePie has not removed an apparent error. His comment, "as always, we're gonna play on 'hard', 'cos that's what we do, no matter what", helps further establish his on-screen persona, even as (noted by some viewers in the comments section) he appears to click the game's "moderate" level (Figure 7.2).

FIGURE 7.2 Insert shot of PewDiePie choosing the game level

Credit: UNBELIEVABLE GAMEPLAY!!! *Uncharted 4* FULL GAME Part 1/Walkthrough/Playthrough, YouTube, Felix Kjellberg/PewDiePie, 2018.

FIGURE 7.3 *Uncharted 4* begins with an action "cinematic"

Credit: UNBELIEVABLE GAMEPLAY!!! *Uncharted 4* FULL GAME Part 1/Walkthrough/Playthrough, YouTube, Felix Kjellberg/PewDiePie, 2018.

FIGURE 7.4 "Flashback" to cutscene with lead character, Nate, as a child

Credit: UNBELIEVABLE GAMEPLAY!!! *Uncharted 4* FULL GAME Part 1/Walkthrough/Playthrough, YouTube, Felix Kjellberg/PewDiePie, 2018.

The game's opening sequence illustrates the way *Uncharted* combines the designs of both games and feature films. It borrows from the conventions of action movies by beginning the story "in media res" (in the middle) before attempting to draw the user's attention to the central storyline. Thus *Uncharted 4* starts with a short action sequence – with sound effects (a storm) and soundtrack (orchestral action/ pirate music) – to engage the audience with the characters and provide genre information. PewDiePie's commentary here is not narrative (he doesn't need to explain the story or his interaction with the game) but evaluative, commenting on the quality of the graphics and effects as would a consumer journalist reviewing the game for a games magazine; "it's like an animated action movie!"

Producing such game sequences is complex, because unlike in film and TV – where the film-maker (not the viewer) decides the order, angle, size and content (characters or objects) of each frame – in a game, the player can choose what appears on screen. Here, the "accelerate" icon in the centre of the screen "cues" the player that the speed of the boat and the positioning of camera can be controlled via the game console controller (Figure 7.3). If the player was given complete control of the screen, the developers would, in theory, have to create an infinite number of graphic images to ensure continuity. To economise on this production cost,

Naughty Dog have produced a type of scene known as an "in-game cinematic". As Cooper (2017) describes, most of what appears on screen is controlled by the animators (it is predominantly a "cutscene", but the player is able to exercise some control of the movement of the protagonist (the character in the boat). In the terms of Chapters 2 and 3 we could see this is as a requirement for much more extensive "blocking" than would be involved in filming live action. To ensure continuity of space, time and motion of the different elements of the scene, the animators create a range of potential shots and "paths" of movement for the boat across the sea. While the background does not change, the software links the boat to the other animated assets in the scene (characters, objects, backgrounds etc.) so that the programme can move these in relation to the movement of the boat. To limit the cost of animation needed, the number of paths available to the player (the degree of task variability for the producers) is subtly limited by the inclusion of obstacles (the waves, enemy boats etc.) that help predict the paths users will take (op. cit.). The game software is then able to produce continuity in the scene in response to the player's decisions about the direction of the boat. To an extent, *Uncharted 4* follows this model throughout the game which is structured around a linear narrative, with multiple optional "paths" for the user to explore, so that the designers can predict the order that players will progress through the events of the game (similar to the limits on uncertainty imposed by the entertainment format in Chapter 6).

The game then uses the movie "flashback" technique to transition to a scene set in an orphanage (Figure 7.4), to provide the "back story" of the central character Nate (Britain Dalton/Nolan North) and to introduce a new central character – his brother Sam (Chase Austin/Troy Baker) – who has not appeared in the previous games but will feature in Nate's quest when the gameplay proper starts. PewDiePie's "as live" commentary enables him to help the user comprehend the narrative events as he experiences them: "What? Have we gone back in time?" This scene is an example of a "cutscene", common in AAA games, which is used to tell the story, rather than to provide gameplay – challenges, tasks or puzzles for the user to solve. The aim of such scenes is to increase the user's sense of "immersion"

FIGURE 7.5 Reverse shot: dialogue between Nate and the nun

Credit: UNBELIEVABLE GAMEPLAY!!! *Uncharted 4* FULL GAME Part 1/Walkthrough/Playthrough, YouTube, Felix Kjellberg/PewDiePie, 2018.

(suspension of disbelief) in the game. This cutscene is produced like a sequence in an animated feature, for the same reasons (viewer/player comprehension), and follows the continuity principles outlined in Chapter 2; 180° lines, shot-reverse-shot coverage of dialogue etc. Thus, the choice of shot sizes reflects the dominant design of film. Here, a close-up is chosen because it helps convey the emotion of the central character. The use of actors and motion capture techniques help the animators render the actor's performance in this detail.

This scene also shows one of the most significant ways in which letsplay videos are edited. The shot combines footage from the face-cam and the game camera. For the majority of the letsplay the face-cam UGC appears as an insert, in the corner of the screen, leaving the majority of the screen to be used for the professional game footage. However, at points, the face-cam insert obscures an important element of the game footage. To resolve this problem, in the editing process PewDiePie cuts to a full screen image of the game footage. The combination of the face-cam and the game footage also creates a potential problem for the user. Should they follow PewDiePie's expression or the game footage. In the main, PewDiePie resolves this by using the techniques used by newsreaders cueing a transition to a film report (see Chapter 5), motivating audiences to expect the transition with a "look" down. Although he does not explicitly observe continuity rules, in the insert PewDiePie's eyeline is directed towards the animated scene. In gameplay sequences, the process of playing the game also ensures his eyeline is directed to the scene rather than the viewer, most of the time. However, there are moments in both types of scene, when he reacts to events by making a joke for example, that his eyeline addresses the audience ("breaking the fourth wall") in the way TV presenters or stand-up comedians address their audiences. The shot also illustrates the way letsplay videos ensure the game subtitling is in vision. This technique follows the conventions of the DVD commentary, in allowing PewDiePie to present his commentary whilst he and his audience can continue to follow the game characters' dialogue.

Figure 7.5 shows an emotional scene; the young Nate is being treated harshly by a nun responsible for his care. PewDiePie is largely silent, performing his own emotional response and also allowing his audience to experience the emotions of the scene without interruption. He uses commentary only to provide comic relief from these emotions, with a few brief humorous comments, "mean!", to differentiate his letsplay video (using the generally humorous subversive tone of the genre) from the darker emotions of this section of the game itself. This section of the video also illustrates how game developers make transitions. The end of this scene in the game – as the character escapes the orphanage – motivates a transition between the "cutscene" and the first opportunity for genuine gameplay.

In the gameplay sections of video games, the player takes over (from the developers) much more control of what appears on screen. At this point, achieving continuity for every potential decision of the player would require the animators to create a potentially infinite number of shots. The solution is provided by the real-time animation generated by the game engine. As the player moves the "camera", the computer software generates the images necessary to create continuity.

FIGURE 7.6 Shot of "platforming" gameplay as Nate escapes the orphanage

Credit: UNBELIEVABLE GAMEPLAY!!! *Uncharted 4* FULL GAME Part 1/Walkthrough/Playthrough, YouTube, Felix Kjellberg/PewDiePie, 2018.

This real-time process of animation is unable to replicate the resolution of professional animation in the cutscenes. The video illustrates the lower quality of some of the animation of the controllable elements of the scene (e.g. in close-ups of the central character's face). In the scene shown in Figure 7.6 the impact of this loss of resolution is reduced by the use of "lighting" and the developer's decision to limit the player's control of camera movement to following the character from behind.

This section also shows the characteristic type of gameplay elements in *Uncharted*, which focus on "platforming" as well as including standard game elements such as using vehicles and weapons to overcome or escape from enemies. In platform games, players are set the challenge of successfully controlling the characters to enable them to jump, swing or climb between a variety of surfaces. In creating this platforming scene, the developers use 3D animation software to automate the creation and animation (movement) of "assets" (characters, backgrounds, objects etc.). These assets and movements are storable and reusable. The animation work involved in creating *Uncharted*'s 3D platforming elements is extensive. In the "booster" sequence in Figure 7.6, many companies might reduce the degree of "blocking", and thus the cost of animation, required by creating different scenes from a single, reusable "boost" package of basic movements, by adding layers of animation to show specific characters and scenery. For *Uncharted 4*, however, Naughty Dog animated each booster scene individually (see Cooper, 2017).

By moving from the narratively focused cutscenes and in-game cinematics to actual gameplay, this scene creates the interactive narrative which drives the letsplay presenter's commentary. The game has departed from a scripted narrative to the more unscripted nature of a sports game or reality show (see Chapter 6). This creates space for commentary, cueing the viewer to look at and understand the most important events occurring. The letsplay commentary differs, however, because the events are not only unscripted, they result from the commentator's own interaction with the game. Rather than providing an "objective" or merely ironic commentary on events, the letsplay commentary has some of the elements of online "reaction" videos, where the face-cam and commentary record the commentator's own spontaneous reactions to actions taken in the game. In sharing this emotional response, PewDiePie's eyeline moves from the game to directly address his audience.

As with the previous scenes, this shot, with the face-cam close-up inset into the wide shot from the game video, illustrates how the letsplay design enables YouTubers to attract audiences used to the quality of film and TV by combining UGC with professional quality game footage. This use of a channel to present professional content created for other platforms parallels the evolution of radio, after the introduction of TV, towards formats based on live presentation of recorded music (see Dwyer, 2013). In many respects the letsplay format finally realised the prediction of radio syndicator Louis Snader, in the 1940s, that TV stations would be hosted by TV jockeys presenting short films (Anderson, 1994). However, unlike the DJ's relationship to the record, the interactive nature of video games enables PewDiePie to become a character in the story, to experience the challenges of the game and to display his skills as a gamer. In this respect his commentary helps users see how he is solving the kinds of puzzles presented by the game; "What does that do? When it's safe . . . to roll out . . . OK I got it."

As PewDiePie completes this level of the game, the game footage includes a call to action, motivating players to continue to the next stage of the mystery and their quest. PewDiePie then makes a transition back to the face-cam in full screen using the classic cinema convention of the fade to black. He then presents his, relatively standard, end sequence. This promotes the next video in the series, which will appear "tomorrow", and also promotes the channel by encouraging viewers to add to his audience metrics by leaving a like or a comment. This sequence also includes routine demonstrations of the authenticity of his relationship with his audience —making a "brofist" and using a version of the classic radio or TV presenter's "trademark" sign-off, which for PewDiePie is, "as always, stay awesome bros".

FIGURE 7.7 PewDiePie signals the end of the episode with a "brofist" salute to his audience

Credit: UNBELIEVABLE GAMEPLAY!!! *Uncharted 4* FULL GAME Part 1/Walkthrough/Playthrough, YouTube, Felix Kjellberg/PewDiePie, 2018.

Market control

The technological changes to recording, editing and post-production and distribution of audio, video, images and text so dramatically reduced the costs of media production and distribution and lowered the barriers to entry to the media market, one commentator summarised the first decade of the twenty-first century with the phrase *Here Comes Everybody* (Shirky, 2008). This new digital competition had an immediate impact on existing media companies. Newspapers were affected first, with US daily average circulation falling from 54.6 million to 31 million between 2004 and 2017 (Barthel, 2017). Despite the newspapers' efforts to develop digital operations, web traffic to newspaper sites declined in 2017 (ibid.). The period 2004 to 2008, alone, saw a 42% fall in the market value of the main US newspaper businesses (Evans, 2009).

US TV ratings were impacted later, but the live TV watched by an average US viewer fell 43%, from 32 to 18 hours, between 2008 and 2018 (Magna, 2018a). In the industry's most important commercial segment, people aged 18–49, the four terrestrial networks' viewing fell 10% in 2017 alone (Magna, 2018b). In the US, all of the conventional media industries saw a fall in advertising sales in 2017, with print sales most affected, falling 15% to $18 billion. By contrast, digital sales grew 18% to $85 billion, more than twice the total sales ($42 billion) of national TV advertising (ibid.). The largest increases in digital sales were in digital video (up 28%) and social media (up 39%) (ibid.).

In the UK, digital media accounted for 50% of all advertising sales in 2015, the first country in the world where this happened. The period 2007 to 2017 saw a 28.6% fall in the price of UK TV advertising (average TV CPMs) (Farey-Jones, 2018). The section of the audience most affected by these changes was millennials. While the rest of the US population watch 34.5 hours of TV each week, millennials watch just over 19 hours, less time than they spend on their smartphones (Cakebread, 2017). For this reason, almost all the rise in digital advertising is occurring on mobile devices. Mobile advertising sales rose 40% to $48 billion and now account for around 30% of all US advertising sales (Magna, 2018b).

Digitisation had enabled real democratisation of media production and distribution. For the first time, the means of producing and distributing content were widely available. Because of the public good characteristics of media products, amateur producers were able to distribute and receive content via websites and peer-to-peer networks. Many of the new entrants to the media market were amateur producers using websites and social media to communicate with global audiences or communities of people interested in the same subjects. Many of the producers and consumers of such UGC were the same young people who were beginning to abandon conventional media. It is estimated that 70% of UGC production is created by people aged 25 to 54 (DMN, 2015). Many of these new entrants are entrepreneurs as well as innovators and enthusiasts, developing new forms of media products and finding new ways to earn income from the process. Cunningham and Craig (2017:72) estimate that there are now "more than 2.5 million YouTube creators globally receiving some level of remuneration from their uploaded content".

But equally, in making content so freely shareable, digitisation has meant media companies – studios, newspapers, broadcast networks – which own the copyright to media products, are unable to prevent audiences from sharing it with peers for free. More importantly, digitisation has brought new entrants to the "informal economy", establishing businesses monetising content whose copyright they don't own. Recent estimates suggest that the leading pirate websites earn around $209 million a year in advertising revenue alone (ACE, 2018).

The emergence of letsplay videos, as a form of UGC, derived from the coevolution of the digital media industry with the film, TV and games industries. The latter, after 20 years of experimentation, began to mature in the late 1990s, with the emergence of the Sony Playstation to compete with the Nintendo console and PC gaming. The dominant design, which would become known as the AAA game, began to stabilise around a defined group of game genres and increasingly big production budgets (DeMaria and Wilson, 2002). While there are similarities between the media and games industries, particularly the way they address "two-sided markets", the games industry developed a "platform" business model which extends the network effects normally associated with media businesses to "lock in" or increase the "switching costs" for individual consumers (Barnett, 2018). This model is common in the computing industry and worked first in the so-called Gillette or razor and blades business model where manufacturers subsidise the cost of the operating system (the razor) to lock in consumers to purchasing compatible software (blades). The main manufacturers – Nintendo, Microsoft and Sony – have subsidised the cost of game consoles in order to lock in a large number of users who can then be persuaded to pay premium prices for the compatible games (Christian, 2018b). The platform (and its owner) is then in a position to act as gatekeeper choosing which companies may use the platform to access the user base and how much to charge them for the privilege. Vertical integration can increase the platform owners' control. At one point both Microsoft and Sony owned the developers of the game franchises which were most important in their respective consoles' (Xbox and Playstation) continued sales (Bungie's *Halo* and Naughty Dog's *Uncharted*). This platform business model, the market power achieved through vertical integration, and the high cost of the dominant design of AAA games has produced consolidation, such that in 2017 77% of the $121.7 billion global games market was shared among 25 companies (Wijman, 2018).

As the games industry matured in the late 1990s, the emergence of the internet facilitated the growth of online gaming communities. A key title in initiating the coevolution or convergence (see Chapter 1) of the two technologies was *Quake* (1996) a multiplayer "shooter" (FPS) with teams of players ("clans") competing online. The game also provided, for the time, a high level of 3D animation and it was this aspect which led to *Quake*'s role in linking games with user generated video. The game software enabled recording of gameplay footage which gamers began to turn into narrative films known as machinima and share online. In 2000,

UK gamer Hugh Hancock created the website machinima.com as a single place for gamers to post their videos and for other gamers to watch (Muncy, 2017).

The emergence of inexpensive and relatively simple technology allowed more gamers to record and edit game footage. In 1999, members of the *Quake* community established the SomethingAwful.com website which would become host for the first of a new genre – the letsplay video (Chouinard, 2017) A second crucial title, this time initiating coevolution of games with film and TV production, was Microsoft's *Halo* franchise which, beginning in 2001, became the main driver of sales for its Xbox console. A group of fans, which later became the company Rooster Teeth, established a website to show a narrative series, *Red vs. Blue*, created from *Halo* footage (Rigney, 2012). This series soon began to attract audiences of around 750,000 for each episode, enabling Rooster Teeth to establish a business based on viewers paying annual subscriptions to download the films before they became free (ibid.). Microsoft took a tolerant view of the use of its copyright material, seeing the series as a legitimate part of the marketing of the game franchise.

"Serial entrepreneur" Allen DeBevoise saw the potential for machinima.com to become the MTV of games videos; "it's not really the game itself, just like the music video isn't really the music itself. We can build an entertainment lifestyle brand out of that culture" (Pollack, 2013:1). A new distribution channel would take gaming videos to a wider audience; "we started thinking of YouTube the way a cable network thinks of a satellite provider" (ibid.). DeBevoise acquired machinima.com, establishing it as a YouTube channel showing a wide range of gaming videos, including *Red vs. Blue*, and videos based on all the hit AAA franchises of the period. The combination of YouTube and the growth in mobile and smartphone viewing of video took machinima.com to a global audience. In 2009, the site launched its subchannel *Respawn*, and signed PewDiePie, who in 2011 began a weekly series *Fridays with PewDiePie*. By 2012 he had reached 1 million subscribers and by 2013 *Respawn* passed 1 billion views (Christian, 2018b).

The games companies had taken a generally tolerant view of gaming videos, believing the copyright infringement involved had only a minor negative impact on game sales (with the video substituting for buying the game) and a potentially positive impact (as a form of sales promotion). The success of machinima.com, and other UGC sites, led the industry to take a more serious commercial interest in gaming videos. Rather than attempting to prevent copyright infringement, they approached gaming videos more in terms of the emerging concept of "influencer" (or "social network") marketing (see Chapter 1). From this perspective, game video producers were not competitors but expert consumer guides, trusted – because they were independent of the industry – to review and recommend products to the gaming community. The opportunity was to try to influence the influencers. In its promotional campaign for 2011, Nintendo attempted a "soft" approach to this through a competition for the best letsplay videos (Chouinard, 2017). Machinina began to sign thousands of contracts to represent gaming video producers, establishing the site as a platform, a one stop shop, to enable sponsors to reach influencers (and vice versa) and through them to reach the gaming community. In 2014 it was reported that Microsoft had made an arrangement with Machinima to "secretly" pay games video producers to promote the Xbox One (Opam, 2014). Such arrangements obviously risked undermining the authenticity which was the basis of the audience's trust in any purchase recommendations (see Regulation and legitimacy, this volume, p. 188).

However, by this stage, Google had encouraged a large number of new entrants to this market – representing UGC creators to brands. When YouTube's application interface was opened to companies wishing to operate "YouTube networks", in 2009, it was a rapid success. That same year, $100 million was invested increasing to $500 million by 2012; "by 2014, $1.65 billion had been invested" (Christian, 2018a:1). Many of the new entrants to this emerging industry, which would come to be called Multichannel Networks (MCNs), followed the Machinima approach of focusing on UGC producers of videos in the genres they believed would attract brands. Companies signed up UGC producers of music (Vevo), beauty (StyleHaul) and dance (DanceOn) videos (Lobato, 2016). While there were many variants of MCN, at the core of the approach was a platform business model (see Chapter 1). Their offer to sponsors was to manage the risk of associating their brands with such uncertain media channels as those of UGC video producers. They would identify and aggregate the best talent, manage their output and charge brands a premium to have a presence on this platform.

In many respects this offer was similar to that of the talent agencies which had acted as independent production companies and representatives for US film and TV talent since the 1940s (see Chapters 2 and 3). Indeed, some MCNs signed YouTubers on contracts similar to those of Hollywood's studio era (see Chapter 2). To realise the value of their initial investment, such MCNs locked their creators into multi-year deals without the option to end the contract early (Graves and Lee, 2017). However, while conventional talent agencies might represent hundreds of professional performers, the MCNs attempted to represent thousands of (mainly young) amateurs. As Lobato (2016) notes, in attempting to monetise UGC, the MCNs effectively had to take on (at least some of) the full range of conventional media management roles. They acted as talent spotters, identifying YouTubers who could attract significant numbers of the target audience, and signed them up to contracts (largely based on sharing advertising and other revenue). Like network executives, they "aggregated" the content of these individual producers into a (often genre-based) network. As producers, they provided technical support, creative advice and production facilities to try to "professionalise" the quality of UGC videos. Like marketing executives, they attempted to promote their networks to global audiences (Vollmer et al., 2014). The next stage was to try to sell advertising on this network, especially through an understanding of the algorithms of Google and YouTube. Like Machinima, they approached brands to try to persuade them to sponsor the network or the channels of individual YouTubers. As Lobato (2016:352) notes; "This model . . . is more lucrative than display advertising because MCNs do not have to split their gross revenues with Google". Finally, they sought ways to monetise the YouTubers' direct relationship with their fans by developing merchandise and books and organising live appearances. Cunningham et al. (2016:378) describe this period of experimentation in the emergence of a UGC "industry" as a "huge, unprecedented experiment in seeking to convert vernacular or informal creativity into talent and content increasingly attractive to advertisers, brands, talent agencies, studios and venture capital investors on a near-global scale". The problem with this model was that it required management techniques which did not exist in the conventional media.

In practice, the MCNs were unable to manage UGC in this way. The fundamental problem was that unlike conventional talent agencies, who dealt with performers who had accommodated to the experience of working for large corporations, the MCNs were attempting to manage UGC producers who had already achieved some success with their target audience, without any involvement with corporations or any experience of being managed, advised or produced. A second order of problem concerned the scale of the operation. While an MCN might bring in successful sponsorship deals for some of their most popular YouTubers, there were no economies of scale which enabled them to achieve this for the mass of their producers. Instead, they attempted to differentiate levels of service between the most popular YouTubers and the rest; Machinima had three levels (red, white and black). The result was that MCNs created a large group of YouTubers whose expectations of fame, wealth and creative support had instead left them tied to arrangements where they had to work tirelessly to produce enough videos to generate an (often very small) income, which they now had to share with an MCN as well as YouTube (Graves and Lee, 2017).

The MCNs began to move away from the platform model of UGC and towards an open innovation model, where their UGC networks effectively became incubators, with low cost ways of developing TV series, formats or performers, which they could turn into professional web series and/or sell to conventional media businesses. This reflected an unfortunate problem with YouTube as a vehicle for UGC producers: YouTube's most popular content is professionally produced.

> Music channels appear prominently in the top ten highest-reach YouTube networks across all comparator countries. With the exception of France and Japan, the "big three" American recording companies (Warner Music, Sony BMG and Universal Music Group) are all in the top five highest-reach YouTube networks in each comparator country.
>
> *Ofcom, 2018b:154*

In 2013 Machinima launched *Prime*, a subchannel based partly on commissioning established Hollywood talent, including Ridley Scott. DeBevoise described its explicit "open innovation" approach to media development; "by combining this unique incubation model together with our powerful partnership of established creative talent and scaled distribution to millions on Machinima, we believe new sci-fi franchises will be born" (Fleming, 2013).

One of the many dissatisfied UGC producers was PewDiePie who legally ended his contract with Machinima and joined a gaming channel (Polaris) run by another MCN, Maker Studios. By 2012 Maker Studios' 2 billion monthly views outstripped Machinima's audience and, by 2013, PewDiePie had become the leading YouTube creator, measured by subscribers, a position he holds to date. However, PewDiePie also took the route all MCNs were promoting, by successfully making the transition to more conventional media production. He partnered with Maker Studios to produce a reality format *Scare PewDiePie* (Constine, 2015 https://techcrunch.com/2015/10/21/youtube-original/?_ga=2.76056208.44629621.1534942839-1708843793.1533679325).

Another MCN to adopt this approach, AwesomenessTV, produced *Royal Crush* a branded content series and two feature films, one a commission for Netflix.

These successes persuaded conventional media organisations to vertically integrate into the digital market and brought consolidation of the MCNs. RTL bought BroadbandTV in 2013 and StyleHaul in 2014, Disney bought Maker Studio in 2014, Warner Brothers bought Machinima in 2016 and Viacom bought AwesomenessTV in 2018. Disney CFO, Jay Rasulo, described this period of experimentation as: "like 50 years ago, when movie studios were trying to make television – it's not completely natural . . . so it made sense to acquire a company that is very good at this" (Rasulo, cited in Lobato, 2016:351).

However, the market control exercised even by giant, global media conglomerates like Disney pales by comparison to that of Google, now easily the world's largest media company (Livemint, 2017). Google has controlled around 70% of search advertising while its subsidiary YouTube dominates online video advertising (Barnett, 2018). In the UK, Google and Facebook control more than half (54%) of the digital advertising market (Bold, 2017).

The coevolution of conventional and digital media industries has created a competition for market control between five US digital "majors" (Google, Apple, Facebook, Amazon and Twitter), the big media conglomerates (Viacom/CBS, 21st Century Fox, Disney etc.) and China's Baidu and Tencent. As Barnett (2018) suggests, the platform model of the digital majors may give them an in-built advantage in this battle. At its most basic level this is a competition for "attention". Chapter 1 outlined the concept of an "attention economy" where apparently "free" media products, like broadcast TV programmes or free newspapers, still follow the market logic of scarce private goods. First, of course, they are not free to produce and distribute. As the previous chapters have shown, they are increasingly expensive to produce on a professional basis.

They are also not free to consume, since although audiences do not pay for these media products, they incur costs, using up their scare attention time to find products they want. These search costs are reduced, in conventional media, by the commissioning practices and linear schedules of broadcasters, the editorial policies and layout of newspapers or the green lighting and release schedules of Hollywood studios. Even as cable and then digital channels proliferated, the electronic programme guide served to economise on scarce attention. Digitisation lowers barriers to entry and so makes available a practically infinite amount of content, broadening choice, but increasing the potential search costs.

The profitability of media companies usually depends on producing a variant of a dominant design to attract the largest (or most valuable niche) audience, while at the same time implementing process innovations to try to keep production costs low. As noted, the low barriers to entry to digital media production suggest that it will be more difficult to arrive at a dominant media product. However, in the absence of such a "hit" product, digitisation enables companies like YouTube to aggregate, to collect together, an almost infinite amount of media content – music, films, TV shows, news reports, UGC etc. This aggregation process effectively makes YouTube a "one stop shop" for video content (and much audio and music). The business activity for YouTube is to develop systems to reduce the costs to audiences of finding content they want. YouTube does this through investing in systems to organise, personalise and recommend media content to viewers. This two-step process – aggregating the greatest possible catalogue of content, and using technology to enable viewers to find content without high search costs – enables YouTube to attract the attention of a huge global audience of 1.5 billion people (Statista, 2018). For a long time, advertisers were sceptical about the figures claimed for internet audiences, which were too small even to register on conventional measurement systems like Nielsen and Comscore (Napoli, 2012). Recent estimates suggest that "the proportion of ads being seen by people in most of the countries around the world is still relatively low, between 40% and 50%" (Bounie et al., 2017:3). These problems with demand, along with the huge volume of content available online, combined to keep the price of advertising to online audiences much lower than for conventional media. It was this which made UGC so hard to develop as an advertising business, both for individual creators and for MCNs.

However, the development of "programmatic" advertising enabled Google and Facebook to bypass the conventional media ratings agencies like Nielsen and give brands detailed data about their audiences, including their online habits, to enable them to target consumers with specific profiles (Christian, 2018b). Automated ad servers could follow individual audience members as they surfed between websites enabling brands to choose the time and place they wanted their advertisement presented to targeted audience demographics or profiles. These systems could also inform the brands if the targeted viewers bought their product or one of their competitors' (Bounie et al. 2017). This form of advertising also introduced another cost to the consumption of apparently "free" online video. Viewers began to pay for content by, knowingly or otherwise, consenting for YouTube to use their data to sell advertising (Gill et al. 2013).

YouTube began to offer programmatic ad sales in 2008 and by 2015 it was generating $1.55 billion in net advertising revenue in the US alone, from the 170 million US users it attracted (Statista, 2018). With this successful advertising model in place, YouTube was able to take advantage of its greatest asset – its catalogue of free content. As Cunningham et al. note (2016:379):

> In marked contrast to traditional film studios and television (TV) networks, YouTube elected to avoid the messy and legally cumbersome traditional media model of owned or shared IP. YouTube also avoided paying fees for content as well as offering backend residual or profit participation. Rather, YouTube entered into "partnership agreements" with their content creators based on a split of advertising revenue.

The reasons YouTube was able to avoid the "messy business" of creating or acquiring IP (intellectual property) are discussed below (see Regulation and legitimacy, this volume, p. 188). The important point to note here is that this makes YouTube's production cost virtually zero. Instead, the company can focus all its investment on maximising its audience to generate behavioural data to sell to advertisers. In contrast to the IP ownership model of media businesses, this platform model provides the digital majors with a firm basis to control their respective markets.

As noted at the beginning of this chapter, the technical barriers to entry to the digital advertising market are low. And this means many new advertising/behavioural data-based businesses may launch each year. The online video sector alone has seen the entry of a range of platforms specifically targeted at the growing audience for video on mobile phones, and often targeting younger audiences looking for a community of peers rather than the older demographics aggregated on existing platforms. However, as Barnett (2018:1109) argues, platform strategies based on the aggregation of content and audiences can achieve very high market shares for the platform owner and produce effective barriers to entry leading to "extreme concentration" in these markets. The first barrier to entry is the zero cost to YouTube of acquiring content. A new entrant, such as a Netflix, is faced with huge, ongoing costs of acquiring or creating content IP – $8 billion in 2018 (Koblin, 2017). Second, as a first mover, YouTube has the benefit of network effects; having used massive content aggregation to reach a huge global audience, its global brand recognition makes it a preferred "one stop shop" for audiences looking for free-to-view online video. Users can minimise their costs (in attention time) by searching YouTube first, before considering competitors. Similarly, advertisers seeking maximum exposure, or even a targeted audience, are likely to gravitate to the market leader. Third, economies of scale favour YouTube over competitors or new entrants. A new entrant seeking to promote itself to audiences faces significant technological and marketing costs to build even a small audience. By contrast, YouTube faces very low to zero marginal costs in serving additional viewers or contributors. Finally, these advantages together give YouTube, and the other digital majors, access to extraordinary financial resources to protect their control of the market by acquiring any new entrants which might pose a potential challenge (Dolata, 2017).

These barriers to entry mean that, to be successful, any new entrant must identify a new section of the audience. But they also increase the likelihood that the new entrant will be acquired by an existing digital major before they aggregate a sufficient audience to become a competitive threat. The pattern of launch and acquisition of new online video platforms is indicative of the strength of the market control exercised by the digital majors. Instagram added video to its photo application in 2013, a year after it was acquired by Facebook. Both Vine (short video) and Periscope (live streaming) were acquired by Twitter around the time they were launched in 2012 and 2015, respectively. Twitch, launched in 2011, is an alternative to Machinima based on gamers streaming their gameplay and commentary live. It was acquired by Amazon in 2014.

The examples of Myspace, Yahoo and Blackberry should remind us that even the digital majors may not achieve permanent market control (Evans, 2017). Furthermore, the other chapters in this book, outlining the struggles of the Hollywood studios, news organisations and broadcast networks, have illustrated the continual cycles of oligopoly and competition in media markets. However, at present, the platform model and aggregation strategies of the digital majors does appear to give them a strong and possibly decisive advantage over those media organisations whose businesses are based on the creation of IP. At this stage, the competition in media markets looks likely to occur *within* this oligopoly of digital majors, rather than between them and media companies or new entrants. The main factor which could change this, at present, would appear to be the threat of regulation, to reduce their market control, or a crisis of legitimacy and loss of public trust in these companies.

Regulation and legitimacy

As Sandoval and Fuchs (2010) note, the idea of audiences producing their own media content – through "community" or "public access" media or "participatory culture" – has long occupied a role in the history of critiques of mass media. As new media technologies have emerged, various forms of decentralised, community or alternative forms of production and governance have been proposed and occasionally supported by regulators; radio (in the 1920s and again with FM in the 1980s), video (in the 1970s) and cable (in the 1980s) (Dwyer, 1989). At various points, mass media organisations have also supported "user" production, for example through the BBC's Community Programmes Unit (1973–2002), which among other things developed *Video Nation* (BBC), which might be considered a forerunner to the YouTube vlog.

The emergence of the internet presented "new possibilities for a cheap, participatory media production . . . for bypassing (mass media) gate-keepers . . . and for reaching a potentially global audience" (Sandoval and Fuchs, 2010:143). As noted above, and in Chapter 5, most of the UGC created does not fulfil the hopes of the critics of mainstream media (Fenton, 2010). A typical example of the paradigmatic YouTube video, this time featuring a baby rather than an animal, illustrates the regulatory issues raised by internet distribution of UGC. In 2007, Stephanie Lenz uploaded a 29-second video she had made of her 13-month old son pushing a baby walker and "dancing" to music (Prince's *Let's Go Crazy*) playing in the kitchen. The owners of the music copyright, Universal Music Group, ordered YouTube to take the video down from their site, as it infringed copyright. Supported by campaigning groups, Ms Lenz issued a counter-notice arguing that YouTube had violated the conditions of the 1998 Digital Millennium Copyright Act, and other laws, which provided that websites should have "safe harbor" from copyright infringement, if the UGC constituted "fair use" (Sawyer, 2009). The case has continued to be argued and reached the US Supreme Court in 2017.

This difficulty in deciding the meaning of fair use has an impact on UGC creation if, as in this case, the copyright owners decide to contest the issue. As noted, in the early days of gaming videos, Microsoft specifically waived its copyright over the *Halo* game footage to permit production of the UGC series *Red vs. Blue*. Other games producers followed suit, including specific and limited permissions to use game footage in the terms of their End-User License Agreements (Haefliger et al., 2010). As noted, the games companies appeared to believe that, in the terms of Chapter 1, a gameplay video would not act as a substitute for purchase of the game itself. Other companies have taken the view that YouTube content does act as a direct substitute for purchase of the media product, and taken legal action, particularly Viacom, who in 2007 sued YouTube for $1billion copyright infringement for hosting 150,000 clips from TV shows including *Spongebob Squarepants* (Sawyer, 2009, Hassanabadi, 2011).

Liebowitz (2018) has argued for a distinction between two types of online content. The first, UGC, would cover the Lenz video, on the grounds that 20 seconds of poor quality background music could not substitute for purchase of Prince's *Let's Go Crazy*. The second, User Uploaded Content (UUC), would cover the uploads of *Spongebob Squarepants*, since viewing these free on YouTube might well substitute for buying a DVD or watching the shows on a pay TV or advertising funded TV channel. Liebowitz (2018:12) argues that the number of copyright infringing files (music, TV shows, movies etc.) annually uploaded to YouTube "could easily be near a billion". Moreover, it is possible that this copyright content could account for much of the audience YouTube attracts. Ding et al. (2011) estimated that 20% of YouTube uploaders attract 97% of the views.

Effectively, the conventional media industries found they were acting as suppliers of content to YouTube, at zero cost to the platform. Their ability to extract a price for their content depended on the ability to control access to it, and their failure to persuade the courts clearly limited their ability to use the law to enforce this. The alternative seemed to be to act as their own content police, devoting huge resources to monitoring YouTube to identify and ensure infringing material was taken down. Each mistake in doing this, such as the demand to take down the Lenz video, undermined the legitimacy of their argument and further weakened their position in relation to YouTube (Sawyer, 2009).

Furthermore, YouTube, and its parent company Google, have not remained passive, but have actively lobbied to prevent legislation which would have made them more responsible for copyright infringements on their platforms (Barnett, 2018).

The economic effect of this was to give YouTube considerable market power in determining the price it would pay for copyright content on its platform. This negotiation happened in 2007 when YouTube announced its Partnership Programme (YPP) and Content ID system. Under this arrangement, copyright owners would not request that their content be taken down and would not receive any up-front payment to license the content (as they would from a broadcaster, cable channel or VOD platform). Instead, the owners would receive a share of any advertising revenue accrued from views of the content. As the content owners joined YPP, they were effectively accepting that they could not prevent the loss of income from the substitution effect of YouTube viewing (e.g. loss of DVD sales) and the loss of potential sales to other channels or platforms. As Liebowitz (2018) shows, this arrangement must have been inferior to any sale they could have made if YouTube were not already in possession of the content, and with a considerable degree of legal force behind them. It also must have affected on-demand platforms (like Netflix) who acquire films and TV shows through normal distribution procedures. YouTube's defence is that its Content ID system either takes down or pays advertising revenue on 99.5% of content identified as infringing, but as Liebowitz notes, this ignores an unknown but potentially significant quantity of content which, for a number of reasons, goes unidentified. To an extent, therefore, the presumed legitimacy of UGC (as democratic or participatory media) has disguised the illegitimacy of much online video which is more properly described as UUC.

It is not only IP where the digital majors enjoy freedom from regulations which apply to conventional media companies. As platforms, rather than publishers, they also escape legal liability under content laws applying to libel, content diversity, hate speech etc. This freedom partly results from the challenge to any conceivable regulatory structure which is posed by global scale of operation and the volumes of content on these platforms (Barnett, 2018). However, rather than no regulation at all, platforms like YouTube impose detailed contractual obligations on all their users. The difference between these rules and those of conventional media is that the platforms choose them (rather than them being imposed by government) and their purpose is largely to ensure that legal liabilities are transferred to the user, who in the case of UGC producers becomes the publisher.

Rather than editorial staff, digital platforms have largely used algorithms to identify and "take down" content which might be deemed offensive – whether legally or ethically. The many failures of these systems to perform this role effectively have been exposed largely by advertisers discovering their brands being promoted next to content promoting terrorism or hate speech (Graves and Lee, 2017). YouTube was forced to act following a social media outcry after PewDiePie and another high-profile UGC producer, Logan Paul, uploaded content considered offensive. Maker Studios (now Disney Digital Networks) terminated its contract with PewDiePie and and YouTube cancelled season 2 of *Scare PewDiePie*. However, when 250 advertisers removed their advertisements YouTube instituted broader measures to regulate content. First, they passed on the commercial imperatives which they were themselves facing. Their systems began to "demonetise" videos which were considered offensive and they raised the barriers to entry (in terms of subscribers and video views) to the YPP. This provoked a further angry response, this time from UGC producers who began to lose some or all of their income from the platform and complained that YouTube's systems were demonetising legitimate content and so limiting freedom of speech. To try to satisfy both of these sides of its platform, and in apparent recognition of the failure of its algorithms, YouTube's parent, Google, announced that, by the end of 2018, it would have more than 10,000 people employed to identify and remove content which was not "advertiser friendly" (Weiss, 2018). Estimates of YouTube's advertising revenues show an increase from around $8 billion to $10–15 billion between 2015 and 2017, demonstrating that it has, thus far, survived these challenges to the legitimacy of its business practices (Jhohnsa, 2018).

Process innovation

There have been no published, academic empirical studies of letsplay production, so the majority of this section is based on communications with letsplayers and internet forums devoted to the subject (especially www.reddit.com/r/letsplay/ and https://creatoracademy.youtube.com/) and also Sylvestre's (2017) "how-to" guide.

It's important to note that UGC production is as old as professional media production. Domestic audio video and print technologies have always been used for UGC. The potential impact of UGC production has been greater at moments when cheaper distribution technology created the opportunity to reach a large audience. This potential has been greatest when media product designs emerged which enabled UGC to compete at the quality level with professional products. Music radio, during its early years and after the development of low cost FM transmitters, combined these three elements, but without a regulatory regime which could permit access to distribution (Dwyer, 1989). Fan video, produced using VHS technology, combined two elements (Jenkins, 1992).

The letsplay video design, produced with digital technology, distributed via the internet, under "safe harbor" and "fair play" regulations, combined the necessary elements for UGC to reach a significant audience (Graves and Lee, 2017). Further, the letsplay design enables UGC producers to achieve the required product at the high volume (both length and number of episodes) and low to zero marginal cost appropriate to the content aggregation logic of the YouTube platform (Barnett, 2018). "Attention economics" suggests that aggregating content at the channel level will attract viewers just as it does at the platform level. Regular addition of new content to a channel builds habitual viewing which retains viewers, helping convert them into subscribers.

Achieving this level of output at such low cost requires most letsplay producers to work at a much more rapid cycle time than the production processes covered in the previous chapters. Although the task decomposition follows the overall steps familiar from film and studio TV production, the design, particularly the use of game footage, allows the UGC producer to limit the content they originate largely to their audio commentary. This enables significant economies in pre-production and production, compared even to other forms of UGC production. Differences in the economies achieved largely reflect the style of commentary adopted for the channel.

Once a game has been selected, the first step is to divide the game narrative or levels into a number of letsplay episodes which will make up a series (Sylvestre, 2017). Efficiencies can be achieved by choosing longer or more complex games which provide source material for a larger number of episodes. Set-up costs are reduced by following the game show model of recording several episodes in a single session. If the style of commentary is based on comic improvisation, there may be no further pre-production work required. Other approaches might require a degree of rehearsal – playing the game a number of times before recording. To capture authentic reactions and improvised humour in the commentary, producers may play the game one or two times. Those who want the commentary to provide background information or highlight subtle details of the gameplay, may rehearse playing the game much more.

Producers also differ in the degree to which they intervene in the process of the gameplay. Each episode may simply involve completing a sequence or level of the game. If a more comedic approach is preferred, players may set themselves challenges, akin to those in a game show format, attempting to play the game "against the clock" (completing a level as fast as possible, or a whole game in one sitting) (Sylvestre, 2017).

If the game has been rehearsed in detail, and the producer has developed an idea of exactly how they want the game footage to look, a final stage might be in blocking out the action of the character(s) and the "camera" movements, to plot out the shot sizes and exactly how the characters should move around the terrain, take on challenges, make decisions etc. This approach (which is closer to the production of machinima films) is unusual, because it privileges quality over the requirements the platform makes for a volume of content to achieve audience aggregation. But at the minimum, this might involve identifying a narrative "end" to the episode (if the level does not have a natural conclusion) rather than simply stopping the game at a randomly chosen point.

Since commentary is the core of the user generated element of production, most producers give some thought to ensuring they make their commentaries sufficiently varied to ensure each episode is individually differentiated. Although writing a detailed script is very rare, many producers plan talking points for the commentary: "make sure you have some interesting conversation points. Make a rough outline (in your head, if not paper) of what you want to say" (EatingSteak, 2018). Engaging in this kind of pre-production may help ensure the quality of the "as live" performance if the unexpected happens: "(if) you die right before a save point and have to replay the level – might be a good time to bring up some history of the series, or what got you into the game in the first place" (ibid.). The alternative to this pre-production is to spend time in post-production recording commentary to cover these sections. In keeping with the series format most letsplays contain a brief introduction to the episode and end with some form of preview or promotion of the next episode and a personalised "sign-off" message.

Most producers record each episode "as live" and, in narrative games, in story order – similar to a sitcom or soap opera. The recording process itself is more akin to a studio recording of a magazine show. Since the design has reduced most of the task variability in the visual elements of studio production, the set-up times of the camera, lighting and set are reduced to a minimum, and this set-up is fixed for the duration of the recording. The focus of the recording section is therefore on the main variable element of the recording – the audio commentary (Sylvestre, 2017). Here, the process resembles that of voice actors recording dialogue for animated films. The set-up therefore has to ensure the quality of the voice recording, setting recording levels to maximise the volume of the voice, compared to the ambient sound (of the room, game equipment, street sounds etc.) without being so loud as to distort the signal. Following the recording, the priority is in editing the audio commentary to include the most entertaining elements and to ensure this sound is as clear and listenable as possible removing "ums" and "ahs" and any problems of microphone technique (lip smacks, "pops" etc.). "A big part of the 'product' that you're selling with a let's play is your audio, your voice. It is worth your while to spend some time on it" (Unclefuz, 2018).

Editing the video involves the potentially complex process of synchronising the various video and audio inputs. On screen, the gameplay footage must link with the input of the face-cam and these video inputs must be synchronised with the audio inputs from the game capture and the commentary recording. The final edit, requires transitions between sections of game and face-cam video, and post-production with the addition of music and graphics. Final quality control involves watching a playback of the whole video before uploading to YouTube.

The final element involves the packaging and promotion of the video to build the audience. This means choosing an appropriate thumbnail image – the still from the video, which viewers will see before they click to play – and giving the video an appropriately attractive title (Sylvestre, 2017).

Clearly many UGC producers take great pride in their videos and their channels. Their choice of games, the way they interact with them, the commentary they provide and the skills they devote to producing the final film are a form of self-expression, a "vernacular creativity" (Burgess, 2006). Letsplay producers are part of a community with other producers and with their own fans. Digitisation has enabled them, rather than passively consuming media games, to become active fans, helping to create a "remix culture" (Lessig, 2008) or "participatory culture" (Jenkins, 1992). For some, this fan activity translates into digital entrepreneurship, as they become start-up media businesses providing niche content to a target audience.

A key question concerns how general this experience is. Many writers have seen successful digital entrepreneurs like PewDiePie as evidence of the broader transition to a "new economy" of niche markets, micro-businesses and peer production (see Leadbeater, 2009). The "crowdsourcing" relationship between the digital majors and these small "producers" (see Tapscott and Williams, 2008) bears strong similarities to the ideas of flexible specialisation (or post-Fordism) often advanced to explain change in other media industries.

However, this captures only parts of the experience of UGC production. As noted, a digital major like YouTube exercises quasi-monopoly power in the digital video advertising market. Their platform model does not rely on a dominant cultural design, instead they exploit any media products which aggregate audiences and so generate audience data. YouTube systems and MCNs encourage digital entrepreneurs to aggregate content to generate audiences and data. YouTube builds this into its contract via the YPP, which requires UGC producers to have achieved 4,000 hours of video views in 12 months, and to have attracted and retained 1,000 subscribers. YouTube's discourse, expressed through its Creator Academy, and that of some of its MCNs, continually encourages producers to output a large volume of videos and to maintain that production on a regular basis. The influence of this discourse is evident in the letsplayers' descriptions of their production practices. Many are working to sustain what is effectively a broadcast schedule, planning their recording days in order to meet the demand to continually produce and upload new videos on regular days at regular times. Most attempt to cover holiday periods and other times of absence by increasing production further, to create an inventory which can then be uploaded on schedule.

Some UGC producers (like Rooster Teeth) generate sufficient revenue, and have sufficient technical and business skills, to escape this dependent relationship and establish their own independent production companies, winning contracts from brands, TV companies and even Hollywood studios. However, the majority remain working on the YouTube platform, attempting to aggregate sufficient content and audiences to generate income. Inevitably, some writers have seen this regularised high-volume production system, not in terms of a "participatory" culture, but in terms of the mass production of culture, controlled by large commercial organisations. Thus Freedman (2012:88) sees "produsage" as a continuation of this system of production irrespective of "whether it is one based on Fordist assembly lines or digital networks". Instead, we might see UGC production for YouTube as an outcome of the coevolution of the platform-based online sector with the media industries, facilitated by the development of digital technologies. UGC producers constitute a vast pool of skilled freelance labour working on a more or less casualised basis.

CONCLUSIONS
Creativity and innovation in media production

In describing exchanges between media theorists and media practitioners, the term conflict is more appropriate than "debate", because each side rejected the competence of the other. Practitioners like Weddle (2003) rejected the obscure language of theorists, holding such theories to be irrelevant to the "nuts and bolts" of media production. Theorists like Hall (1982) argued that it is precisely this "nuts and bolts" knowledge of practice which is the problem. The purpose of media theory, from this perspective, is to demonstrate the ideological role of media production techniques – through the presence of discourses in texts, or through the process of "reception". From this perspective the purpose of teaching media production, if it must be taught, is to deconstruct the ways these production techniques ("signifying practices") produce ideology.

If we accept Maras's (2005) analysis, that this conflict is a problem which media and film schools need to address, then a necessary first step is to move from this state of conflict to one of constructive debate. To do this requires a theoretical explanation of the role of production knowledge which goes beyond portraying media producers as either cogs in a mass production machine or unwitting proponents of a dominant ideology. As Cottle (2007:5) noted, in relation to news reporting, "too often, it seems, journalists are patronised by academics who assume that they alone have an omniscient insight into such difficult representational issues and/or who fail to recognise the range of practitioner's views on offer". This book has attempted to articulate a theory which recognises the competence of both theorists and practitioners. The aim has been to provide a set of concepts and an explanatory theory which can enable a critical debate – on campuses, in production studios and newsrooms and in industry and academic publications – about changes in media industries, regulations, products and production practices. This concluding chapter tries to show how theorists and practitioners could begin to debate some of the key issues – particularly creativity, innovation, convergence and precarity of employment – in media production.

The theories of media production described in the introduction and Chapter 1 have a range of different implications for creativity in media production. The introduction outlined a number of theories of creativity in media production (but for a fuller review see Dwyer, 2015a) including those arguing that media products are homogenised, standardised commodities produced through mass production or bureaucratic organisation. Further accounts suggested a transformation from this mass media production to the production of innovative media products by networks of small businesses. The introduction also briefly addressed theories which argue that media producers are unwittingly engaged in the production of ideology. To outline an alternative to these theories of media production, this book began by drawing on economic theory, to highlight the apparent paradox that where media theorists see standardisation, homogenisation and ideological conformity, economists see media products as highly differentiated, unlike the products and services produced by almost any other industries. Evolutionary economics and rhetorical text type theory then provided the basis for an alternative account, which described the emergence not of standardised products, or purely unique products, but dominant designs providing broad and general guides for producers and audiences. The individual chapters have detailed how these designs formed the basis for the evolution of the media industries, becoming central to the business strategies of media organisations, institutionalised in regulations and technologies and adopted as the core knowledge of media producers.

The standard elements of these dominant designs were explained neither as the capitalist process of standardising commodities for mass production nor as the role of state apparatuses in ensuring ideological conformity. Instead, following rhetorical text type theory, it was argued that the standardisation of some elements of these "coherence structures" was crucial in their effectiveness as means of communication. The chapters illustrated that a key element in the success of a new media product design was its ability to communicate meaning and hold the attention of audiences in ways which audiences judge to be superior to available alternatives. Thus, the design of the feature film succeeded, in part, because French and Italian film-makers innovated a media product which audiences judged superior to the alternatives (live theatre and one-reelers). While the established US film industry (the MPPC) sought to protect their market in nickelodeon films, a group of entrepreneurs recognised the market demand for the feature and built an industry around this design.

This is not to suggest that the standardised designs and the related production techniques were determined solely by the concerns of communicative coherence. In the evolution of each of the media industries, after a period of innovation and experimentation, the adoption of one or more dominant designs became the basis for volume production of media products. In each case (one-reelers, features, B-movies, radio and TV soaps, sitcoms, filmed series, cable and online news, TV formats and letsplay videos) media organisations have attempted to retain audience attention by establishing "habitual viewing" practices, often through the creation of long-running series. The means of achieving such volume production has been explained as the result of a focus, after the adoption of the dominant design, on process innovation. Rather than explaining the resulting production routines as outcomes either of scientific management, or of "ideological state apparatuses", this book has followed Feldman and Pentland (2003) and Nelson and Winter (1982) in proposing an alternative conception of "routines". In this account, routines are understood as a necessary element in the creation of production knowledge. Media businesses and producers learn techniques, templates and "cognitive schema" in the process of solving problems and completing tasks. The spread of such knowledge occurs as a social process ("institutional isomorphism") through which knowledge is codified by media organisations, regulators, industry and professional associations, formal and informal training and the publication of "how to" guides and manuals.

This theory enables an alternative conception of creativity in media production based on a crucial distinction between the dominant design concept, advanced here, and the notions of standardisation, homogeneity and production routines proposed by mass production and cultural studies theories. While a dominant design establishes an overall production task, the individually differentiated nature of media products means this design does not specify how this task should be decomposed, how individual subtasks should be completed, or the necessary inter-dependencies between these subtasks. Process innovations like the continuity script and the format "bible" have reduced task variability compared to their predecessors (the scenario and the ad hoc observational documentary) and provided methods for making the task decomposition more explicit rather than tacit. But these techniques are such a long way from the manufacturing blueprint as to be different in kind. The components of media products – the shot, the headline, the action, the sounds – cannot be specified like the components of a manufactured product. They cannot be produced using "scientific management", but only through the application of (largely tacit) specialist conventions, routines and skills. They cannot be managed through supervision and discipline, only through a discourse. It is this continuing task variability which establishes the continuing importance of creativity in media production. While media producers may not be subverting and replacing the existing dominant designs, their creativity is crucial in realising each new individually differentiated variant. Unlike in a factory, even the most senior media producer cannot specify how a task should be executed. Thus, in every task, even the most junior media producer is required to exercise creativity in the way they apply the skills and knowledge routines they possess. A media worker can produce their *interpretation* of the shot, the performance, the headline, the lighting or sound they believe is required. But only through trial and error and discourse can a senior producer decide if this is the interpretation they want, or if they want changes or a completely new version.

This suggests ways in which theorists, practitioners and students can debate both the effectiveness of the dominant design and the creativity with which producers have approached individual instances. Within the context of journalism education Pöttker (2003:502) begins from the argument that "the inverted pyramid is neither a fortuitous development without real significance nor a straitjacket used merely to discipline the writer, but rather a suitable means of disseminating information in the field of mass communication". The role of debate, therefore, would be to critically explore and assess the "communicative quality and function" of this dominant design. This focus on creativity in applying production knowledge, particularly in achieving various forms of coherence, does not suggest that debates about media production should not address the processes of creating or sustaining ideology. The accounts of production processes given have attempted to show that simply because media production cannot be organised according to "scientific management", creation of media products will always involve a process of discourse. Further, it has been emphasised that this is not a democratic discourse, but takes place within a hierarchical structure.

The short analyses of examples of media products in each of the chapters in this book give a very brief outline of how such study and debate might be conducted. In particular, the aim has been to enable comparisons between different forms of media production. Studying the production of a range of media product types enables comparisons which can help explain the particular nature of each form of production. Thus, the similarities between the production of features and filmed series relate primarily to the similarities in the underlying text type and thus the ability to apply feature techniques to the production of filmed series. This explanation applies to news, documentaries, entertainment formats and some online videos, whose similar text types lead to similar techniques for recording the authentically dramatic or humorous actions of ordinary people or animals. Comparison of radio and TV studio shows, however, illustrates the importance of the original technology, and specifically the inability to edit first audio and then videotape. This necessitated the development of the "as live" method of production, in contrast to the continuity system used for features and filmed series.

A second key subject for debate concerns the question of innovation. Cultural theory does more than "problematise" media practice, it also attempts to identify alternatives – Eisenstein's montage or the French "New Wave" – which might be oppositional to the dominant ideology. This moves the discussion from the question of creativity – in the application of knowledge routines in the creation of features or TV formats – to the potential for subversion of the dominant design and the innovation of alternatives. This book has examined three theories of innovation (as opposed to standardisation) of media products. The first, FS, argues that large media organisations have increased innovation of media products by dismantling mass production and outsourcing (vertical disintegration) to a large number of independent producers, suppliers or freelancers. The evidence supporting this argument in each of the media industries was addressed. It was argued that media production never remotely resembled mass production or Fordism. For example, the studios did not only use their own "in-house" stars, or refuse to contract out their stars to other companies. Nor did they show only their own features at their "owned" cinemas. Further, it was noted that no historic moment of change (from integration to disintegration of media production) can be identified. For example, just as UK broadcasters were disintegrating production to independents, the US networks were merging with Hollywood studios to create vertically integrated producer-broadcasters. Finally, no evidence was found that outsourcing produced superior innovation of media products than vertical integration. Rather than creating a "marketplace of ideas", vertical disintegration in the UK presented these US corporations with an opportunity to enter the UK TV production market by integrating independent producers into their global production and distribution networks.

The second theory suggested an economic logic for outsourcing particular forms of creative work. Transaction cost economics begins from the premise that disintegrated production, because it follows market signals, is more efficient than integrated production. Caves (2000) argues that "simple creativity", the creative work of individual writers or composers etc., is easier to capture in outsourcing contracts than "complex creativity", the creative work of production teams. Some support for this argument was found in the use of freelance correspondents and columnists throughout the history of newspaper production. The disintegration of the production of features, studio shows, filmed series and TV formats also provides some support in the tendency for star "talent" (especially on-screen) to form independent supply companies. This phenomenon has also quickly appeared in UGC production. As we have noted, however, many of these companies have been talent agencies, or have had strong relationships with talent agencies, principally engaged in negotiating ("simple creativity") contracts for star clients, rather than independent producers ("complex creativity").

Rather than a general trend towards more innovative media industry structures, based on outsourcing, the evidence suggests media organisations have used outsourcing and disintegration of production in response to uncertainty about the volume of demand for the dominant design. This argument follows Barrera (2014) in suggesting that when media organisations are faced with an urgent need to produce products in volume (often in the early period after the adoption of the dominant design) they are likely to produce "in-house". In periods when this demand declines (often after the emergence of a potential substitute), media organisations face greater uncertainty, they are more likely to outsource. Rather than achieving innovation by outsourcing to a large number of small producers (a "marketplace of ideas"), the pattern – in both UK and US TV for example – was to outsource to large companies, most of whom became integrated into Hollywood-based global media corporations. Rather than innovation, the key advantage of outsourcing media production, has been the ability to achieve "numerical flexibility", using freelance or casualised staff to match labour costs more closely to peaks and troughs in production.

This book has proposed evolutionary economics, and the industry life cycle, as an alternative to these theories of innovation. This theory suggests that opportunities for successful innovation in the media industries are more limited than might be apparent from a theoretical analysis of their texts. The account of the evolution of these industries has attempted to show how the adoption of a dominant design forms the basis of market control strategies which create barriers to entry by producers with innovative alternative designs. This means that dominant designs may continue to be successful even if they are inferior to available alternatives. As Ryfe (2006:140) notes, in connection with the "inverted pyramid" and its associated techniques;

> it is perfectly possible for an inefficient set of routines to take hold very early on over time, these routines generate identities, behaviors, roles, and values that are seen as appropriate. These norms may crowd out alternative ways of practicing journalism – even if those alternatives might respond more efficiently to exogenous pressures.

The industry life cycle approach suggests historical moments when innovation is most likely to succeed. During periods of disruption (particularly following technological discontinuities), large businesses producing dominant designs have fewer advantages over small competitors with alternative innovations. Efforts to innovate a new dominant design may encourage greater use of "functional flexibility" – bringing in bespoke production skills or technologies and putting new teams together – which may give small firms a temporary advantage. Thus, French and Italian producers successfully innovated the feature design, against the resistance of the dominant film producers.

In addition to the industry life cycle, an alternative avenue for innovation was the coevolution of two media industries. Chapters 3 and 5, for example, outlined occasions when US commercial media were the drivers of innovation in UK broadcasting and newspapers respectively. But coevolution often occurs after the emergence of a new competitor industry. This book has traced the ways each of the media industries has been impacted by technological discontinuities facilitating the rise of new industries, causing substitution and disruption. This has then been followed by innovation in the existing industry. The emergence of film caused audiences to substitute film for live entertainment, TV substituted for film and radio, cable and satellite substituted for TV, internet and social media substituted for TV and newspapers. Each of these substitutions has prompted innovations (the blockbuster film, the TV format) in the impacted industry.

These industry level comparisons can also illuminate debates about ideology. For example, Kompare (2006), Crisell (2012) and others have suggested that the broadcasters and their regulators subscribed to an "ideology of liveness" preferring live studio shows to available recorded programming. Chapters 3 and 4 presented an alternative account, arguing that decisions about live or recorded production reflect technological potentials and the state of evolution of the industry. The limitations of video camera and transmission technologies gave early broadcasting many of the characteristics of a "live" communication system, like the telephone. In the UK, the industry lacked a local film industry to supply recorded dramas. In the US, although the networks were unwilling to take on the costs of production, their market control strategies favoured the "toll booth" model, enabling oligopolistic control of a national advertising market, without the potential for producers of recorded programming to develop competitor networks. As the potential for videorecording and editing increased, production of many studio shows converted to a recorded model, whilst retaining the "as live" production process. Even filmed TV series production, which followed the continuity system for recording features, has largely combined this with the weekly cycle time of studio shows. The technical characteristics of other industries, like film and newspapers, favoured recorded production. While the dominant design of the feature has continued to favour recording, the design of the news report was easily adapted to live TV. The technical characteristics and market control strategies of digital media distributors have moved production of written news reports and UGC forms, like letsplay videos, closer to live or "as live" production. TV formats like *Love Island* attempt to attract audiences to both linear TV and on-demand digital platforms through a hybrid production process which incorporates recording, "as live" and live production.

This conception of coevolution offers an alternative to the idea of a linear process of digital "convergence" in understanding the current changes in media industries. Like previous technological discontinuities, digitisation has enabled coevolution of the media industries with each other, with other cultural industries (such as live entertainment) and with digital industries (such as games and information technology). As in earlier eras, this creates the potential for innovation and also integration or disintegration of media production. This too creates the potential for small companies and startups to become new entrants to the industry, or to suffer a "shake-out" as large companies gain market control. Thus, the oligopolistic market control exercised by the MPPC was undermined by the ability of a group of entrepreneurs (Zukor and others) to recognise the potential of a superior product (the feature film), build a market share and create economic barriers, enabling the studios to establish their own oligopolistic control. A similar process occurred as the US networks lost market share to new cable channels before re-establishing oligopolistic control through vertical integration with the studios and the cable channels. The extent to which digitisation has so reduced barriers to entry as to enable permanent innovation in the media industries is a further central area for debate. It remains to be seen whether the current oligopolistic control of online advertising, exercised by the digital majors, will face successful new entrants. A crucial element here may be the continuing challenges to the legitimacy of the digital majors – whether over intellectual property, privacy, editorial control or taxation.

This account of media production is, necessarily a work-in-progress, the start of a debate, an aid to future research, rather than a definitive account. The aim has been to develop an explanation of media production which connects the different analytical levels outlined in the introduction: micro (production studies/ethnography), meso (organisational studies) and macro (industries/economy) (see Murdock and Golding, 2016). This has limited the space available for more detailed study of production processes. The potential exists for future research to engage in detailed studies (of individual productions, series, newsrooms etc.) which can identify the relationships with organisational and industry levels, without requiring detailed accounts of these elements. By engaging in debate with practitioners, such production studies would add to the integration of theory and practice and thus extend the breadth and depth of the education offered by media and film schools.

REFERENCES

ACE (2018) *The Threat of Online Piracy* The Alliance for Creativity and Entertainment

Abernathy, P. (2016) *The Rise of a New Media Baron* Center for Innovation and Sustainability in Local Media, University of North Carolina Chapel Hill

Adler, M. (2006) 'Stardom and Talent' in Ginsberg, V. and Throsby, V. (Eds.) *Handbook of the Economics of Art and Culture* (Vol. 1), 895–906. Amsterdam: Elsevier

Adorno, T. (2001) *The Culture Industry* Abingdon: Routledge

Aksoy, A. and Robins, K. (1992) 'Hollywood for the 21st Century' *Cambridge Journal of Economics*, *16*(1), 1–22

Albarran, A. (2016) *The Media Economy* London: Routledge

Albarran, A., Chan-Olmsted, S. and Wirth, M. (Eds.) (2006) *Handbook of Media Management and Economics* Mahwah: Lawrence Erlbaum

Albera, F. (2012) 'First Discourses on Film and the Construction of a "Cinematic Episteme"' in Gaudreault, A., Du Lac, N. and Hidalgo, S. (Eds.) *A Companion to Early Cinema*, 119–40. Hoboken: John Wiley & Sons

Allen, L. (1952) 'Filming the I Love Lucy Show' *American Cinematographer* January Available from www.lucyfan.com/filmingthe.html (Accessed 5/1/19)

Allen, R. (1985) *Speaking of Soap Operas* Chapel Hill: University of North Carolina Press

Althaus, S. (2010) 'The Forgotten Role of the Global Newsreel Industry in the Long Transition from Text to Television' *The International Journal of Press/Politics*, *15*(2), 193–218

Alvarado, M., Buonanno, M., Gray, H. and Miller, T. (Eds.) (2014) *The Sage Handbook of Television Studies* London: Sage

Alvarado, M. and Stewart, J. (1985) *Made for Television* London: Thames Methuen British Film Institute Publishing

Alvarado, M. and Buscombe, E. (1982) *Hazell: The Making of a Television Series* London: British Film Institute

American Film Institute (1988) *Catalog of Motion Pictures 1911–1920* Berkeley: University of California Press

Anderson, C. (2007) *The Long Tail* London: Random House

Anderson, C. (1994) *Hollywood TV* Austin: University of Texas Press

Andrejevic, M. (2014) 'When Everyone Has Their Own Reality Show' in Ouellette, L. (Ed.) *A Companion to Reality Television*, 40–56. Hoboken: John Wiley & Sons

Anello, D. and Cahill, R. (1963) 'Legal Authority of the FCC to Place Limits on Broadcast Advertising Time' *Journal of Broadcasting & Electronic Media*, 7(4), 285–303.

Arnold, D. and Bongiovi, J. R. (2013) 'Precarious, Informalizing, and Flexible Work' *American Behavioral Scientist*, 57(3), 289–308

Aslama, M. and Pantti, M. (2006) 'Talking Alone: Reality TV, Emotions and Authenticity' *European Journal of Cultural Studies*, 9(2), 167–84

Bakewell, J. and Garnham, N. (1970) *The New Priesthood* London: Allen Lane

Bakker, G. (2012a) 'The Quality Race' in Neale, S. (Ed.) *The Classical Hollywood Reader*, 31–42. Abingdon: Routledge

Bakker, G (2012b) 'How Motion Pictures Industrialized Entertainment' *The Journal of Economic History*, 72(4), 1036–63

Bakker, G. (2005) 'The Decline and Fall of the European Film Industry: Sunk Costs, Market Size, and Market Structure, 1890–1927' *The Economic History Review*, 58(2), 310–51

Balio, T. (1993) *Grand Design: Hollywood as a Modern Business Enterprise, 1930–1939* (Vol. 5) New York: Scribner

Balio, T. (Ed.) (1990) 'New Producers for Old' in Balio, T. (Ed.) *Hollywood in the Age of Television* Boston: Unwin Hyman

Balshofer, F. and Miller, A. (1967) *One Reel a Week* Berkeley: University of California Press

Banks, M. (2010) 'Craft Labour and Creative Industries' *International Journal of Cultural Policy*, 16(3), 305–21

Banks, M., Gill, R. and Taylor, S. (Eds.) (2014) *Theorizing Cultural Work* London: Routledge

Bantz, C., McCorkle, S. and Baade, R. (1980) 'The News Factory' *Communication Research*, 7(1), 45–68

Barker, D. (1991) 'The Emergence of Television's Repertoire of Representation, 1920–1935' *Journal of Broadcasting & Electronic Media*, 35(3), 305–18

Barnatt, C. and Starkey, K. (1997) 'Flexible Specialization and the Reconfiguration of Television Production in the UK' *Technology Analysis & Strategic Management*, 9(3), 271–86

Barnett, J. (2018) 'The Costs of Free' *Journal of Institutional Economics*, 14(6), 1097–120

Barnhurst, K. G. (2005) 'News Ideology in The Twentieth Century' in Høyer, S. and Pöttker, H. (Eds.) *Diffusion of the News Paradigm 1850–2000*, 239–62. Göteborg: Nordicom

Barnouw, E. (1968) *A History of Broadcasting in the United States: The Golden Web: 1933 to 1953* (Vol. 2) New York: Oxford University Press

Barrera, C. (2014) 'Skill, Job Design, and the Labor Market Under Uncertainty' PhD dissertation Harvard University

Barthel, M. (2017) 'Despite Subscription Surges for Largest U.S. Newspapers, Circulation and Revenue Fall for Industry Overall' *Fact Tank* Pew Research Center 1 June www.pewresearch.org/fact-tank/2017/06/01/circulation-and-revenue-fall-for-newspaper-industry/ (Accessed 7/9/18)

Batchelor, J. (2017) 'Uncharted Series Sales Pass 41 Million' Gamesindustry.biz 11 December www.gamesindustry.biz/articles/2017-12-11-uncharted-series-sales-passes-41-million (Accessed 14/2/19)

Baudry, J. and Williams, A. (1974) 'Ideological Effects of the Basic Cinematographic Apparatus' *Film Quarterly*, 28(2), 39–47

Baughman, J. (2007) *Same Time, Same Station* Baltimore: John Hopkins University Press

Baughman, J. (1997) 'Show Business in the Living Room' *Business and Economic History*, 26(2), 718–26

Beattie, K. (2004) 'Up Close and Personal' in Beattie, K. (Ed.) *Documentary Screens* London: Palgrave

Bechky, B. (2006) 'Gaffers, Gofers, and Grips' *Organization Science*, *17*(1), 3–21

Becker, H. (1982) *Art Worlds* Berkeley: University of California Press

Beckert, J. (2010) 'Institutional Isomorphism Revisited' *Sociological Theory*, *28*(2), 150–66

Benedict, M. and Ogden, J. (2002) 'Market Structure and Employee Relations: An Analysis of the Newspaper Industry' *Journal of Legal Studies in Business*, *9*, 99–134

Bennett, J., Kerr, P. and Strange, N. (2013) 'Cowboys or Indies?' *Critical Studies in Television*, *8*(1), 108–30

Berlyne, D. (1974) *Studies in the New Experimental Aesthetics* New York: Hemisphere

Berry, D. (1993) 'USA Today, the London Free Press and the Rationalization of the North American Newspaper Industry' PhD dissertation Concordia University

Bielby, D. and Harrington, C. L. (2008) *Global TV* New York: New York University Press

Bielby, W. and Bielby, D. (2003) 'Controlling Prime-Time' *Journal of Broadcasting & Electronic Media*, *47*(4), 573–96

Bielby, W. and Bielby, D. (1994) 'All Hits Are Flukes' *American Journal of Sociology*, *99*(5), 1287–313

Bignell, J. (2009) *The Police Series* London: Wallflower

Bignell, J. (2005) *Big Brother: Reality TV in the Twenty-First Century* Basingstoke: Palgrave Macmillan

Biressi, A. and Nunn, H. (2005) *Reality TV* London: Wallflower Press

Biskind, P. (2007) 'An American Family' *Vanity Fair* April 2007 www.vanityfair.com/news/2007/04/sopranos200704 (Accessed 5/1/19)

Boddy, W. (1993) *Fifties Television* Urbana: University of Illinois Press

Boddy, W. (1985) 'The Studios Move into Prime Time' *Cinema Journal*, *24*(4), 23–37

Bold, B. (2017) 'Google and Facebook Dominate over Half of Digital Media Market' *Campaign* 18 September 2017_www.campaignlive.co.uk/article/google-facebook-dominate-half-digital-media-market/1444793 (Accessed 13/1/19)

Boltz, I. and Clemen, W. (2013) *Shakespeare's Soliloquies* London: Methuen

Bordwell, D., Staiger, J. and Thompson, K. (Eds.) (1985) *The Classical Hollywood Cinema* London: Routledge

Born, G. (2004) *Uncertain Vision* London: Secker & Warburg

Bounie, D., Valérie, M. and Quinn, M. (2017) 'Do You See What I See?' *SSRN Electronic Journal* Available from SSRN: https://ssrn.com/abstract=2854265 (Accessed 5/1/19)

Boyd-Barrett, O. and Rantanen, T. (Eds.) (1998) *The Globalization of News* London: Sage

Boyle, E. (2003) 'When Industry Recipes Change, Who Gets Cooked?' Submitted to the Strategic Management/Entrepreneurship Track of the *Southern Management Association* 2003 Meeting

Braverman, H. (1974) *Labor and Monopoly Capital* New York: New York University Press

Briggs, A. (1965) *Golden Age of Wireless* Oxford: Oxford University Press

Brook, V. (1998) 'Checks and Imbalances' *Journal of Film and Video*, *50*(3), 24–39

Brookey, R. (2010) *Hollywood Gamers* Bloomington: Indiana University Press

Budzinski, O. and Gaenssle, S. (2018) 'The Economics of Social Media Stars' *Ilmenau Economics Discussion Papers*, *21*(112), 1–37

Bughin, J., Doogan, J. and Vetvik, O. (2010) 'A New Way to Measure Word-of-Mouth Marketing' *McKinsey Quarterly*, *2*, 113–16

Burch, N. (1979) 'Film's Institutional Mode of Representation and the Soviet Response' *October, 11 (Winter)*, 77–96

Burgess, J., Green, J. and Jenkins, H. (2013) *YouTube* Oxford: Wiley

Burgess, J. (2006) 'Hearing Ordinary Voices' *Continuum, 20*(2), 201–14

Butler, J. (2012) *Television: Critical Methods and Applications* London: Routledge

Butler, J. (2007) *Television Style* London: Routledge

Cakebread, C. (2017) 'Millennials Watching Less TV than Previous Generations' *Business Insider* http://uk.businessinsider.com/millennials-watching-less-tv-than-previous-generations-chart-2017-8 (Accessed 7/9/18)

Caldwell, J. (2008) *Production Culture* Durham: Duke University Press

Caldwell, J. (2006) 'Critical Industrial Practice' *Television & New Media, 7*(2), 99–134

Caldwell, J. (1995) *Televisuality* New Brunswick: Rutgers University Press

Campbell-Kelly, M., Garcia-Swartz, D., Lam, R. and Yang, Y. (2015) 'Economic and Business Perspectives on Smartphones as Multi-Sided Platforms' *Telecommunications Policy, 39*(8), 717–34

Campling, J. (1995) 'From Rigid to Flexible Employment Practices in UK Commercial Television' *New Zealand Journal of Industrial Relations, 20*(1), 1–22

Camporesi, V. (1990) 'We Talk a Different Language' *Historical Journal of Film, Radio and Television, 10*(3), 257–74

Camporesi, V. (1989) 'Mass Culture and the Defence of National Traditions' PhD dissertation European University Institute

Cantor, M. (1982) 'The Organization and Production of Primetime Television' in Pearl, D., Bouthilet, L. and Lazar, J. (Eds.) *Television and Behavior*, 349–62. Bethesda: National Institute of Mental Health

Cardwell, S. (2007) 'Is Quality Television Any Good?' in McCabe, J. and Akass, K. (Eds.) *Quality TV*. London: IB Tauris

Casau, G. and Garin, M. (2015) 'Between Film and Television. An Interview with Lodge Kerrigan' *Comparative Cinema, 3*(7), 28–34

Cater, D. and Adler, R. (Eds.) (1975) *Television as a Social Force* New York: Praeger

Cattani, G., Ferriani, S., Frederikse, L. and Taube, F. (2011) *Project-Based Organizing and Strategic Management* Bingley: Emerald Group Publishing Limited

Caves, R. (2006) 'Organization of Arts and Entertainment Industries' in Ginsberg, V. and Throsby, V. (Eds.) *Handbook of the Economics of Art and Culture* (Vol. 1), 533–66. Amsterdam: Elsevier

Caves, R. (2005) *Switching Channels* Cambridge: Harvard University Press

Caves, R. (2000) *Creative Industries* Cambridge: Harvard University Press

Chalaby, J. (2016a) *The Format Age* Cambridge: Polity Press

Chalaby, J. (2016b) 'Drama Without Drama' *Television & New Media, 17*(1), 3–20

Chalaby, J. (2012) 'At the Origin of a Global Industry' *Media, Culture & Society, 34*(1), 36–52

Chalaby, J. (2011) 'The Making of an Entertainment Revolution' *European Journal of Communication, 26*(4), 293–309

Chalaby, J. (2015) 'The Advent of the Transnational TV Format Trading System' *Media, Culture & Society, 37*(3), 460–78

Chandler, D (2007) *Semiotics: The Basics* London: Routledge

Chapman, J. (2002) *Saints and Avengers* London: IB Tauris

Chase, D. (2009) *The Sopranos* New York: Warner Books

Chirita, A. (2017) 'Competition and Regulatory Trends in Digital Markets' *Competition Law Review, 12*(2) 119–30

Chisholm, D. C. (1993) 'Asset Specificity and Long-Term Contracts' *Eastern Economic Journal, 19*(2), 143–55

Chinoy E. (1982) 'Control and Resistance on the Assembly Line' in Giddens, A. and Mackenzie, G. (Eds.) *Social Class and the Division of Labour*, 87–100. Cambridge: Cambridge University Press Archive

Chouinard, A. (2017) 'From Fan Videos to Crowdsourcing' PhD dissertation Concordia University

Chris, C. (2002) 'All Documentary, All the Time?' *Television & New Media*, *3*(1), 7–28

Christensen, C. (1997) *The Innovator's Dilemma* Boston: Harvard Business Review Press

Christian, A. (2018a) 'How YouTube Blew It' *LA Review of Books* 19 January https://lareviewofbooks.org/article/how-youtube-blew-it/ (Accessed 7/9/18)

Christian, A. (2018b) *Open TV* New York: New York University Press

Christopherson, S. (2011) 'Hard Jobs in Hollywood' in Winseck, D. and Jin, D. (Eds.) *The Political Economies of Media*, 23–141. London: Bloomsbury Publishing

Cinemetrics.lv www.cinemetrics.lv/movie.php?movie_ID=7472 (Accessed 7/9/18)

Citywire ITV plc http://citywire.co.uk/money/share-prices-and-performance/share-factsheet.aspx?InstrumentID=79321 (Accessed 8/1/18)

Cohen, S. and Young, J. (Eds.) (1981) *The Manufacture of News* London: Constable

Conor, B. (2014) 'Hired Hands, Liars, Schmucks' in Banks, M., Gill, R. and Taylor, S. (Eds.) *Theorizing Cultural Work*, 58–69. London: Routledge

Constine, J. (2015) 'YouTube Red Subscription Will Include Original Series from PewDiePie, CollegeHumor, And More' *TechCrunch* https://techcrunch.com/2015/10/21/youtube-original/?_ga=2.76056208.44629621.1534942839-1708843793.1533679325 (Accessed 13/2/19)

Cooper, J. (2017) Interactive Cinematics in *Uncharted 4* Twitch Animation Exchange February 2017 Available from www.gameanim.com/2018/03/09/interactive-cinematics-in-uncharted-4/ (Accessed 7/9/18)

Copeland, G. (2007) 'A History of Television Style' in Butler, J. (Ed.) *Television Style*, 253–84. London: Routledge

Coppola, S. (1991) *Hearts of Darkness* (American Zoetrope)

Corner, J. (1999) *Critical Ideas in Television Studies* Oxford: Clarendon Press

Corner, J. (1996) *The Art of Record* Manchester: Manchester University Press

Cornfield, D. (Ed.) (1987) *Workers, Managers, and Technological Change* Boston: Springer

Cottle S. (2007) 'Ethnography and News Production' *Sociology Compass*, *1*(1), 1–16

Courtney, J. C. and Smith, D. E. (Eds.) (2010) *The Oxford Handbook of Canadian Politics* New York: Oxford University Press

Couldry, N. and Curran, J. (Eds.) (2003) *Contesting Media Power* Lanham: Rowman & Littlefield

Cox, J. (1999) *The Great Radio Soap Operas* Jefferson: McFarland

Crisell, A. (2012) *Liveness and Recording in the Media* Basingstoke: Palgrave Macmillan

Crisell, A. (2002) *An Introductory History of British Broadcasting* London: Routledge

Cunningham, S. and Craig, D. (2017) 'Being "Really Real" on YouTube' *Media International Australia*, *164* (1), 71–81

Cunningham, S., Craig, D. and Silver, J. (2016) 'YouTube, Multichannel Networks and the Accelerated Evolution of the New Screen Ecology' *Convergence*, *22*(4), 376–91

Curran, J., Fenton, N. and Freedman, D. (Eds.) (2012) *Misunderstanding the Internet*, 73–98. Abingdon: Routledge

Curran, J. and Seaton, J. (2009) *Power Without Responsibility* London: Routledge

Curtin, M. and Sanson, K. (2014) 'The Division of Labor in Television' in Alvarado, M., Buonanno, M., Gray, H. and Miller, T. (Eds.) *The Sage Handbook of Television Studies*, 133–43. London: Sage

Darlow, M. (2004) *Independents Struggle* London: Quartet Books

Davis, J. (1991) *TV UK: A Special Report* Peterborough: Peterborough Knowledge Research

DCMS (2006) *A Public Service All: The BBC in The Digital Age* White Paper London: DCMS

DCMS (2005) *Review of the BBC's Royal Charter* London: DCMS

Department of National Heritage (DNH) (1995) *Media Ownership: The Government's Proposals* London: HMSO

Deakin, S., Lourenço, A. and Pratten, S. (2004) 'The Liberalisation of British Television Production', Centre for Business Research, Judge Institute of Management, University of Cambridge July

DeFillippi, R., Grabher, G. and Jones, C. (2007) 'Introduction to Paradoxes of Creativity' *Journal of Organizational Behavior, 28*(5), 511–21

DeMaria, R. and Wilson, J. (2002) *High Score!* Berkeley: McGraw-Hill/Osborne

Dertouzos, J. and Quinn, T. (1985) *Bargaining Responses to the Technology Revolution* Rand Corporation

De Vany, A. (2004) *Hollywood Economics* London: Routledge

Ding, Y., Du, Y., Hu, Y., Liu, Z., Wang, L., Ross, K. and Ghose, A. (2011) 'Broadcast Yourself' *Proceedings of the 2011 ACM SIGCOMM Conference on Internet Measurement Conference* ACM

DMN (2015) '10 Stats That Show Why User Generated Content Works' www.dmnews.com/content-marketing/blog/13042512/10-stats-that-show-why-usergenerated-content-works (Accessed 7/9/18)

Dolata, U. (2017) *Apple, Amazon, Google, Facebook, Microsoft* (No. 2017–01) SOI Discussion Paper

Dopfer, K. and Potts, J. (2008) *The General Theory of Economic Evolution* Oxford: Routledge

Dosi, G. (1982) 'Technological Paradigms and Technological Trajectories' *Research Policy, 11*(3), 147–62

Downing, J. D., McQuail, D., Schlesinger, P. and Wartella, E. (Eds.) (2004) *The SAGE Handbook of Media Studies* Thousand Oaks: Sage

Doyle, G. (2002) *Understanding Media Economics* London: Sage

Dubrofsky, R. (2014) 'The Bachelorette's Postfeminist Therapy' in Ouellette, L. (Ed.) *A Companion to Reality Television*, 189–207. Hoboken: John Wiley & Sons

Dwyer, P. (2016) 'Understanding Media Production: A Rejoinder to Murdock and Golding' *Media, Culture & Society, 38*(8), 1–4

Dwyer, P. (2015a) 'Managing Creativity in Media Organizations' in Lowe, G. and Brown, C. (Eds.) *Managing Media Firms and Industries*, 343–65. Cham, Switzerland: Springer

Dwyer, P. (2015b) 'Theorizing Media Production: The Poverty of Political Economy' *Media, Culture & Society, 37*(7), 988–1004

Dwyer, P. (2013) 'Online Radio: A Social Media Business' in Friedrichsen, M. and Muhl-Benninghaus, W. (Eds.) *Handbook of Social Media Management*, 455–75. Heidelberg: Springer

Dwyer P. (1989) 'Community Radio' Doctoral Thesis, Imperial College London

EatingSteak (2018) 'Let's Talk About Preproduction' www.reddit.com/r/letsplay/comments/zeg31/lets_talk_about_preproduction/ (Accessed 7/9/18)

Eddy, W. (1945) *Television: The Eyes of Tomorrow* New York: Prentice-Hall

Elliott, P. (1972) *The Making of a Television Series* London: Constable

Ellis, G. (2011) 'A Ghost in the Chair' PhD dissertation University of Auckland

Eng, J. (2018) 'Friends: "The One with the Oral History of the Trivia Game Episode"' *TV Guide* www.tvguide.com/news/friends-oral-history-trivia-game-embryos-episode/ (Accessed 29/8/18)

Esser, A. (2010) 'Television Formats' *Popular Communication, 8*(4), 273–92

Evans, D. (2017) 'Why the Dynamics of Competition for Online Platforms Leads to Sleepless Nights but Not Sleepy Monopolies' *SSRN Abstracts* Available from SSRN: https://ssrn.com/abstract=3009438

Evans, D. (2009) 'The Online Advertising Industry' *Journal of Economic Perspectives, 23*(3), 37–60

Evans, P. and Green, J. (2017) *Eyes Half Shut* (BECTU)

Falkinger, J. (2008) 'Limited Attention as a Scarce Resource in Information-Rich Economies' *The Economic Journal, 118*(532), 1596–620

Farey-Jones, D. (2018) 'TV Hit By First Ad Revenue Drop for Seven Years' *Campaign* 6 March www.campaignlive.co.uk/article/tv-hit-first-ad-revenue-drop-seven-years/1458679 (Accessed 7/9/18)

Faulkner, S., Leaver, A., Vis, F. and Williams, K. (2008) 'Art for Art's Sake or Selling Up?' *European Journal of Communication, 23*(3), 295–317

Feldman, M. and Pentland, B. (2003) 'Reconceptualizing Organizational Routines as a Source of Flexibility and Change' *Administrative Science Quarterly, 48*(1), 94–118

Fell, J. L. (Ed.) (1983) *Film before Griffith* Berkeley: University of California Press

Fenton, N. (Ed.) (2010) *New Media, Old News* London: Sage

Feuer, J., Kerr, P. and Vahimagi, T. (1984) *MTM: Quality Television* London: British Film Institute

Feuer, J. (1983) 'The Concept of Live Television' in Kaplan, E. (Ed.) *Regarding Television* (Vol. 2), 12–22. Frederick: University Publications of America

Fishman, M. (1998) 'Television Reality Crime Programs' in Fishman, M. and Cavender, G. (Eds.) *Entertaining Crime*, 11–24. New York: de Gruyter

Fishman, M. and Cavender, G. (Eds.) (1998) *Entertaining Crime* New York: de Gruyter

Fleming, M. (2013) 'Ridley Scott Partners with Machinima to Develop Episodic Sci-Fi Web Programming' *Deadline Hollywood* 11 March https://deadline.com/2013/03/ridley-scott-partners-with-machinima-to-develop-episodic-sci-fi-web-programming-450812/ (Accessed 13/2/19)

Fligstein, N. and McAdam, D. (2012) *A Theory of Fields* Oxford: Oxford University Press

Fludernik, M. (2000) 'Genres, Text Types, or Discourse Modes?' *Style, 34*(2), 274–92

Forbes (2018) 'Global 2000: The World's Largest Public Companies' *Forbes* 6 June www.forbes.com/global2000/#16d913d335d8 (Accessed 7/9/18)

Freedman, D. (2012) 'Web 2.0 and the Death of the Blockbuster Economy' in Curran, J., Fenton, N. and Freedman, D. (Eds.) *Misunderstanding the Internet*, 73–98. Abingdon: Routledge

Friedrichsen, M. and Muhl-Benninghaus, W. (Eds.) (2013) *Handbook of Social Media Management* Heidelberg: Springer

Fuchs, C. (2016) 'Against Theoretical Thatcherism: A Reply to Nicholas Garnham' *Media, Culture & Society, 38*(2), 301–11

Funk, J. (2012) 'The Unrecognized Connection Between Vertical Disintegration and Entrepreneurial Opportunities' *Long Range Planning, 45*(1), 41–59

Gans, H. (1979) *Deciding What's News* New York: Pantheon

Garnham, N. (2016) 'Review of Fuchs, C. "Digital Labour and Karl Marx"' *Media, Culture & Society, 38*(2), 294–300

Garnham, N. (2011) 'The Political Economy of Communication Revisited' in Wasko, J., Murdock, G. and Sousa, H. (Eds.) *The Handbook of Political Economy of Communications*, 41–61. Chichester: Wiley-Blackwell

Garud, R., Tuertscher, P. and Van de Ven, A. H. (2013) 'Perspectives on Innovation Processes' *Academy of Management Annals*, 7(1), 775–819

Gaudreault, A., Du Lac, N. and Hidalgo, S. (Eds.) (2012) *A Companion to Early Cinema* Hoboken: John Wiley & Sons

Geuens, J. P. (2000) *Film Production Theory* New York: State University of New York Press

Giddens, A. and Mackenzie, G. (Eds.) (1982) *Social Class and the Division of Labour* Cambridge: Cambridge University Press Archive

Gill, P., Erramilli, V., Chaintreau, A., Krishnamurthy, B., Papagiannaki, K. and Rodriguez, P. (2013) 'Follow the Money' *Proceedings of the 2013 Conference on Internet Measurement Conference* ACM, 141–8

Ginsberg, V. and Throsby, V. (Eds.) (2006) *Handbook of the Economics of Art and Culture* (Vol. 1) Amsterdam: Elsevier

Gitlin, T. (1983) *Inside Prime Time* New York: Pantheon

Gleich, J. (2012) 'The Lost Studio of Atlantis' *The Velvet Light Trap, 70*(Fall), 3–17

Goldman, W. (1983) *Adventures in the Screen Trade* London: Futura

Golding, P. and Elliott, P. (1979) *Making the News* London: Longman

Gomery, D. (2007) 'Talent Raids and Package Deals' in Hilmes, M. (Ed.) *NBC: America's Network*, 153–68. Berkeley: University of California Press

Gomery, D. (1996) 'The Hollywood Studio System' in Nowell-Smith, G. (Ed.) *The Oxford History of World Cinema*, 43–53. Oxford: Oxford University Press

Graves, F. and Lee, M. (2017) 'The Law of YouTubers' *Landslide Magazine* May/June ABA Section of Intellectual Property Law Available from SSRN: https://ssrn.com/abstract=2966793

Griffin, N. (2007) 'Inside HBO's *The Wire*' Cinematography Creative COW.net. https://library.creativecow.net/articles/griffin_nick/hbo_the_wire.php (Accessed 7/9/18)

Grindstaff, L. (2002) *The Money Shot* Chicago: University of Chicago Press

Guardian (2018) 'Love Island Did Not Breach Rules Showing Dani Dyer's "Distress"' *The Guardian* 16 July www.theguardian.com/tv-and-radio/2018/jul/16/love-island-did-not-breach-rules-showing-dani-dyer-distress-ofcom-tears-video (Accessed 7/9/18)

Guardian (2007) 'Pact Deputy Fights Suspension' *The Guardian* 14 March www.theguardian.com/media/2007/mar/14/broadcasting.television2 (Accessed 7/9/18)

Gunning, T. (1994) *DW Griffith and the Origins of American Narrative Film* Urbana: University of Illinois Press

Gurevitch, M., Bennett, T., Curran, J. and Woollacott, J. (Eds.) (1982) *Culture, Society, Media* London: Methuen

HMSO (1988) *Broadcasting in the '90s* White Paper London: HMSO

Habermas, J. (1989) *The Structural Transformation of the Public Sphere* Cambridge: MIT Press

Hadida, A. L. (2009) 'Motion Picture Performance' *International Journal of Management Reviews, 11*(3), 297–335

Haefliger, S., Jäger, P. and Von Krogh, G. (2010) 'Under the Radar' *Research Policy, 39*(9), 1198–213

Hall, A. (2014) *Compete and Compare* (BBC) www.bbc.co.uk/mediacentre/speeches/2014/dg-city-university (Accessed 8/1/18)

Hall, S. (1982) 'The Rediscovery of Ideology' in Gurevitch, M., Bennett, T., Curran, J. and Woollacott, J. (Eds.) *Culture, Society, Media*, 52–86. London: Methuen

Hand, R. (2015) *Listen in Terror* Oxford: Oxford University Press

Hannan, M. and Carroll, G. (1992) *Dynamics of Organizational Populations* Oxford: Oxford University Press

Hanson, O. and Morris, R. (1931) 'The Design and Construction of Broadcast Studios' *Proceedings of the Institute of Radio Engineers, 19*(1), 15–34

Harjo, I., Frandsen, T. and Hsuan, J. (2016) 'Servitization, Services and Managing Complexity' in *The 23rd International Annual EurOMA Conference 2016* Available from www.forskningsdatabasen.dk/en/catalog/2349714247

Hark, I. (Ed.) (2002) *Exhibition, the Film Reader* London: Routledge

Harrington, C., Scardaville, M., Lippmann, S. and Bielby, D. D. (2015) 'Soap Operas and Artistic Legitimation' *Communication, Culture & Critique, 8*(4), 613–31

Hartley, J. (2007) 'The Evolution of the Creative Industries', *Proceedings Creative Industries Conference, Asia-Pacific Weeks*, Berlin Available from https://eprints.qut.edu.au/12647/

Harvey, S. (1989) 'Deregulation, Innovation and Channel Four' *Screen, 30*(1–2), 60–79

Hassanabadi, A. (2011) 'Viacom v. YouTube – All Eyes Blind' *Berkeley Technology Law Journal, 26*(1), 405–40

Hawes, W. (2001) *Live Television Drama, 1946–1951* Jefferson: McFarland

Henderson, S. (2017) *The Hollywood Sequel* London: British Film Institute

Hensher, P. (2014) 'So You Want to Be a Writer?' *The Guardian* 14 March www.theguardian.com/books/2014/mar/14/creative-writing-courses-advice-students (Accessed 15/8/18).

Hesmondhalgh, D. and Baker, S. (2011) *Creative Labour* New York: Routledge

Hill, A. (2014) *Reality TV* London: Routledge

Hilmes, M. (2012) *Network Nations* New York: Routledge

Hilmes, M. (Ed.) (2007) *NBC: America's Network* Berkeley: University of California Press

Hilmes, M. and Loviglio, J. (Eds.) (2002) *Radio Reader* New York: Routledge

Hilmes, M. (1999) *Hollywood and Broadcasting* Urbana:University of Illinois Press

Hirsch, P. M. (1972) 'Processing Fads and Fashions' *American Journal of Sociology, 77*(4), 639–59

Hobday, M. (1998) 'Product Complexity, Innovation and Industrial Organisation' *Research Policy, 26*(6), 689–710

Hobson, D. (1982) *Crossroads* London: Methuen

Holloway, H. (1987) 'IT and the UK Newspaper Industry' *Journal of Information Technology, 2*(3), 135–50

Holmes, D. (2006) 'The "Give-Away" Shows – Who Is Really Paying?' *Journal of British Cinema and Television, 3*(2), 284–303

Holmes, S. (2014) 'You Don't Need Influence . . . All You Need Is Your First Opportunity!' *Critical Studies in Television, 9*(1), 23–42

Holt, J. (2011) *Empires of Entertainment* Piscataway: Rutgers University Press

Holt, J. and Perren, A. (Eds.) (2011) *Media Industries* London: John Wiley & Sons

Honthaner, E. (2013) *The Complete Film Production Handbook* Amsterdam: Focal Press

Horwitz, J. (2013) 'Visual Style in the "Golden Age" Anthology Drama' *Cinémas, 23* (2–3), 39–68

Hoskins, C. and Mirus, R. (1988) 'Reasons for the US Dominance of the International Trade in Television Programmes' *Media, Culture & Society, 10*(4), 499–515

House of Lords (2005) Review of the BBC's Royal Charter Stationery Office Ltd

Høyer, S. and Pöttker, H. (2005) *Diffusion of the News Paradigm 1850–2000* Göteborg: Nordicom

Hyatt, W. (2010) *A Critical History of Television's The Red Skelton Show* Jefferson: McFarland

Iosifidis, P. (2016) 'Media Ownership and Concentration in the United Kingdom' in Noam, E. (Ed.) *Who Owns the World's Media?* New York: Oxford University Press

Isaacs, D. (2017) 'Comedy and Corned Beef: The Genesis of the Sitcom Writing Room' in Renov, M. and Brook, V. (Eds.) *From Shtetl to Stardom: Jews and Hollywood* West Lafayette: Purdue University Press

ITV (2019) *2018: A Triumphant Year for Telly* https://www.itvmedia.co.uk/news/2018-a-triumphant-year-for-telly (Accessed 13/2/19)

Jacobs, J. (2000) *The Intimate Screen* Oxford: Oxford University Press

Jacobs, R. (1996) 'Producing the News, Producing the Crisis' *Media, Culture & Society*, *18*(3), 373–97

Jacobson, B. (2011) 'The Black Maria' *History and Technology*, *27*(2), 233–41

Jaske, J. (1981) 'Collective Bargaining Issues in Newspapers' *Hastings Communication and Entertainment Law Journal*, *4*(4), 595–604

Jenkins, H. (2006) *Convergence Culture* New York: New York University Press

Jenkins, H. (1992) *Textual Poachers* New York: Routledge

Jhohnsa, E. (2018) 'How Much Could Google's YouTube Be Worth?' *The Street* 12 May www.thestreet.com/investing/youtube-might-be-worth-over-100-billion-14586599 (Accessed 7/9/18)

Jucker, A. (2005) 'News Discourse' in Skaffari, J., Peikola, M., Carroll, R., Hiltunen, R. and Wårvik, B. (Eds.) *Opening Windows on Texts and Discourses of the Past*, 7–22. Amsterdam:John Benjamins Publishing

Kalleberg, A., Wallace, M., Loscocco, K., Leicht, K. and Ehm, H. (1987) 'The Eclipse of Craft' in Cornfield, D. (Ed.) *Workers, Managers, and Technological Change*, 47–71. Boston: Springer

Kaplan, E. (Ed.) (1983) *Regarding Television* (Vol. 2) Frederick: University Publishers of America

Karlsson, C. and Picard, R. (Eds.) (2011) *Media Clusters* Cheltenham: Edward Elgar Publishing

Kaul, A. (1986) 'The Proletarian Journalist' *Journal of Mass Media Ethics*, *1*(2), 47–55

Keane, M. and Moran, A. (2008) 'Television's New Engines' *Television & New Media*, *9*(2), 155–69

Keith, S. (2015) 'Horseshoes, Stylebooks, Wheels, Poles, and Dummies' *Journalism*, *16*(1), 44–60

Kemper, T. (2010) *Hidden Talent* Berkeley: University of California Press

Kepley Jr V. (1990) 'From "Frontal Lobes" to the "Bob-and-Bob" Show' in Balio, T. (Ed.) *Hollywood in the Age of Television*, 41–62. Boston: Unwin Hyman

Kerrigan, S. and McIntyre, P. (2010) 'The Creative Treatment of Actuality' *Journal of Media Practice*, *11*(2), 111–30

Kerttula, T. (2016) "What an Eccentric Performance" *Games and Culture* (Online First)

Klepper, S. (1997) 'Industry Life Cycles' *Industrial and Corporate Change*, *6*(1), 145–82

Koblin, J. (2017) 'Netflix Says It Will Spend Up to $8 Billion on Content Next Year' *New York Times* 16 October www.nytimes.com/2017/10/16/business/media/netflix-earnings.html (Accessed 7/9/18)

Kolker, R. (Ed.) (2008) *The Oxford Handbook of Film and Media Studies* New York: Oxford University Press

Kompare, D. (2006) *Rerun Nation* New York: Routledge

Koszarski, R. (1994) *An Evening's Entertainment* (Vol. 3) Berkeley: University of California Press

Küng, L. (2008) *Strategic Management in the Media* London: Sage

Lampel, J. (2011) 'Institutional Dynamics of Project-Based Creative Organizations' in Cattani, G., Ferriani, S., Frederikse, L. and Taube, F. (Eds.) *Project-Based Organizing and Strategic Management*, 445–66. Bingley: Emerald Group Publishing Limited

Lampel, J., Shamsie, J. and Lant, T. (2006) 'The Genius Behind the System' in Lampel, J., Shamsie, J. and Lant, T. (Eds.) *The Business of Culture*, 57–72. Mahwah: Lawrence Erlbaum

Lanham, R. (2006) *The Economics of Attention* Chicago: University of Chicago Press

Leadbeater, C. (2009) *We-Think* London: Profile

Leblebici, H., Salancik, G. R., Copay, A. and King, T. (1991) 'Institutional Change and the Transformation of Inter-Organizational Fields' *Administrative Science Quarterly, 36*(3), 333–63

Lee, D. (2012) 'Precarious Creativity' *Creative Industries Journal, 4*(2), 155–70

Lehner, J. (2009) 'The Staging Model' *International Journal of Project Management, 27*(3), 195–205

Lessig, L. (2008) *Remix* New York: Penguin

Levine, E. (2001) 'Toward a Paradigm for Media Production Research' *Critical Studies in Media Communication, 18*(1), 66–82

Liebowitz, S. (2018) *Economic Analysis of Safe Harbor Provisions* Center for the Analysis of Property Rights and Innovation, University of Texas at Dallas

Lin, D. (2007) 'Asset Specificity and Network Control of Television Programs' Doctoral Thesis George Mason University

Lindsay, J. (2018) 'Does Love Island Film Scenes Twice?' *Metro* 13 July https://metro.co.uk/2018/07/13/love-island-film-scenes-twice-7713164/ (Accessed 7/9/18)

Livemint (2017) 'The World's Media Giants, as Far as Ad Revenue Is Concerned' *Livemint* https://www.livemint.com/Companies/QDlyspOkJsdbKmEXXR7IJO/The-worlds-media-giants-as-far-as-ad-revenue-is-concerned.html (Accessed 13/2/19)

Lobato, R. (2016) 'The Cultural Logic of Digital Intermediaries' *Convergence, 22*(4), 348–60

Logan, R. (1986) 'USA Today's Innovations and Their Impact on Journalism Ethics' *Journal of Mass Media Ethics, 1*(2), 74–87

Lotz, A. (2007) *The Television Will Be Revolutionized* New York: New York University Press

Lotz, A. (2004) 'Textual (Im)Possibilities in the U.S. Post-Network Era' *Critical Studies in Media Communication, 21*(1), 22–43

Lowe, G. and Brown, C. (Eds.) (2016) *Managing Media Firms and Industries* Cham, Switzerland: Springer

Lowrey, W. (2012) 'Journalism Innovation and the Ecology of News Production' *Journalism & Communication Monographs, 14*(4), 214–87

McCabe, J. and Akass, K. (Eds.) (2007) *Quality TV: Contemporary American Television and Beyond* London: IB Tauris

McChesney, R. (1995) *Telecommunications, Mass Media, and Democracy* New York: Oxford University Press

McCormack, P. (2017) 'New York to Hollywood' *Senior Projects* Spring 2017, Bard College Available from digitalcommons.bard.edu

McKercher, C. (2002). *Newsworkers Unite* Lanham: Rowman & Littlefield

McKernan, L. (Ed.) (2002) *Yesterday's News* London: Wallflower Press

McKinlay, A. and Quinn, B. (1999) 'Management, Technology and Work in Commercial Broadcasting 1979–98' *New Technology, Work and Employment, 14*(1), 2–17

McKinney, A. (2018) 'Making It Pay to Be a Fan' Doctoral Thesis, The City University of New York

McLeod, E. (2005) *The Original Amos 'n' Andy* Jefferson: McFarland

McNaughton, D. (2014) 'Video Film Recording' *Historical Journal of Film, Radio and Television, 34*(3), 390–404

McNichol, T. and Carlson, M. (1985a) 'A Developer Remodels US News' *Columbia Journalism Review, 24*(2), 31

McNichol, T. and Carlson, M. (1985b) 'Al Neuharth's Technicolor Baby, Part II' *Columbia Journalism Review*, *24*(1), 44

Magna (2018a) 'US TV Industry at a Crossroads' https://magnaglobal.com/us-tv-industry-at-a-crossroads/ (Accessed 7/9/18)

Magna (2018b) *Magna Advertising Forecasts* 21 March 2018 New York

Maier, E. (2013) 'Coordinating Over Time' Doctoral Thesis University of Western Ontario

Maloney, M. (2018) 'General Hospital Turns 55' *Variety* 29 March https://variety.com/2018/tv/features/general-hospital-55th-anniversary-steve-burton-jacklyn-zeman-frank-valentini-interview-1202735231/

Maras, S. (2005) 'The Problem of Theory and Practice' *Journal of Media Practice*, *6*(2), 93–103.

Marengo, L. and Dosi, G. (2005) 'Division of Labor, Organizational Coordination and Market Mechanisms in Collective Problem-Solving' *Journal of Economic Behavior & Organization*, *58*(2), 303–26

Marjoribanks, T. (2000) *News Corporation, Technology and the Workplace* Cambridge: Cambridge University Press

Mashon, M. (2007) 'NBC, J. Walter Thompson, and the Struggle for Control of Television Programming' in Hilmes, M. (Ed.) *NBC: America's Network*, 135–52. Berkeley: University of California Press

Mayer, V. (2009) 'Bringing the Social Back In' in Mayer, V., Banks, M. and Caldwell, J. (Eds.) (2009) *Production Studies*, 15–24. New York: Routledge

Mayerle, J. (1989) 'A Case Study of *Newhart*' *Journal of Popular Film and Television*, *17*(3), 100–12

Mediatique (2017) *Content Market Dynamics in the UK* 2 November Final Report

Mediatique (2015) *TV Production Sector Evolution and Impact on PSBs* (Ofcom)

Mediatique (2008) *All Grown Up* Mediatique

Mendel, R. (1991) 'Cooperative Unionism and the Development of Job Control in New York's Printing Trades, 1886–1898' *Labor History*, *32*(3), 354–75

Merritt, R. (2002) 'The Nickelodeon Theater, 1905–1914' in Hark, I. (Ed.) *Exhibition, the Film Reader*, 21–31. London: Routledge

Meyers, C. (2011a) 'The Problems with Sponsorship in US Broadcasting, 1930s–1950s' *Historical Journal of Film, Radio and Television*, *31*(3) 355–72

Meyers, C. (2011b) 'From Sponsorship to Spots' in Holt, J. and Perren, A. (Eds.) *Media Industries* London: John Wiley & Sons

Meyers, C. (1997) 'Frank and Anne Hummert's Soap Opera Empire' *Quarterly Review of Film & Video*, *16*(2), 113–32

Mezias, S. and Boyle, E. (2002) *The Organizational Dynamics of Creative Destruction* Basingstoke: Palgrave Macmillan

Mezias, S. and Kuperman, J. (2001) 'The Community Dynamics of Entrepreneurship: The Birth of The American Film Industry, 1895–1929' *Journal of Business Venturing*, *16*(3), 209–33

Miller, D. and Shamsie, J. (1996) 'The Resource-Based View of the Firm in Two Environments' *Academy of Management Journal*, *39*(3), 519–43

Mindich, D. (2000) *Just the Facts* New York: New York University Press

Mindich, D. (1993) 'Edwin M. Stanton, the Inverted Pyramid, and Information Control' *Journalism & Communication Monographs*, *140*, 1–31

Mittell, J. (2015) *Complex TV* New York: New York University Press

Mittell, J. (2002) 'Before the Scandals' in Hilmes, M. and Loviglio, J. (Eds.) *Radio Reader*, 319–42. New York: Routledge

Moore, B. (1980) 'The Cisco Kid and Friends' *Journal of Popular Film and Television*, *8*(1), 26–33

Mordden, E. (1988) *The Hollywood Studios* New York: Knopf

Morris, R. (2007) 'The End of the Networks' *FIU Law Review*, *2*(1), 55

Morroni, M. (2014) 'Production of Commodities by Means Of Processes' *Structural Change and Economic Dynamics*, *29*(C, June), 5–18

Morroni, M. (1992) *Production Process and Technical Change* Cambridge: Cambridge University Press

Mosco, V. (2011) 'The Political Economy of Labor' in Wasko, J., Murdock, G. and Sousa, H. (Eds.) *The Handbook of Political Economy of Communications*, 358–80. Chichester: Wiley-Blackwell

Muncy, J. (2017) 'Once the Darling of YouTube, Machinima Still Lives On – for Some' *Wired* 23 April www.wired.com/2017/04/red-vs-blue-machinima/ (Accessed 7/9/18)

Musser, C. (1994) *The Emergence of Cinema* Berkeley: University of California Press

Murdock, G. (2018) 'Keynote Address' *Media Industries: Current Debates and Future Directions*, Conference, 18–20 April, King's College London

Murdock, G. and Golding, P. (2016) 'Political Economy and Media Production: A Reply to Dwyer' *Media, Culture & Society*, *38*(5), 763–69

Murdock, G. (1982) 'Large Corporations and the Control of the Communications Industries' in Gurevitch, M., Bennett, T., Curran, J. and Woollacott, J. (Eds.) *Culture, Society, Media*, 114–47. London: Methuen

NAO (2017) *Managing the BBC's Workforce* (National Audit Office)

Napoli, P. (2012) 'Audience Evolution and the Future of Audience Research' *International Journal on Media Management*, *14*(2), 79–97

Neale, S. (2012) *The Classical Hollywood Reader* Abingdon: Routledge

Neale, S. (1980) *Genre* London: BFI

Nelson, R. (1997) *TV Drama in Transition* London: Macmillan

Nelson, R. (1995) 'Recent Evolutionary Theorizing About Economic Change' *Journal of Economic Literature*, *33*(1), 48–90

Nelson, R. and Winter, S. (1982) *An Evolutionary Theory of Economic Change* Cambridge: Belknap Press

Nerone, J. (2017) 'The Labor History of News in the US before World War I' *Medijska Istraživanja: Znanstveno-Stručni Časopis Za Novinarstvo I Medije*, *23*(2), 83–105

Nerone, J. (2008) 'Newswork, Technology, and Cultural fFrm, 1837–1920' in Zelizer, B. (Ed.) (2008) *Explorations in Communication and History* 136–56. London: Routledge

Nerone, J. and Barnhurst, K. (2003) 'US Newspaper Types, the Newsroom, and the Division of Labor, 1750–2000' *Journalism Studies*, *4*(4), 435–49

Newcomb, H. (2004) 'Narrative and Genre' in Downing, J. D., McQuail, D., Schlesinger, P. and Wartella, E. (Eds.) *The SAGE Handbook of Media Studies* Thousand Oaks: Sage

Newman, M. (2006) 'From Beats to Arcs' *The Velvet Light Trap*, *58*(1), 6–28

Nichols, B. (1991) *Representing Reality* Bloomington: Indiana University Press

Nielsen, M. (1989) 'The Devaluation of Labor-Power in Broadcasting and Cable' *Journal of Film and Video*, *41*(3), 23–33

Noam, E. (Ed.) (2016) *Who Owns the World's Media?* New York: Oxford University Press

Nowell-Smith, G. (Ed.) (1996) *The Oxford History of World Cinema* Oxford: Oxford University Press

Ofcom (2018a) *Media Nations Report* (Ofcom)

Ofcom (2018b) *The International Communications Market 2017* (Ofcom)

Ofcom (2004) *Review of Public Service Television Broadcasting* (Ofcom)

Oliver and Ohlbaum (2015) *TV Producer Consolidation, Globalisation and Vertical Integration: Myths and Realities A Report for PACT* (PACT)

Oliver and Ohlbaum (2014) *The Evolution of The TV Content Production Sector* (Ofcom)

Oliver and Ohlbaum (2011) *The Role of Terms of Trade* (PACT)

Opam, K. (2014) 'Microsoft Reportedly Paying YouTube Personalities to Promote Xbox One' *The Verge* 20 January 2014 www.theverge.com/2014/1/20/5328766/ microsoft-reportedly-paying-youtube-personalities-to-promote-xbox-one (Accessed 7/9/18)

Örnebring, H. (2018) 'Journalists' Thinking About Precarity' *Journal Details*, 8(1), 109–27

Örnebring, H. (2013) 'Journalism as Institution and Work in Europe, circa 1860' *Media History*, 19(4), 393–407

O'Sullivan, S. (2017a) 'Epic, Serial, Episode' *Narrative Culture*, 4(1), 49–75

O'Sullivan, S. (2017b) 'Broken on Purpose' in Rivkin, J. and Ryan, M. (Eds.) *Literary Theory: An Anthology*, 42–54. Hoboken: John Wiley & Sons

Ouellette, L. (Ed.) (2014) *A Companion to Reality Television* Hoboken: John Wiley & Sons

Owen, B. and Wildman, S. (1992) *Video Economics* Cambridge: Harvard University Press

Parks, P. (2017) 'Crisis Continued' *Journalism Studies*, 18(10), 1–22

Pautz, M. C. (2002) 'The Decline in Average Weekly Cinema Attendance, 1930–2000' *Issues in Political Economy, 11*(July), 54–65

Peacock, A. (1986) *Report of the Committee on Financing the BBC* (Vol. 9824). London: HMSO

Pearl, D., Bouthilet, L. and Lazar, J. (Eds.) (1982) *Television and Behavior* Bethesda: National Institute of Mental Health

Pearson, R. (1996) 'Early Cinema' in Nowell-Smith, G. (Ed.) *The Oxford History of World Cinema*, 13–22. Oxford: Oxford University Press

Pekurny, R. (1980) 'The Production Process and Environment of NBC's "Saturday Night Live"' *Journal of Broadcasting & Electronic Media*, 24(1), 91–9

Percival, A. (2018) 'Love Island Behind the Scenes Secrets' *Huffington Post* 31 May www.huffingtonpost.co.uk/entry/love-island-behind-the-scenes-secrets-villa_ uk_5b0fbe9ae4b05ef4c22b133c (Accessed 7/9/18)

Perebinossoff, P., Gross, B. and Gross, L. (2012) *Programming for TV, Radio & the Internet* New York: Routledge

Perren, A. (2004) 'Deregulation, Integration and a New Era of Media Conglomerates' PhD Dissertation University of Texas at Austin

Perrow, C. (1967) 'A Framework for the Comparative Analysis of Organizations' *American Sociological Review*, 32(2), 194–208

Phalen, P. and Osellame, J. (2012) 'Writing Hollywood: Rooms with a Point of View' *Journal of Broadcasting & Electronic Media*, 56(1), 3–20

Phillips, W. (2005) 'Television Sitcom Production at the BBC 1973–1984' PhD dissertation University of Westminster

Picard, R. (2008) 'Shifts in Newspaper Advertising Expenditures and Their Implications for the Future of Newspapers' *Journalism Studies*, 9(5), 704–16

Picard, R. (2005) 'Unique Characteristics and Business Dynamics of Media Products' *Journal of Media Business Studies*, 2(2), 61–9

Picard, R. (2002) 'US Newspaper Ad Revenue Shows Consistent Growth' *Newspaper Research Journal*, 23(4), 21–33

Pickard, V. (2013) 'The Air Belongs to the People' *Critical Studies in Media Communication*, 30(4), 307–26

Piore, M. and Sabel, C. (1984) *The Second Industrial Divide* New York: Basic Books

Poell, T., Nieborg, D., Duffy, B. E., Prey, R. and Cunningham, S. (2017) 'The Platformization of Cultural Production' *Selected Papers of #AoIR2017* The 18th Annual Conference of Internet Researchers

Pollack, N. (2013) 'You Are Watching Machinima, the Future of TV' *Wired* 12 February www.wired.com/2013/02/ff-you-are-watching-machinima/ (Accessed 7/9/18)

Pooley, J. (2008) 'The New History of Mass Communication Research' in Park, D. W. and Pooley, J. (Eds.) *The History of Media and Communication Research*, 43–69. New York: Peter Lang.

Porter, M. E. (1985) *Competitive Advantage* New York: Free Press

Potschka, C. (2012) *Towards a Market in Broadcasting* Basingstoke: Palgrave Macmillan

Pöttker, H. (2005). 'The News Pyramid and its Origin from the American Journalism in the 19th Century Inquiry' in Høyer, S. and Pöttker, H. (Eds.) *Diffusion of the News Paradigm 1850–2000*, 51–64. Göteborg: Nordicom

Pöttker, H. (2003) 'News and Its Communicative Quality' *Journalism Studies*, 4(4), 501–11

Quinn, B. (2007) 'Management, Restructuring and Industrial Relation' PhD dissertation University of St. Andrews

Quinn, M. (2001) 'Distribution, the Transient Audience, and the Transition to the Feature Film' *Cinema Journal*, 40(2), 35–56

Raphael, C. (1997) 'The Political Economy of Reali-TV' *Jump Cut*, 41, 102–9

Rathmell, J. M. (1966) 'What Is Meant by Services?' *Journal of Marketing*, 30(4), 32–6

Ravage, J. (1977) '. . . Not in the Quality Business' *Journal of Broadcasting & Electronic Media*, 21(1), 47–60

Redden, J. and Witschge, T. (2010) 'A New News Order?' in Fenton, N. (Ed.) *New Media, Old News* London: Sage

Redfern, N. (2014) 'The Structure of ITV News Bulletins' *International Journal of Communication*, 8, 1557–78

Regev, R. (2016) 'Hollywood Works' *Enterprise & Society*, 17(3), 591–617

Renov, M. and Brook, V. (2017) *From Shtetl to Stardom: Jews and Hollywood* West Lafayette: Purdue University Press

Rhomberg, C. (2012) *The Broken Table* New York: Russell Sage Foundation

Rigney, R. (2012) 'How Rooster Teeth Won the Internet with Red vs. Blue' *Wired* 25 May www.wired.com/2012/05/rooster-teeth-red-vs-blue/ (Accessed 7/9/18)

Riverol, A. (1992) *Live from Atlantic City* Bowling Green: Popular Press

Rivkin, J. and Ryan, M. (2017) *Literary Theory: An Anthology* Hoboken: John Wiley & Sons

Robins, J. (1993) 'Organization as Strategy' *Strategic Management Journal*, 14(S1), 103–18

Rock, P. (1981) 'News as Eternal Recurrence' in Cohen, S. and Young, J. (Eds.) *The Manufacture of News*, revised edition, 64–70. London: Constable

Rock, P. (1973) 'News as Eternal Recurrence' in Cohen, S. and Young, J. (Eds.) *The Manufacture of News*, 226–43. London: Sage

Rodowick, D. N. (1995). *The Crisis of Political Modernism* Berkeley: University of California Press Roman, J. (2005) *From Daytime to Primetime* Westport: Greenwood Publishing Group

Rooney, B. and Belli, M. (2013) *Directors Tell the Story* New York: Focal Press.

Rose, J. and Nesbitt-Larking, P. (2010) 'Politics and the Media' in Courtney, J. C. and Smith, D. E. (Eds.) *The Oxford Handbook of Canadian Politics*, 281–300. New York: Oxford University Press

Rosse, J. and Dertouzos, J. (1978) 'An Economist's Description of the Media Industry' *Proceedings of the Symposium on Media Concentration*, 40–192. Washington, DC: FTC

Ryfe, D. (2006) 'Guest Editor's Introduction' *Political Communication*, 23(2), 135–44

Sachsman, D. and Bulla, D. (Eds.) (2017) *Sensationalism* Abingdon: Routledge

Saferstein, B. (1992) 'Collective Cognition and Collaborative Work' *Discourse & Society*, *3*(1), 61–86

Saltzis, K. (2006) 'Media Convergence in News Organisations' Doctoral Thesis, University of Leicester

Sandoval, M. and Fuchs, C. (2010) 'Towards a Critical Theory of Alternative Media' *Telematics and Informatics*, *27*(2), 141–50

Sarrina Li, S. and Lee, C. (2010) 'Market Uncertainty and Mimetic Isomorphism in the Newspaper Industry' *Asian Journal of Communication*, *20*(3), 367–84

Sawyer, M. (2009) 'Filters, Fair Use & Feedback' *Berkeley Technology Law Journal*, *24*(1), 363–404

Schatz, T. (2012) 'Hollywood: The Triumph of the Studio System' in Neale, S. (Ed.) *The Classical Hollywood Reader*, 167–78. Abingdon: Routledge

Schatz, T. (1996) *The Genius of The System* New York: Pantheon

Schatz, T. (1990) 'Desilu, I Love Lucy, and the Rise of Network TV' in Thompson, G., Thompson, R. J. and Burns, G. (Eds.) *Making Television*, 117–35. New York: Praeger

Schlesinger, P. (1978) *Putting 'Reality' Together* London: Constable

Schlosberg, J. (2013) 'Modelling Media Ownership Limits' LSE Media Policy Project Series

Schudson, M. (2001) 'The Objectivity Norm in American Journalism' *Journalism*, *2*(2), 149–70

Schudson, M. (1978) *Discovering the News* New York: Basic Books

Schumpeter, J. (1942/2010) *Capitalism, Socialism and Democracy* London: Routledge

Scott, A. J. (2004) 'The Other Hollywood' *Media, Culture & Society*, *26*(2), 183–205

Shoemaker, P. and Reese, S. (1996) *Mediating the Message* White Plains: Longman

Sendall, B. (1983) *Independent Television in Britain: Volume 2 Expansion and Change, 1958–68* London: Macmillan

Sewell, P. (2010) 'From Discourse to Discord' *Television & New Media*, *11*(4), 235–59

Sexton, M. (2013) 'Celluloid Television Culture' PhD dissertation Birkbeck, University of London

Shirky, C. (2008) *Here Comes Everybody* London: Penguin

Simon, H. and March, J. (1976) *Administrative Behavior and Organizations* New York: Free Press

Skaffari, J., Peikola, M., Carroll, R., Hiltunen, R. and Wårvik, B. (Eds.) (2005) *Opening Windows on Texts and Discourses of the Past*, 7–22. Amsterdam: John Benjamins Publishing

Skillset (2016) *2015 Employment Survey: Creative Media Industries* (Skillset)

Slater, G. and Spencer, D. (2000) 'The Uncertain Foundations of Transaction Costs Economics' *Journal of Economic Issues*, *34*(1), 61–87

Smith, A. (1776) *The Wealth of Nations*, Books 1–3, London: Penguin

Smith, T. J. (2012) 'The Attentional Theory of Cinematic Continuity' *Projections*, *6*(1), 1–27

Staiger, J. (1985) Parts 2, 5 and 7 in Bordwell D., Staiger, J. and Thompson, K. (Eds.) *The Classical Hollywood Cinema*, 88–231, 548–79 and 660–71. London: Routledge

Staiger, J. (1979) 'Dividing Labor for Production Control' *Cinema Journal*, *18*(2), 16–25

Starkey, K. C., Barnatt, C. and Tempest, S. (2000) 'Beyond Networks and Hierarchies' *Organization Science*, *11*(3), 299–305

Statista (2018) 'YouTube Viewers United States' www.statista.com/statistics/469152/number-youtube-viewers-united-states/ (Accessed 7/9/18)

Stedman, J. W. (1996) *WS Gilbert* London: Routledge

Steemers, J. (2004) *Selling Television* London: British Film Institute

Stempel, T. (2000) *Framework* Syracuse: Syracuse University Press

Stensaas, H. (1986). 'Development of the Objectivity Ethic in US Daily Newspapers' *Journal of Mass Media Ethics*, *2*(1), 50–60

Storper, M. (1993) 'Flexible Specialisation in Hollywood: A Response to Aksoy and Robins' *Cambridge Journal of Economics*, *17*(4), 479–84

Storper, M. (1989) 'The Transition to Flexible Specialisation in the US Film Industry' *Cambridge Journal of Economics*, *13*(3), 273–305

Storper, M. and Christopherson, S. (1987) 'Flexible Specialization and Regional Industrial Agglomerations' *Annals of the Association of American Geographers*, 77(1), 104–17

Sylvestre, S. (2017) *Morjax's YouTube Creator's Guide* Kindle Books

TRP Research (2014) UK Television Exports FY 2013/2014 www.thecreativeindustries. co.uk/media/354136/tv-exports-survey-fy-13-14-1-.pdf (Accessed 7/9/18)

TVB (2008) Broadcast-Only, Satellite and Wired-Cable Households www.tvb.org/ (Accessed 7/9/18)

Tapscott, D. and Williams, A. (2008) *Wikinomics* London: Atlantic Books

Taves, B. (2012) *Thomas Ince* Lexington: University Press of Kentucky

Taylor, F. W. (1914) *Scientific Management* New York: Harper & Row

Taylor, J. (2002) 'Beating the Press?' in McKernan, L. (Ed.) *Yesterday's News* London: Wallflower Press

Tempest, S. (2003) 'Intergenerational Learning' *Management Learning*, *34*(2), 181–200

Thompson, G., Thompson, R. J. and Burns, G. (Eds.) (1990) *Making Television* New York: Praeger

Thompson, J. D. (1967) *Organizations in Action* New York: McGraw-Hill

Tibbetts, J. (1985) *The American Theatrical Film* Bowling Green: Bowling Green State University

Tschmuck, P. (2006) *Creativity and Innovation in the Music Industry* Heidelberg: Springer

Tuchman, G. (1973) 'Making News by Doing Work: Routinizing the Unexpected' *American Journal of Sociology*, *79*(1), 110–31

Turner, S. and Lourenço, A. (2010) 'Competition and Public Service Broadcasting' Centre for Business Research, University of Cambridge Working Paper No. 408

Turnock, R. (2007) *Television and Consumer Culture* London: IB Tauris

Ulrich, K. (2016) 'A Short Look at the Long Take' *ASBBS Proceedings*, *23*(1), 535–9

Unclefuz (2018) 'Serious Audiorecording Issues' www.reddit.com/r/letsplay

Uricchio, W. (2008) 'Television's First Seventy-Five Years' in Kolker, R. (Ed.) *The Oxford Handbook of Film and Media Studies*, 286–306. New York: Oxford University Press

Van de Ven, A. (1976) 'A Framework for Organization Assessment' *Academy of Management Review*, *1*(1), 64–78

Van Kranenburg, H. and Hogenbirk, A. (2006) 'Issues in Market Structure' in Albarran, A., Chan-Olmsted, S. and Wirth, M. (Eds.) *Handbook of Media Management and Economics*, 325–44. Mahwah: Lawrence Erlbaum

Vianello, R. (1985) 'The Power Politics of "Live" Television' *Journal of Film and Video*, *37*(3), 26–40

Vollmer, C., Blum, S. and Bennin, K. (2014) *The Rise of Multi-Channel Networks* PWC: New York

Von Hippel, E. (2005) *Democratizing Innovation* Chicago: MIT Press

Voorhees, L. (1930) 'Acoustics of Radio Broadcasting Studios' *Journal of the AIEE*, *49*(3), 210–17

WAN-IFRA (2016) *World Press Trends 2016* World Association of Newspapers and News Publishers

Wasko, J., Murdock, G. and Sousa, H. (Eds.) (2011) *The Handbook of Political Economy of Communications* Chichester: Wiley-Blackwell

Wasko, J. (1994) *Hollywood in the Information Age* Cambridge: John Wiley & Sons

Weaver, P. (1975) 'Newspaper News and Television News' in Cater, D. and Adler, R. (Eds.) *Television as a Social Force*, 81–94. New York: Praeger

Weddle, D. (2003) 'Lights, Camera, Action. Marxism, Semiotics, Narratology' *Los Angeles Times Magazine* 13 July, 14 http://articles.latimes.com/2003/jul/13/magazine/tm-filmschool28/1 (Accessed 15/8/18).

Weiss, G. (2018) 'YouTube Alters Partner Program Eligibility' *tubefilter* 16 January www.tubefilter.com/2018/01/16/youtube-alters-partner-program-google-preferred/ (Accessed 15/8/18)

White, D. (1950) 'The Gatekeeper: A Case Study in the Selection of News' *Journalism Quarterly*, 27(4), 383–90

White, T. (2015) *Blue-Collar Broadway* Philadelphia: University of Pennsylvania Press

Wijman, T. (2018) 'Top 25 Public Game Companies Earn $94.1 Billion in 2017' *Newzoo* 9 May https://newzoo.com/insights/articles/top-25-public-game-companies-earn-94-1-billion-in-2017/ (Accessed 7/9/18)

Wilke, J. (1998) 'The Struggle for Control of Domestic News Markets' in Boyd- Barrett, O. and Rantanen, T. (Eds.) *The Globalization of News* 49–60. London: Sage

Williamson, O. E. (1985) *The Economic Institutions of Capitalism* New York: Free Press

Wilson, K. (2000) 'Talent Agents as Producers' *Loyola LA Entertainment Law Review*, 21(3), 401–15

Wilson, J. M. and McKinlay, A. (2010) 'Rethinking the Assembly Line' *Business History*, 52(5), 760–78

Winseck, D. and Jin, D. (Eds.) (2011) *The Political Economies of Media* London: Bloomsbury Publishing

Winston, B. (2002) *Media, Technology and Society* London: Routledge

Wyver, J. (2012) 'Dallas Bower: A Producer for Television's Early Years, 1936–9' *Journal of British Cinema and Television*, 9(1), 26–39

Ytreberg, E. (2001) 'Moving Out of the Inverted Pyramid' *Journalism Studies*, 2(3), 357–71

Zelizer, B. (Ed.) (2008) *Explorations in Communication and History* London: Routledge

INDEX